SPIRITUAL ALCHEMY

ABOUT THE AUTHOR

Jenny Tyson is a registered nurse living in rural Nova Scotia, Canada. She has devoted the past twelve years to intensive spiritual studies in a variety of traditions, including shamanism, Paganism, and Enochian magic. She is clairaudient and knowledgeable in scrying and dowsing. Together with Dr. Dee and Edward Kelley, she developed the system of electronic spirit communication known as the jukebox. She is involved with the Atlantic Fellowship Conference, the Atlantic Dowsing Association, and the Applied Precognition Project.

AN INITIATION EXPERIENCE WITH EDWARD KELLEY

SPIRITUAL ALCHEMY

SCRYING, SPIRIT COMMUNICATION AND ALCHEMICAL WISDOM

JENNY TYSON

Llewellyn Publications
Woodbury, Minnesota

FIRST EDITION
Fifth Printing, 2021

Book design by Rebecca Zins
Cover design by Kevin R. Brown
Cover dragon: Shutterstock.com / 128142638 / ©Eugene Ivanov
Interior dragon: iStockphoto.com / 70238885 / ©Dezmond55
Photos, homunculus illustration, and seals by Jenny Tyson

Library of Congress Cataloging-in-Publication Data
Names: Tyson, Jenny, author.
Title: Spiritual alchemy : scrying, spirit communication, and alchemical wisdom / Jenny Tyson.
Other titles: At head of title: An initiation experience with Edward Kelley.
Description: FIRST EDITION. | Woodbury : Llewellyn Worldwide, Ltd, 2016. | Includes bibliographical references and index.
Identifiers: LCCN 2016029330 (print) | LCCN 2016038334 (ebook) | ISBN 9780738749761 | ISBN 9780738750842
Subjects: LCSH: Spiritualism. | Enochian magic. | Hermetism. | Kelly, Edward, 1555–1595.
Classification: LCC BF1261.2 .T97 2016 (print) | LCC BF1261.2 (ebook) | DDC 133.9/1—dc23
LC record available at https://lccn.loc.gov/2016029330

Llewellyn Publications
A Division of Llewellyn Worldwide Ltd.
2143 Wooddale Drive
Woodbury, MN 55125-2989

www.llewellyn.com
Printed in the United States of America

Contents

PART TWO: **Practical Applications . . . 171**

Foreword

‡

A UNIQUE BOOK OF PRACTICAL SPIRIT INITIATION

This is Jenny's book. All of the text, apart from a few notes that I've added, was written by her or received by her from spirits through scrying or clairaudience. My wife is not a professional writer, so she asked me to edit it. I was happy to do so because I regard it as a unique document in the history of Western magic. Nothing quite like this book exists elsewhere. It is based entirely on Jenny's actual experiences over the course of a full year of intense esoteric practice. I can attest to the integrity of that practice. Every day for a year she spent several hours in ritual meditation or trance. Although she didn't know it at the time, she was preparing herself for the extended ordeal of alchemical initiation that forms the heart of the book.

This intense year-long course of magical practice to facilitate communication with spirits was entered into without any prior expectations. In the beginning, Jenny merely sought to contact the spirit of the great Elizabethan magician Dr. John Dee, due to her ongoing interest in Enochian magic. After experimenting with various methods of communication, she succeeded in forming a link not only with Dee, but with Dee's partner, the alchemist Edward Kelley, and with other spirits who came to be her teachers.

The spirits she contacted told Jenny what to do in her daily magical practice, and she did it. She allowed them complete control over her development. In the course of her training, she acquired the faculties of clairaudience, clairvoyance, and channeling. The results are recorded here in her own words. For twelve months, she believed she was developing her psychic perceptions as a trance medium. It was only later that she came to realize how during that period of intense training she was being prepared by her spirit teachers for a ritual of initiation that, when successfully completed, resulted in a perfect state of oneness with the highest spiritual principle.

The successful completion of the alchemical initiation ritual had practical as well as spiritual consequences. When you realize on a very deep level that mind and body are one, it becomes possible to cure the ills of the body with the mind. The ways in which Jenny healed herself of medical problems are described in the text. Jenny would say these cures were of small importance compared to the spiritual wisdom she acquired. I think they have value in indicating the practical benefits of spiritual enlightenment.

A DEDICATED MAGICIAN

Jenny's interest in Western magic began before I even met her. It was her study of my writings on magic that caused us to get to know each other. We corresponded, found we had common interests, got together, and eventually married. Jenny moved from Maine to Nova Scotia and obtained her Canadian citizenship. I have been able to help her in some of her esoteric work in the years since we came together, but the impulse to undertake that work did not come from me. It arose from her own deep fascination with magic and spirituality.

For five years prior to even beginning the year of training described in these pages, Jenny made an intense study of all the major currents of Western esotericism. Her study was not confined to books. She practiced what she learned on a daily basis. Some of the disciplines she mastered include modern witchcraft, Nordic mythology, ritual magic in the Golden Dawn tradition, tarot, Kabbalah, astrology, and Enochian magic.

The Enochian magic of the Elizabethan sage Dr. John Dee held a particular fascination for her. For two years prior to beginning her year of preparation, she devoted herself wholly to the study and practice of Enochian magic. The house is filled with the Enochian ritual furniture and instruments she constructed for her work. No one who watched, as I did, while she painstakingly carved the *Sigillum Dei Aemeth*, or Seal of the Truth of God, into disks of genuine beeswax that she had cast herself could ever doubt her complete dedication and commitment.

I emphasize the practical side of Jenny's study of magic because so often books on magic are written by those who get their knowledge only from other books. They are library magicians who never actually do any magic, but Jenny is not one of them. Everything she has written here is based on her actual experience; there is nothing theoretical or derivative.

POINTS OF VALUE

Readers will find great value in Jenny's unique analysis of the ancient alchemical text known as the Emerald Tablet of Hermes Trismegistus, the sentences of which have never before been explained as the stages of spiritual evolution.

They will welcome the detailed practical instructions she gives on the use of the spirit box, an electronic device for communicating audibly with spirits that is enjoying an enormous popularity at this time due to the wonders of electronics, which have made this device both inexpensive and simple to use.

They will be fascinated by her complex initiation ritual, an ordeal of faith and endurance that involved the rising of her consciousness through the esoteric centers of the self under the guidance of her spirit teachers.

The description of how to use an alchemical homunculus in training to open the heart to the entry of spirits is, so far as I am aware, completely unique. It was conveyed directly to Jenny by the spirit of Edward Kelley and has great utility in enabling the student to learn the skills needed for mediumship and channeling.

SPIRIT TEACHERS

All these teachings stemmed from Jenny's initial desire to make contact with the spirit of Dr. John Dee. There is an old saying in magic that when the student is ready, the teacher appears. This was certainly true for Jenny. In her case the teacher turned out not to be John Dee but his friend and crystal gazer, the alchemist Edward Kelley, who received the system of Enochian magic we have today from spirits while scrying into a crystal globe. Through his expert guidance of Jenny's magical training, Kelley proved that he was as gifted a teacher after death as he had been a scryer during his earthly life.

It has long been my personal contention that the only true teachers in magic are spiritual beings. Many of the grimoires of Western magic consist either of a method for contacting a spirit who will then teach the magician a system of magic or a description of a system of magic that has already been taught to the author of the grimoire by a spirit.

Sometimes the two are combined—the first part of the grimoire gives a method for contacting the spirits, and the second part gives a portion of their secret teachings. This is the case with the grimoire known as *The Book of the Sacred Magic of Abramelin the Mage*, which played a key role in the Golden Dawn tradition of magic and its offshoots.

Samuel Mathers, who translated the *Abramelin* text and who was a gifted psychic and spirit medium, received the complex magical system of the Golden Dawn from spirits known as the Secret Chiefs. They dictated various rituals and techniques to him, and he wrote them down as he received them.

One of Mathers's students was the infamous magician Aleister Crowley, who was for a time a student of the Golden Dawn system of magic. Crowley's *Book of the Law*, the central text of his cult of Thelema, was dictated to him by a spirit named Aiwass. Crowley regarded Aiwass as his Holy Guardian Angel, which he had received after successfully completing the *Abramelin* procedure. In this way the thread of Western magic unspools itself through time.

In contacting Dee and Kelley, and having these spirits agree to teach her, Jenny was continuing a tradition in magic that predates recorded history—all shamans, from the earliest beginnings of humanity down to the present day, have been instructed by spirits with whom they make psychic contact. Modern magic is a direct descendant of shamanism.

Where Jenny's book differs from many of the books on magic that have been conveyed by spirits to human students is its focus on personal spiritual development. This is not a book of spells or rituals or sigils, but a book of techniques for developing actual skills in scrying and spirit communication. It will teach you how to make contact with your own spiritual teachers. Once you have established communication with a spiritual teacher, you hold the key to the kingdom of magic.

KELLEY'S COMMENTARY

Throughout the book you will find illuminating comments by Edward Kelley and sets of dialogues that took place between Jenny and Kelley. The spirit gave Jenny strict instructions that his words should not be altered by her or by me, except to modernize the punctuation and sentence structure so that it would be more easily comprehended by readers. I have been true to these instructions. These are Kelley's own words exactly as he spoke them to Jenny, with minor changes in punctuation.

You will notice that Kelley's literary voice is quite different from Jenny's voice. He tends to use archaic constructions, which I have let stand. His writing is very concentrated and focused so that he is able to pack a great deal of meaning into a small amount of text. His commentaries should be read slowly and with care to avoid missing the teachings he wished to convey.

ALCHEMICAL INITIATION

The ritual of alchemical initiation that is the heart of this book was the natural culmination of Jenny's year of study. It was truly a peak experience, more intense emotionally and more profound spiritually than any other event in her life. Even as a mere onlooker, I found it almost overwhelming to watch her work her way through this ritual, which is fully described in the text. Let me only say here that it provides a means of direct personal communion with the very highest spiritual entities and transcends the boundaries both of philosophy and religion.

At the highest level, all enlightenment is the same. There are many men and women throughout history who have achieved this clarity, and there are many paths to its attainment. Kelley, having been an alchemist during life, chose a system of enlightenment that is based on alchemical principles. It is completely unique, and it is practical. I witnessed its success with my own eyes. This book is a testament to the power of magic to expand and transform human consciousness. It is also the amazing story of one woman's journey of the soul, through all doubts and trials, and her ultimate successful attainment of higher consciousness.

Let Jenny's story serve as a beacon to other seekers—proof that such attainment is possible without decades of religious study. This is the Western way, the way of magic. No, it is not quick or easy. Nothing of value in life is quick or easy. But it is within the abilities of anyone who has a serious desire to transcend the limits of ordinary consciousness and undergo a personal life-altering transformation. The greatest magic is the magic that transforms the self.

—***Donald Tyson***

Part One

MY TRAINING AND INITIATION

Chapter 1

‡

MY PREVIOUS EXPERIENCE

I had a frustrating start to my attempt to learn the arts of spirit evocation and mediumship. In fact, you might even say I fell flat on my face. I initially had little to no psychic perception, though it was not for lack of discipline or effort. I worked very hard on meditation and other exercises that were supposed to open those abilities, but I could not perceive anything at first. This is the story of how that changed. In this book I will disclose the system of establishing spirit communication that was taught to me by the spirits who helped me and acted as my teachers. I believe it will help those facing the same difficulties I experienced early on in my experiments.

FIFTEEN YEARS AGO

My quest for spirit communication started a few years before I came to Nova Scotia. I was living in Maine at this time. It was a difficult time in my life financially, physically, and spiritually. I felt lost and alone and was heading down a self-destructive path. I was in crisis and trying to find my way out.

This crisis was the turning point that led to my marriage to Donald and moving to Nova Scotia. It was a period of closing old doors as new ones were getting ready to open. I was isolated, stripped of material wealth, and emotionally detached from my social roots and networks. I suffered severe emotional wounds, and like a wild thing I sought solace in lonely, isolated places as I started to heal.

I wandered down to Booth Bay Harbor one day as I was exploring the coastal towns and beaches of midcoast Maine. I found an interesting bookstore called Enchantments. This bookstore is the most complete Pagan and New Age bookstore on the face of the planet. I do not think that a tarot deck or book that has ever been published was missing from their inventory. It was a perfect place for someone who was spiritually searching. I sought a way to get a handle on the slippery slope that I found myself on. I picked out the book *The Golden Dawn* by Israel Regardie. It looked substantial enough to keep me busy for awhile. I picked out the book based on its physical size and because it appeared to be complex and meaty. I had never heard of the Golden Dawn.

It was through Regardie's book that I first learned about evocation. I worked on the exercises, following the directions as precisely as I could. There was no Internet in the location where I lived, so I had no opportunity to seek out answers to my questions online. After a year or so, I attempted my first evocation in the woods of an island off the coast of Maine, where I was living at the time. The ritual did not succeed. I felt as if nothing had happened. There was no sign or sense that any spirit was present with me during the ritual. I was very disappointed. I closed the circle in tears, wondering what I had done wrong.

I went back to the bookstore as often as I could, seeking books that might provide answers to the question of how to evoke and converse with a spirit. It became my personal quest. However, I lived on an island. Trips to the mainland were infrequent and required significant preparation, especially in summer. A ferryboat trip was required to take the car to the mainland. In summer, spots were mostly taken up by tourists, requiring island residents to wait in line for days to obtain a spot on the boat.

Wintertime was also difficult, as the storms that racked the Maine coast often closed down the ferry service. Trips in winter on the boat with the car were risky. Storms came up quickly and often without much warning. Maine does not have kind winters by any stretch of the imagination. My trips were limited to once or twice a year.

Eventually I moved back to the mainland. I was healing and moving forward in my life again. By now my book collection on spirit evocation had grown to fill a modest bookshelf. I made attempts at scrying, tarot, dowsing, and other means of interacting with spirits. In spite of my increasing knowledge, my lack of psychic ability was constantly creating a stumbling block.

The breakthrough started in the spring of 2007. I had not had access to the Internet for nearly ten years. I bought my first cell phone, a necessity for work. I could access email using the phone. I had the opportunity to ask questions that I had never been able to ask.

I purchased a book called *Familiar Spirits* by Donald Tyson. I had been following his work, and at that point he was my favorite author. I watched the mail order catalogs for new books coming out and grabbed them up as fast as they were published. I felt like I was making a little bit of progress with the information I was using from those books, or at least that the sense of failure had lessened a little bit. I had many questions about evocation still unanswered, but I felt the answers were closer at hand than they had been before.

I decided to try mailing a letter to Donald. The publisher offered to forward the mail to the author in the books that they published. The letter was a work of art. I used illuminated lettering and embellishments. Donald still has that first letter, and yes, it did get his attention. I followed up a few months later with an email. I was on the island doing some work at the time. The email exchange that day changed both of our lives.

In three months' time we were dating, and in seven months we were married. I moved up to Nova Scotia. I had found my love and healing in the new relationship. I wondered if my one-way communication with spirits had exerted a positive effect.

When I first came to live in Canada, in 2007, it was six months before I was able to work in my profession of nursing. I had to take a series of competency tests and sit for the College of Nursing exams. During this time I was not allowed to work, and Donald and I were not yet married.

I occupied myself doing illustrations for Donald. Before moving to Canada, studying art was one of the few hobbies that I enjoyed. One of my coworkers was an accomplished painter and offered lessons in her spare time. I had only a small number of illustrations to do for the books he was writing at the time, which were the *Fourth Book of Occult Philosophy* and *The Thirteen Gates of the Necronomicon*. This left me with time to do some heavy-duty spiritual work.

Donald encouraged me. He said to use the books I had studied as a guide and allow my intuition to lead me along my own path, rather than following the instructions in the book verbatim. This excellent advice eventually led to my incredible experiences with Edward Kelley that I describe in these pages. His advice led me to grant myself the freedom to find the path to success.

I owned a copy of Dr. Dee's *Five Books of Mystery*, edited by Joseph Peterson, a well-known and respected occult author. I had always wanted to explore this earlier part of the Enochian system of magic described in Peterson's book. Dr. Dee called it the Heptarchy. It is a complicated book, written in a mixture of sixteenth-century English and Latin. Before the move to Canada, I had been too busy to sit down and work with the material. I decided to follow in Dr. Dee's footsteps and try to communicate with the angels using the same methods he had used.

I spent about two years exploring the *Five Books of Mystery*, which make up the first half of the Enochian diary material. The experience was worthwhile. The angels seemed interested in my attempts to communicate with them. I was not able to hear or see them, but sometimes I could feel a touch, like a hand laid on my shoulder or arm. I had dream encounters where I would wake up knowing something that I had not known when I went to sleep. The results were subtle and laid the groundwork for my work with Edward Kelley. I could feel something as I worked through this grimoire and realized later that I was starting to open a little at this point. The sparks of perception were present, even though I did not recognize them until much later.

It was also at this time that I had a lucid dream encounter with Dr. Dee. It was in a beautiful green English grove. Dr. Dee sat under the trees. He looked much the same as he looks in his portrait, except that his appearance was younger. His beard and hair were brown rather than silver. He was not wearing his iconic scholar's skullcap. He wore a plain green robe. I asked him if he was Dr. Dee, and he told me yes, he was. I realize now that this was an astral projection, not an ordinary dream, and that it foreshadowed my later work with Dr. Dee and Edward. Beyond the greeting, I do not remember anything else.

I attempted to invoke all the angels listed in the Heptarchy. I did not see them, but I was able to work through intuition. The angels did not appear to my intuition as Edward described them in Dr. Dee's diaries (Edward scried them in a crystal and described them to Dr. Dee, who wrote down their descriptions in his books). I was mildly surprised at this. It made me a little uneasy at first.

Later I came to understand that the nature of spirit vision is such that every seer's vision is unique. Each seer will see spirits in different ways. Edward's vision was relevant to his culture and time, and my intuited perceptions were relevant to me. Angels have no physical appearance of their own. Their interactions with Edward's mind are what created their appearances as described in the diaries.

One notable experience that occurred during my early experiments with the Heptarchy is that my strained relationships with members of my family were healed. I returned home after a long estrangement from my parents, accompanied by my new husband. We rediscovered our bond, and our family became strong and whole once more. I believe the angels played a major role in this recovery, even though I was not able to determine at that time exactly how they were working with me. I only knew that they were there, and my trust in them began to build.

After two years of working with the angels of the Heptarchy, there was a misunderstanding on my part that caused me to think that they did not want to continue to interact with me. The incident happened during an astral projection. I dreamed that I was shot and killed in my sleep. I astrally projected from this dream, and the experience became lucid. I thought I was dead and tried to call Bynepor, one of the angels of the Heptarchy, for help. He came and explained to me that I was not dead but only dreaming. I was confused and did not want to return to my body. I started to argue with him. I left and tried to run away.

When I woke up, I felt ashamed of what I had said to the angel. I was unable to contact the angels of the Heptarchy after that incident. I stopped the work with the Heptarchy at that point. I felt as though I had been on the verge of success but once again had fallen flat on my face.

After the experiments with the Heptarchy, I still felt frustrated with my lack of ability to make the critical spiritual connection. I decided to try a different approach. I had read a book called *Magical Use of Thought Forms* by Dolores Ashcroft-Nowicki and J. H. Brennan, and was interested in the evocation of the Yidam, a Tibetan deity, and the story of Pema Tense, a Tibetan Buddhist monk who is seeking enlightenment. He finds a teacher and is sent to a cave to perform a ritual to conjure one of the fierce Tibetan deities. He accomplishes the goal of the exercise and then learns from the deity he has conjured. After a period of time, he realizes that he is generating the entire experience. Upon gaining the insight of the true nature of the evoked entity, he wins control over it and develops a true understanding of the illusional nature of the universe.

This account inspired me. I believed if I could accomplish this kind of ritual, I would be able to gain true insight to the spiritual and physical world. I felt that the deity would be the most competent teacher on the path to seek spiritual truth. In 2012 I decided to attempt a variation on this ritual. I had also studied accounts of tulpa making and incorporated the concepts into my own experiment.

I worked for several months on the evocation. I attempted to evoke the Norse god of the sea, Njord. The deity fascinated me, and I thought he would be an interesting spirit to interact with. I have a strong ancestral connection with Norway through my mother's side of the family, and that connection was a major influence on my faith at that time.

The ritual met with little to no success. Occasionally I had a glimmer of a connection or sense of a presence with me. Day after day I stared into the darkness with an ever-growing frustration and belief that I was a psychic dud.

This was the eve of the great breakthrough. The years of frustrated failure were about to end.

Chapter 2

‡

FIRST CONTACT WITH JOHN DEE

During the last week in May 2013, my husband and I decided to attempt to contact the spirit of the Elizabethan magician and alchemist Dr. John Dee using a spirit communication board.

We believed we would find it easier to communicate with a spirit with whom we feel a personal connection. Dr. Dee is a spirit who shares many interests and values in common with us. My husband and I both have the same fascination for Hermetic philosophy, alchemy, and angelic magic that Dr. Dee had during his lifetime. Were he still alive today, we would eagerly seek him out as a teacher. We also share similar life values with Dr. Dee.

In particular, we had a keen interest in Dr. Dee's esoteric work, particularly the secret diaries in which he described his communications with angels. I had studied the earlier portion of the Enochian magic system that is described in the diaries for about two years. Donald had written a book about the later magical material in the diaries received by Edward Kelley from the angels (*Enochian Magic for Beginners*, Llewellyn, 1987) and more recently had been writing occult adventure stories about Dr. Dee and Edward Kelley (*The Ravener and Others*, Avalonia, 2011). We hoped to gain more information about Dee's life and work through the communication board.

These common interests led to the first successful experiment in communication with Dr. Dee. But before I describe it in more detail, I have asked Donald to write a brief account of Dr. Dee and Edward Kelley so that those readers unfamiliar with these two men will understand who they are and what they did.

A HISTORICAL NOTE

by Donald Tyson

Jenny has asked me to write something about the extraordinary pair of men who play such a central role in this book, the Elizabethan scholar Dr. John Dee and his scryer, the alchemist Edward Kelley. Both men are astonishing historical figures, their lives filled with adventure, romance, intrigue, and magic. They have been badly treated by popular writers, who have mischaracterized them as conniving and evil, but nothing could be further from the truth.

Today Dee and Kelley would be called scientists. Both men sought to acquire knowledge, not merely through book study but through experimentation. Dee hoped to learn the magic of heaven that the angels were reputed to have taught to the patriarch Enoch after his ascent to heaven while Enoch was still alive in the flesh. Kelley, for his part, burned with a lifelong passion to unravel the alchemical mystery of the philosopher's stone, which would transform base metals into gold.

Dr. John Dee

The uncommonly long life of Dr. John Dee (1527–1609) spanned the entire Elizabethan Age. As a boy he witnessed the dissolution of the Catholic monasteries under Henry VIII, and as a very old man he saw the hysterical witch persecutions under James I. In his prime he served Elizabeth I throughout her reign as her trusted political advisor, physician, and espionage agent. He is best remembered by historians as a cartographer and a mathematician, but he was also an astrologer, an alchemist, and a ceremonial magician.

During his own lifetime he was universally regarded as one of the greatest mathematicians in all of England, and his reputation as a scholar extended across the channel to continental Europe. It was Dee who coined the term "British Empire." He was in the forefront of the exploration of the New World by English ships. The captains of those ships relied on Dee's nautical charts to avoid being wrecked on hidden reefs. His personal library was the largest in England. Men came from all over Europe to consult with him and his books at his home in Mortlake, which at the time was a small village on the River Thames just outside of London (it has since then been absorbed into the growing city).

Queen Elizabeth I would sometimes stop at his house when she took her royal barge up the Thames from her palace at Hampton Court or when she traveled across her realm on horseback with her courtiers. Dee was her special favorite. Their friendship began while the young princess Elizabeth was being held under house arrest by her half sister, Queen Mary Tudor. Mary was Catholic, and both Elizabeth and Dee favored the Protestant cause of the Anglican Church created by Elizabeth's father, Henry VIII.

As a demonstration of his loyalty to Elizabeth, Dee drew up a horoscope that predicted her ascent to the English throne and her long and prosperous reign. He did so at great personal risk because such an astrological chart could have been considered treason against the reigning monarch, Mary Tudor. It was also Dee who chose the most astrologically auspicious date for young Elizabeth's coronation as queen following the death of her half sister.

In later years Elizabeth never forgot Dee's loyalty toward her during her time of peril. Their friendship remained steadfast throughout her life. She consulted him as a physician when she suffered medical complaints that her own royal physicians were unable to cure. She also used Dee as a spy when he traveled from England to continental

Europe and as an astrologer when some dire portent such as a comet appeared in the heavens.

Her most significant mark of regard toward Dee was her private assurance to him, repeated several times, that his occult experiments would never be called into question during her lifetime. She gave Dee carte blanche to do whatever he wished in his studies of magic and alchemy without having to worry that he would be imprisoned or executed.

One of Dee's preoccupations was his desire to establish communication with angels so that he could learn angelic magic. His purpose was twofold. He wanted this esoteric knowledge for its own sake, on the principle that knowledge is its own reward, but he also intended to use it in a practical way to advance the supremacy of England on the high seas and to extend the lands of the British Empire.

It was said in the Bible and other holy texts such as the book of Enoch that the patriarch Enoch had been elevated to heaven while still living. He was one of only two men accorded this honor by God, the other being Elijah. When in heaven the angels taught Enoch all the magical arts that were forbidden for mankind to know at that time. Dee wanted to learn the same magic that had been taught to Enoch.

He began his attempts to contact the angels by scrying into various crystal globes. Crystal gazing was well known and commonly used in England in Dee's time and was not in itself against the law. Communications with angels were also perfectly legal. The scrying only became illegal when it was used to communicate with spiritual beings other than angels. The assumption was that all non-angelic spirits were demonic.

Dee had only middling success in his solitary experiments with crystal scrying. This led him to hire several professional scryers to help him in his work. Even with these paid scryers, his success was mixed until March 8, 1582, when a man calling himself Edward Talbot came to visit his Mortlake house.

Edward Kelley

This mysterious visitor was Edward Kelley (1555–1597), who for reasons of his own choosing introduced himself to Dee under an assumed name. It is possible that Kelley first went to Dee's house for the purpose of entrapping Dee into performing spirit magic before witnesses who would testify against Dee in a court of law. Kelley may even have been paid to fulfill this role. In spite of the protection of Queen Elizabeth, Dee had his enemies at the English court.

Kelley tried to induce Dee to show him some of Dee's mastery of magic. When Dee declined, Kelley offered to display to Dee his own skill in spirit evocation. Dee professed to be horrified at such a proposal and said he wanted no part in such unholy work, but on a later day he asked Kelley if he would care to assist him in his attempt to communicate with the angels of God by scrying into a crystal, a perfectly lawful activity. Kelley readily accepted.

The first scrying session between Dee and Kelley was immensely productive. Almost at once Kelley made contact with spirits who would later identify themselves as the angels who had instructed Enoch in the magic of heaven. Dee sat at his desk and copied down verbatim everything Kelley described seeing in the crystal and every word the angels spoke to Kelley. This became part of Dee's meticulous written record of the angelic scrying sessions, which is often known as the Enochian diaries.

In his own way, Edward Kelley was even more extraordinary than John Dee. Born to an apothecary in the city of Worcester, his fascination with chemistry began early in life. It is a reasonable speculation that he must have helped his father mix the various chemicals that went into the making of the medicines prescribed by physicians. While still in his teens, he attended Oxford University but left without obtaining a degree.

He was a wild young man given to drunkenness, lawlessness, and a fascination for alchemy and necromancy. He is said to have earned a living for a while by drawing up false land-title deeds and also from "coining," which was the Elizabethan equivalent of counterfeiting. Coiners made coins out of base metal, which looked like gold or silver but was almost worthless, and exchanged them for the real thing.

There is a rumor that he was put in the stocks at Worcester, and even that he had his ears "cropped"—the tops of the ears of criminals were snipped off with a pair of shears to mark them for the rest of their lives. There is little on which to base this story. It is probably false.

What is not in dispute is that Kelley also earned money by putting on displays of necromancy in which he called from their graves the spirits of dead men and questioned them regarding the locations of hidden treasure. For this work he was paid by noblemen seeking buried gold or sometimes secret information from the dead. This was a serious crime, which is why John Dee pretended to be horrified when Kelley suggested at Mortlake that he would display to Dee his prowess as a necromancer.

Kelley was an enormously gifted scryer. Dee recognized this instantly and proposed that Kelley should stay at his house in Mortlake and scry for him. Having no better prospects, Kelley accepted. He immediately betrayed the men who had employed him to entrap Dee, revealing them to be Dee's enemies. The two formed a bond of friendship that endured until Kelley's death. They worked closely together on the Enochian communications from 1582 until 1589, when they were parted. In spite of their separation, their regard for each other never wavered.

Kelley's primary interest throughout his life was alchemy. He sought with a burning passion the secret of transforming base metals into gold. For a period while they lived in Bohemia, both Dee and Kelley worked together at practical alchemy. They each had their own separate alchemical furnaces, but they exchanged information freely.

It was alchemy that got Kelley killed. When Dee returned home to England from Bohemia, Kelley stayed behind to make gold for the

Holy Roman Emperor Rudolf II. By some accounts he was successful. He enjoyed great acclaim and great wealth for a few years, and was given lands and a noble title by the emperor that was equivalent to a knighthood, but in the end he fell out of favor with Rudolf, was imprisoned on two occasions, and died by falling from a wall while trying to escape his second imprisonment.

Enochian Magic

Dee's secret diaries from the years 1582 to 1608 record his experiments in communication with the hierarchy of spiritual beings identifying themselves as the angels who had instructed the biblical patriarch Enoch in the magic of heaven. For this reason these spirits are commonly known as the Enochian angels. Dee sought to learn this system of heavenly magic from the angels by repeatedly invoking them into his scrying crystals during ritual séances. The Enochian diaries in which Dee recorded the scrying sessions he worked in partnership with Kelley from 1582 to 1589 contain the most fascinating information on the system of Enochian magic.

This system is incomplete, and the angels never revealed to Dee the exact manner of its working or its ultimate purpose. They prohibited Dee from using the magic during his lifetime. Over the past century Enochian magic has become popular among modern magicians, who have evolved different ways of using it. Enochian magic has acquired a reputation as the most powerful system of magic that exists, but some magicians also say that it is the most dangerous.

A matter that is often overlooked by modern magicians but was of great significance to John Dee is that Enochian magic is an angel magic. Dee believed it to have a holy purpose. The spirits involved are either angels or lesser spirits subjected to the authority of angels. To use it for base or evil purposes would be to subvert its very nature.

Some magicians believe that John Dee deliberately omitted details of Enochian magic to prevent its defilement by those who were unfit to work it. My own opinion is that it was the angels themselves who deliberately omitted portions of the magic in order to insure it would never be worked during Dee's lifetime.

Part of the problem with the Enochian diaries was Edward Kelley's attitude toward the angels. He was never sure what to make of them. At times he accepted that they were the holy angels of God, but at other times he accused them of being demons and refused to tell Dee what they were doing or saying. John Dee's faith in the Enochian angels never wavered, but Kelley's attitude toward the angels was at best ambivalent and much of the time was outright hostility.

The angels, for their part, treated Kelley like a telephone. They didn't care about his opinion and were only concerned about conveying their system of magic accurately to John Dee so that Dee could write it down. At times the angels spoke to Kelley with scathing contempt, and their general disgust and irritation at his waywardness is often expressed throughout the Enochian record. To his credit, Kelley reported what they said even when they were insulting him.

Kelley's main bone of contention with the angels was that they were not yielding up any information that he could put to practical use. The angels promised him the secret of alchemy as a reward for his faithful service to them and to John Dee. At the very end of their partnership, the angels claimed to have made good on their promise, and it is certainly true that eyewitnesses reported that Kelley was able to manufacture gold while he was living in Bohemia. Dee's eldest child, Arthur, later wrote that, much as a child would play with a toy set of wooden blocks, as a young boy he had played with the ingots of gold Kelley had made in his alchemical furnace.

In modern times, magicians have used various parts of the Enochian system for mundane purposes, and they claim it is highly effective. This can only be regarded as a misuse of the magic from the angels' point of view, but perhaps it is flexible enough to tolerate misuse. Only a relatively small part of Enochian magic is used by most modern magicians, the portion based around four complex squares of letters known as the four Watchtowers, combined with the beautiful poetry of the invocations known as the Enochian Keys and the Call of the Thirty Aethyrs. This comprises no more than around 10 percent of Enochian magic as it was recorded by Dee.

Jenny's book is not directly concerned with Enochian magic, but it is because of the system of Enochian magic that survived in Dee's diaries that both John Dee and Edward Kelley possess the status they presently enjoy as two of the greatest magicians who ever lived.

Until very recently mainstream historians downplayed Dee's occult studies, just as they downplayed the similar devotion to alchemy by another great English scholar, Sir Isaac Newton. Magic was looked upon by them as a silly delusion, so Dee's study of magic was dismissed as unimportant. Over the last few decades Dee's historians and biographers have begun to realize that we cannot understand John Dee without understanding his passion for spirit communication. It was a huge part of his daily life, a part he hid from prying eyes because it could so easily be misinterpreted by others as illegal. He knew he had the protection of Queen Elizabeth, but he did not want to push his luck further than necessary, so all of his scrying sessions are contained in diaries that he carefully hid away.

It is something of a miracle that his diaries were not lost forever following his death. Dee had divided the diaries into two parts. The later portion he buried in the field next to his house at Mortlake. The other, earlier portion of the diaries he concealed in a secret drawer of one of his travel chests. Shortly after his death the buried portion of the diaries was dug up by the antiquarian Sir Robert Cotton and published in 1659 by Meric Casaubon. The other part remained in its secret drawer for decades, then was finally found in 1662 by the owner of the chest and sold ten years later to the antiquarian Elias Ashmole.

Jenny believes that it was not mere chance that preserved the Enochian diaries but purposeful design on the part of the angels. I am inclined to agree that something more purposeful was going on.

When you consider how easily either half of the record might have been lost, yet both were discovered and preserved, it does seem that there was a higher providence at work.

—Donald Tyson

THE SPIRIT BOARD

The system of ritual magic communicated by the angels to Dr. Dee and Kelley is called the Enochian system. It is widely practiced by those who are serious about the study of Western esotericism. It is regarded by modern Western magicians as the most powerful system of magic that exists in the world. However, there are many unanswered questions about the content of Dr. Dee's diaries. Some of the information appears to be incomplete. We decided that by contacting the spirit of Dr. Dee directly, we might be able to obtain answers to some of the mysteries in the Enochian system that have never been fully explained.

In a sense, we were following John Dee's own approach to occult wisdom. When Dr. Dee sought to learn the secrets of heaven, he asked the angels of heaven directly in a series of spirit séances with Edward Kelley. We sought to learn the unwritten mysteries of Enochian magic by asking the spirit of John Dee directly through the spirit communication board.

The spirit board is a device that has been used for centuries to communicate with spirits. In its simplest form, the spirit board consists of twenty-six slips of paper, each with a letter of the alphabet written on it and arranged in a circle on the smooth surface of a table. An inverted glass sliding across the table indicates letters of words in the response of the spirits.

Almost everyone is familiar with the present commercial form of the board, which is called a Ouija Board and has been sold by Parker Brothers since 1966. The original Ouija Board was patented by Elijah Bond in 1891. Bond was the first person to combine a planchette, or pointer, with a board on which were printed the letters of the alphabet. However, the general concept of selecting letters of the alphabet by means of a pointer moved by spirits has been in use since the time of the ancient Greeks.

The Ouija is a rectangle of pressboard, smooth and glossy on its upper surface. Letters of the alphabet are evenly spaced in two crescents, along with the words yes, no, and goodbye. A wooden triangle on three legs, called a planchette or pointer, slides over the board to indicate letters of words or yes-no answers to questions.

The spirit communication boards that my husband and I use are spirit-specific. If we use a communication board that is not constructed specifically for the spirit we are contacting, then other additions are made to the setup to assist our focus on the spirit we are attempting to communicate with. The photo on the following page shows the communication board used to talk to Dr. Dee.

THE SÉANCE

In this séance to achieve contact with John Dee we did not consider astrological factors or hours of the day. In traditional magic this is known as the use of times. It is common to take the hours of the day assigned to the planets into account in communications with nonhuman spirits, but in Spiritualist operations, where one is working with a human spirit who has passed on, it is generally not a vital consideration.

When using the communication board, we sat on plain wooden chairs facing each other with our knees almost touching. The board rested between us, on our knees. It was oriented sideways so that it was not upside down from the perspective of either of us. We each rested one finger on the base of the inverted shot glass that served as the planchette.

We focused on Dr. Dee's portrait and sigil intensely for several minutes to assist him in finding us, and we graciously invited him to talk with us. We explained to the spirit that we desired communication to

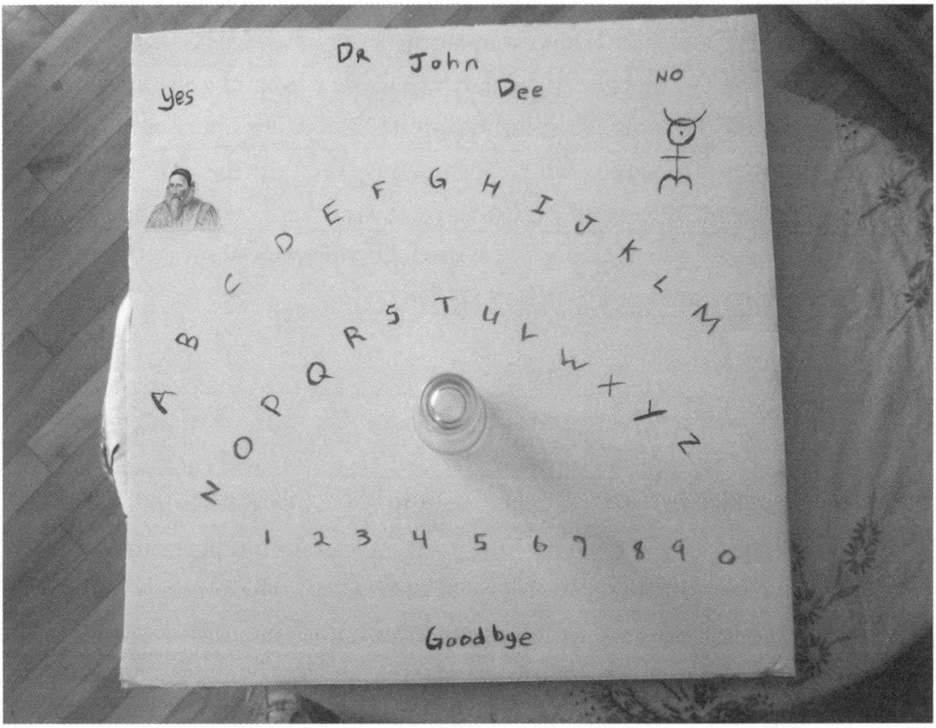

This is the board and glass we used for the initial contact.

be made through the spirit board by influencing our hands to move the shot glass to the letters that would spell out his responses.

Our invitations to spirits are always polite and gracious. We remember that spirits can feel our emotions and hear our thoughts as easily as we hear and respond to spoken voices. We never attempt to force a spirit to appear.

It is a common misconception that spirits move the pointer on the spirit board. In reality, to communicate with us Dr. Dee influenced the movement of our hands on the board. Our hearts, minds, and bodies had to be open to the influence of the spirit of Dr. Dee in order for the pointer to move.

Once the formal invitation was made, we moved the planchette in a clockwise circular direction. I find that using my non-dominant hand sometimes works better for this sort of thing, as I have less control and it makes it somewhat easier for the spirit to influence its movement, so I used my left hand. Donald used his right hand on the planchette.

The touch of a spirit is gentle and light, so we had to be quiet, open, and responsive to his suggestions. Dr. Dee's touch was clear enough to be discernable. We were working in good harmony with him. Neither Donald or I felt as though our hands or bodies were being possessed. There was no violence and almost no intrusiveness, only the calm, light touch. We knew Dr. Dee would never attempt to disrupt our bodies in any harsh way just for the sake of communicating a few words.

The touch of a spirit is very subtle and can take a few tries to pick up. In the past, with other spirits, I had found it more difficult to feel the influence of the spirit and had to try multiple times before getting any results.

The spirit board can be operated by only one person if that person has a high degree of mediumistic ability and uses a voice or video recorder to make a record of the letters selected by the spirit. However, it is usually easier to have good communication sessions when two or more people operate the board. If a solitary operator is nervous, a second person should be present or the séance should be postponed until the operator is calm. I have occasionally operated a spirit board solo. The results were not nearly as interesting as they were when Donald assisted the operation.

We attempted to voice record the communication session. However, I ran into a problem with the voice recorder. The battery was not at full charge when the session was started, and the instrument failed. Though spirits sometimes are believed to drain electronic devices when they are attempting to contact the physical plane, I think in this case it was my own fault. I did not check the recorder's battery prior to the communication.

The time of the operation was about 7:00 PM. In Nova Scotia in late spring we have light in the sky until after ten o'clock, so the sun was still well up. The light in the séance room needs to be bright enough to see the board. If the operator wished to work at night, an oil lamp would be appropriate to insure enough ambient light to easily see the letters. We don't feel that electric lights are conducive to spirit work, and candles have to be monitored constantly and are distracting.

We did not use a protective ritual circle during this procedure. The room in which we worked is closed with a set of double doors, making the walls of the room itself a kind of circle. Both of us are accomplished magicians, and we felt comfortable with our ability to focus our attention with sufficient strength of will to prevent distractions. In the past we have used circles to help the focus of a ritual operation, but we did not feel it was necessary in this particular case as we both had a high level of motivation. The use of prayer and meditation can be just as effective as a ritual circle to focus the content of the séance.

The response to our attempted contact with John Dee was immediate. He responded yes to the question "Are you here with us?" Making contact took less than a minute from the initiation of the communication to the first movements of the planchette. His responses were firm and clear. We kept the séance short; it lasted about ten minutes. The questions were geared toward confirming his identity.

The most memorable response came when we asked for a word in Latin that would confirm that we were actually in contact with Dr. John Dee. Latin was used as the universal language of scholarship in the sixteenth century, and we reasoned that Dr. Dee would be able to give us a word in the Latin language that we could translate using an online translator, since our knowledge of Latin is limited.

The response of the spirit was immediate but at first extremely puzzling. He moved the pointer to the letters I and V. This made no sense to either of us at the time. After receiving this response, we closed the session. We had achieved our main objective—establishing communication with Dr. Dee. We were disappointed that our request for some kind of Latin verification word had failed, but overall the effort was successful for a first attempt.

When Dr. Dee indicated the session was over by selecting *goodbye*, we asked if he would allow us to contact him again. He indicated that he would. We thanked him with a brief blessing and closed the session.

It was about two hours later when Donald finally realized what Dr. Dee meant by the letters I and V. The letters IV are the Roman numeral for the number 4, and the fourth letter of the Latin alphabet is D, which is the initial letter of John Dee's last name. Dee's name and the letter D sound the same. This caused Dee to sign his name in personal letters and in his private diary entries with a triangle. Why a triangle? Because the fourth letter of the Greek alphabet is delta, which is the Greek equivalent to the Latin letter D, and the Greek delta is shaped like a triangle. It was a kind of pun on the sound of his last name that Dee had used throughout his life when signing letters—a triangle to represent the Greek letter delta, and the Greek delta to represent the Latin letter D.

It was a simple but very clever code the spirit had given us, and it met the requirements we had specified. The Roman numeral IV was, in a sense, a Latin word. Perhaps it was intended by the spirit as a kind of test of his own—a test he applied to us to see if we were serious and bright enough to be worth talking to. We had asked the spirit to provide proof that he was who he claimed to be, and he, in turn, tested us to determine if we were worth his effort.

Once Dr. Dee's code was broken, it gave us a confirmation that our operation had been successful. We had indeed managed to achieve communication with the spirit of the great John Dee, and on the first attempt.

THE JOURNEY BEGINS

At this point I decided to begin a more serious, long-term effort to improve communication with the spirit of John Dee. Donald continued to lend his support for the work as it progressed, but the effort to learn the secrets of Enochian magic from the spirit of John Dee became my personal obsession.

Little did I realize at that time that this simple experiment with the spirit board would result a year later in a life-transforming and completely original alchemical initiation—the Great Work that is the ultimate goal of spiritual alchemy. I never would have suspected that my teacher and guide in this Great Work would be not John Dee but his friend and partner, Edward Kelley.

Chapter 3

‡

EXPERIMENTS WITH THE RADIO

A NOTE FOR THE READER
by Donald Tyson

During the year of training, Jenny communicated with Kelley and her other spiritual teachers by means of a technique of audio scrying known as radio tuning. She soon found this method more fruitful than the spirit board. At first she manually tuned the radio back and forth across the dial to produce a rapid series of words and word fragments. It was not long before she purchased an automatic tuner known as a spirit box. This yielded very good results. Here Jenny gives extensive instructions on how to use radio tuning, both manual and automatic, for communicating with spirits. In my opinion, this is one of the most useful aspects of her book.

Over the course of this year she was not only learning the techniques of concentration and focus that were necessary to open herself to the communication of spiritual beings, but the spirits instructing her were, in effect, rewiring her brain and nervous system. I have observed this process in my own work with spirits. Perception of spiritual beings does not simply occur all at once; the nervous system must be adapted to allow it to occur, and this takes months or years of work on the part of both the scryer and the spirit teachers.

There are, of course, natural mediums who are in communication with spirits from early childhood, but I refer to the rest of us, those without strong or developed innate mediumistic gifts. As the spirits rewire the nervous system, it is possible to feel what they are doing and to trace their movements along the nerves and through the body. It is a fascinating—and, to some, a disturbing—experience. I remember feeling the touches of spirits on the surface of my brain, inside my skull—not all over its surface, but on certain specific spots. When the nerves are stimulated, they feel as though they are conducting electricity. All these things Jenny experienced and endured during her year of training.

—Donald Tyson

After the initial encounter with Dr. Dee, I decided to attempt to find a more substantial and quicker method of communication. The communication board was okay, but it was very slow and not very accurate when I worked with it alone. I found ghost-hunting equipment and techniques to be a fertile ground for developing my initial ideas. These tools have not been used much in traditional Western magical evocation and invocation. The electronic ghost-hunting tools are not specific to any spirit and, like the spirit board, are easy to adapt to individual spirits and situations.

The general term for electronic communication is Instrumental Transcommunication or the abbreviation ITC. I prefer the term Electronic Spirit Communication or ESC. I feel it is a better description of what you are trying to accomplish. A spirit box is any sound device that is used in spirit communication. They fall basically into two categories. The first category is radio based. Radio stations are rapidly scanned, and the sounds resulting from the scanning are recorded and examined for messages. The second category includes apps that are random sound generators. These apps are mostly for cell phones. They work like a random number generator, only with phonetic sounds. The words seemingly put themselves together when you record and play back the sounds. The content of the recording, when played back to the operator, is the spirit's message.

EXPERIMENTS WITH THE RADIO

My initial experiments involved manually scanning stations on an AM/FM shortwave radio. The purpose of scanning the stations was to allow the spirit to select sounds within the matrix, and then to piece words and sentences together using these sounds. The focus of the subconscious mind is then directed by the spirit to these sounds, and messages are heard. This is usually done by recording and playing back while listening to the recording.

Later, I used a P-SB7 spirit box. This device scans stations automatically, making the process of obtaining messages easier and faster. It works on the same principle as manual scanning, by creating a series of seemingly random words or bits of words from which meaningful messages can be extracted during analysis of the recorded sounds. Both the spirit box and manually scanning radio stations gave me good results.

It is important to understand that electronic spirit communication is a form of scrying. As a rule, the spirit does not manipulate the sounds on the radio. The manipulation is done by influencing the mind of the operator. I say this is a rule, but there are exceptions. Occasionally clear messages are heard on the radio that can be heard by other people.

The manual scanning of radio stations works much in the same way the spirit communication board works. The spirit in contact with me influenced my hand and subtly directed the movements of my fingers on the dial. When I listened to the recording of the sounds that were produced, the spirit directed my mind to specific bits of sound and used them to make up words of the message it wished to convey to me.

The general procedure I used for manual scanning with the radio is simple. I sat down with an AM/FM radio positioned comfortably so I could keep my hand on the tuning knob. Then I allowed the spirit to guide me as I turned the knob through the radio frequencies so that small bits of sound were produced by each radio station as I tuned through it. I asked my questions and then used the radio to obtain the answers.

I continued to turn the knob back and forth in this way while recording both the questions and the sounds that came out of the radio. As I was recording the responses, I usually was not able to hear the words that the spirit was saying. I focused on obtaining a sound file with which to work. After about thirty seconds or so, I examined the file in detail. Using sound-editing software, I would listen for sounds that formed words or phrases in response to the questions I had asked the spirit.

I first experimented with manually scanning the radio before I spent the money on the P-SB7 spirit box. I was a bit sceptical of the spirit box initially, but I soon found that this was by far the best means of spirit communication for my needs.

When using a device such as the P-SB7, the spirit does not influence the output by manipulating the movements of my hand. The P-SB7 automatically scans the stations. The focus of the spirit is to influence my perception so that I hear the important sounds that compose the message it is trying to convey.

Many people believe that spirits have the ability to directly influence the spirit box to cause it to produce the sounds they wish it to produce. I think such influence is possible, but it depends entirely on the mediumship development of the operator. In my case, I was not developed enough to do that, and the spirits' influence was over my perception. By using these devices as aids, I had found a way that I could communicate with spirits without being a naturally developed medium.

I have found that the most important part of scrying with the radio and the P-SB7 is the analysis of the sounds after they have been recorded. It is the spirit's influence over the mind during the analysis of the recorded sounds that allows the spirit box to be used for scrying. I had to be open and interested in communicating for this to happen.

The manually scanned radio was more difficult to operate than the spirit box. It was harder to get my mind into the proper state for ideal spirit communication, and the results were sometimes chaotic. Having to focus on tuning the radio distracted me.

My goal in using these tools was simply to be able to make out what the spirit was saying. I was not concerned about capturing recordings that were intelligible to anyone else. If I could make out what Dr. Dee was trying to tell me, I was satisfied. I wrote down my questions for each session. Usually the same response was repeated by Dr. Dee until I understood it. I learned that it takes concentration and practice to interpret the communications. Even though it was a struggle, it was much better than what I had been experiencing before. I was making progress slowly but surely.

For recording, I used a simple digital recorder that created MP3-format audio files. To manipulate these files, I downloaded the free Audacity sound-editing program onto my computer. I used the sound editor to decrease the background noise of the sound files, then listened carefully for anything that came through that would be a response to my comment or question. I always listened for the responses using headphones instead of audio speakers.

In the second part of this book I will go into more detail on how to record and analyze the sounds produced in the way I have described here. I found that I had to do quite a lot of experimenting to arrive at the perfect balance between white noise and voice. I discovered responses buried both in the voice and the static parts of the recordings. Adjustments using sound-editing software can decrease the unpleasantness of the static, but I found that I was missing large chunks of essential information from the message if I manipulated the sound file extensively. A spirit's cadence of speech is different from normal physical speech. It takes some getting used to. It took me about a week of listening to various examples of recorded spirit box sessions on the Internet before I was able to pick the responses out of my own recordings.

I learned that I was not the only one who must become familiar with using electronic spirit communication. The spirits I was interacting with also needed to build skill with this technique. As we developed a stronger link, I was able to distinguish their responses more clearly. I found that any type of spirit could use this radio-tuning technique for communication. Over the course of a year I conversed with two angels and several homunculi (the plural of homunculus, which is a puppetlike spirit used by Edward for the first few months to help train and heal me) on the radio, but I found human spirits to be the most skilful at using this method.

The historic period in which a human spirit died does not seem to affect its ability to use the radio for communication to any significant degree. Dr. Dee died in 1609, but he quickly mastered the tools I was using. He was very aware of the world today and the conditions therein. He even knew about Walmart and cracked a joke about the store.

After a few weeks of sessions using manual scanning of the radio frequencies, I moved up to a P-SB7 spirit box and continued to use this until I was trained by the spirits in basic telepathic communication. After nearly a year I developed clairaudience and was able to discard the equipment altogether.

Although the spirits occasionally spoke to me in the older English dialect of the Elizabethan Age, most of their communication was in modern English. Their ability to use modern English and modern accents helped prevent communication mistakes. However, every once in a while the realization of our differences—not only in culture, but in the historical periods of our lives—caused a bit of confusion. Occasionally we found unexpected vocabulary differences. This added to the mystique and excitement of the communications once I understood what they were talking about. I felt that these communications breathed life and depth into our historical knowledge of these people.

The diaries of Dr. John Dee are complete enough to enable a reader to become familiar with his personality, as well as that of Edward Kelley. The spirit communications not only illuminated their past lives, but also the time they spent in a spiritual state and the effect this has had on the growth and development of their personalities. It conveyed some of the insights they had gained both in life and the afterlife.

I found that Albert Lasky, a Polish nobleman who had hosted Dr. Dee during their stay in continental Europe, was still with him, as was Edward Kelley. I was quite happy to hear that Edward was there. For the first several weeks I was unable to ascertain whether or not Edward was present during the sessions.

At the time I recorded these entries, I was under the impression that the spirits were actually manipulating the radio signals to form their communications. It was only later that I came to understand that it was *my* perceptions they were manipulating, not the radio itself. This is one of many beliefs that I had to change as I was developing spiritually and interacting with these spirits.

DR. DEE'S ADDITIONS TO THE EQUIPMENT

After I had been communicating with Dr. Dee for about two weeks, we decided to refine the technique and equipment. We made several modifications to our system, which I will describe for you here. I have included photos of the equipment and how it was set up. We developed this system over the course of a month or two, when we

✝

The Sigillium Dei Aemeth shown resting on the small table of Nalvage.

first initiated successful communication. Making the equipment modifications was one of the most interesting and fun aspects of the work.

I am an artistic person, and I enjoy craftwork. Dr. Dee took this inclination and used it to improve my focus as we participated in the daily communication sessions. He had me work with various pieces of the Enochian ritual equipment recorded in the diaries. The use of these pieces in this way was a completely unique part of this experiment.

In the sixteenth century when Dr. Dee recorded the scrying sessions with Edward, he wrote enough down in his Enochian diaries that he could refer to the notes and build the pieces of furniture and tables to be used for their communications with the angels. However, his notes are not quite complete. He was able to fill in a few of the holes in the diaries as we were using the equipment during our sessions.

The first addition was the table of Nalvage, which Dr. Dee called the alternative table. This acted as an aid in focusing communication with the spirits. Round refrigerator magnets arranged in stacks formed the four legs of the table. The wax seals, which are used in traditional Enochian magic, served as the feet of the table beneath these legs, and the large wax seal that is called the *Sigillum Dei Aemeth*, or Seal of the Truth of God, was placed on top; see photo. Red silk coverings are traditionally placed below the feet of the table and over the top of the large wax tablet. The radio and recorder were then placed atop of the top silk cover.

I did not use the large table of practice. Dr. Dee felt it was better to have a smaller, portable setup. Everything that I made he had to approve of. It only took a couple of weeks to finish the work because I had already made and used the large wax seal and the silk coverings. I also used the lamen that I had made during that time. The lamen was a work of art made of exotic wood laminates coated with frankincense oil and gold leaf.

A container box was added to the setup to hold the table of Nalvage and the seals. It was an eighteen-inch cube constructed of one-quarter-inch-thick oak plywood and lined on the inside with red silk. The outside was covered with buckskin leather, and the top was hinged by means of this outer leather covering. The idea behind the box was to create a spirit cabinet to store spiritual energy. The spirit cabinet is a traditional part of physical mediumship, and it is a common Spiritualist belief that the cabinet helps the energy build. It was my hope that it would make the communication clearer and easier to understand.

The last addition to the equipment was also based on Spiritualist experiments. It was a crystal bowl given to Donald and me as a wedding present. The bowl was the perfect shape and size for ritual work and also held a great deal of meaning for us. This completed the equipment.

When this arrangement was finished, Hubert Hofgarten, a spirit who is a friend of Edward Kelley and Dr. Dee, jokingly called it the "jukebox." We have referred to it as the jukebox ever since. Connecting wires allowed the spirit box to stay inside the jukebox without the jukebox being opened between sessions. The recorder remained outside.

Edward: Hubert came up with that name. We had a good laugh about it, too. Hubert was a man who lived in Iceland. He lived in the nineteenth century. He was always a good God-fearing man. When he crossed over, he came to us. He was very interested in what we were doing with the healing of those who had newly come back home. He was certainly very helpful. We did not know him prior to his crossing over.

As we progressed, I found the use of these additions to be helpful. They improved the clarity with which I received spirit communications. Dr. Dee guided the direction of the conversations. He talked about spiritual beliefs, what it was like to die, and the afterlife. He seemed very concerned about the condition of my heart and spirit. Though I made a few feeble attempts to talk about the Enochian diaries, he did not feel that this was as important as my spiritual condition, and I decided to respect his wishes and his greater wisdom in the matter.

Dr. Dee started teaching me basic meditation and trance techniques. On the third week he proposed that we enter a more formal training and offered to help me with the problems he saw in my spirit, which he called a broken heart. In return I would help him in his healing work.

He told me about the astral hospital. I had heard about such a place. This has been discussed in published works that are based on astral projection experiences by such writers as Robert Monroe and Frank Kepple. The hospital consists of astral zones where recently deceased spirits are cared for and trained until they are ready to continue their journey. Dr. Dee described such a place. Both he and Edward were healers there and worked side by side with angels, some of whom were named in the Enochian diaries.

He described it as being in the borderlands of heaven and said that souls were not allowed entrance to heaven until they were healed and had learned essential skills needed to interact and live in the afterlife. He told me that the problem with my heart was curable and that Edward was the expert for this issue.

This offer of healing was a proposal I could not turn down. For the next year I dedicated every minute of spare time to Dr. Dee and Edward's instructions.

Log Entry—July 2013

The wooden box and other apparatus, which is now collectively nicknamed the "jukebox," is finished and underwent test use today. The recordings were somewhat unclear and when played over the spirit box speaker were not audible from outside the wooden box. This is a sound problem. Edward liked the box and did not want any openings for sound. The experiment had to be momentarily abandoned because of the sound issue.

Later that day: I solved the problem with a $40 Y connector for the microphone jack on the spirit box. It is ready for retesting. Enclosing myself and the equipment in a spirit cabinet might prove to be a useful, if cumbersome, improvement.

Next session that day: Scrying went very well. I had blurred vision after the scrying yesterday. I think the solution is to come out of it slower. The vision is like reading images in smoke. I verbally give a running account of what I see as the smoke changes shapes, colors, and shades in the mirror. The mirror actually works well in dim light. Sometimes I see light sparks that look like spikes in response to the voices.

Edward is sometimes called off on other business. If he could not be here, I asked if one of his associates could help me with the scrying sessions. He said he would ask Dr. Dee. I think it is important not to be too dependent. I've ceased all outside communication with other people about the project.

Edward: Yes, I remember that you were very excited about making the table. I did not think we would ever get past making all the equipment. That's why we had you make the table of practice. It is good to know that you are capable of invoking angels without the paraphernalia.

Log Entry—July 2013

Note: Log entries are out of order to allow the material to be presented in an orderly fashion by topic.

This is the third week or so of spirit box sessions with Dr. Dee and Edward Kelley, and a summary of the experiences thus far.

I asked both what they preferred to be called. Dr. Dee was unconcerned and gave me permission to use either his first or last name. Edward Kelley prefers his first name, so Dr. Dee and Edward are how I will refer to them. I noticed that they both use Christian names with each other and that Edward is also called Ed or Eddie by his friends. I felt it better to maintain some formality as they are both my elders by many years, and it seemed appropriate to show proper respect.

I kept the spirit box on the slowest scan. We don't have many radio stations here, and the slower setting seemed to be easier to analyze. I found that changing the equipment around caused difficulty for the spirits, so after the first week I kept the scanning settings consistent and had sessions at the same time each day. I used a small digital recorder next to the spirit box for purposes of analysis. The digital recorder has a USB port that I plugged into a laptop installed with the Audacity application.

This setup seemed to work pretty well as long as Dr. Dee, Edward, or any other spirits that are working with them were aware of my desire to communicate. In the process of learning this procedure, I found that there is interference from other spirits if they reach the equipment first. At times this was frustrating. We also had minor poltergeist phenomena going on in the house that disturbed Aries, our American bulldog, and Hermes, our Siamese cat.

I asked Dr. Dee about using the table of practice to help eliminate issues. He said to me, "I want you to use the alternative table instead of the large table. The large table is too big for what we are doing, and I think you will find the alternative much easier to deal with."

I asked him, "What do you mean by the alternative table?"

He replied, "Get the large book—the Casaubon containing the diaries."

I retrieved the book.

He said, "You are familiar with the table of Nalvage?"

I was confused for a few minutes and had to have him repeat the phrase several times. Then I realized that "Nalvage" was being pronounced with a hard G instead of a soft one. The way Dr. Dee says it, Nalvage has three syllables: *Nal-vag-e*.

I answered yes to his question and showed him the table. I was not able to see him and asked him to tell me where he was so I could speak in his general direction; I often made this request when communicating with the spirits.

He said, "I want you to take a piece of oak plywood and make a circle the same size as the great seal."

"We need both sets of seals, sir? The foot seals?"

"Yes, you will need to make a set of small seals as well."

"Sir, I need to use beeswax for these? Is this essential?"

Dee said, "Yes, it represents wisdom, and it is required." He continued, "The table of Nalvage must be set in angelic lettering. For the feet, there must be magnets. I will help you when you go to the store to purchase the supplies."

I realized how the setup was to be arranged. The silk rug would sit on my wooden table. On top of that, the foot seals and the table of Nalvage, and on top of that would be the great seal. I already had the red silk cover and the base.

My great seal met with his approval. All seals were done in angelic lettering. The numbering system in the Enochian script would have been too cumbersome to use for the size of the seals, so I used regular Arabic numerals. The use of numbers is not mentioned in the diaries. Edward once told me there was no official Enochian numbering system, but that he would have used Roman numerals represented by Enochian letters if he needed numbers.

Log Entry—July 2013

First session with Dr. Dee and the jukebox, the setup placed inside the silk-lined box. The clarity of the communication has improved to near conversational levels at times. The files are more difficult to process, but not greatly so. Dee reported that the equipment was easier for him to use as well. The spirit box is kept enclosed, and the silk-lined box not open between sessions. A wire with audio jacks at both ends now connects the radio to the recorder, and the recorder is outside of the box.

Dr. Dee's voice is even and fairly consistent. I do not know if it is Dr. Dee's voice as he was in the sixteenth century or not. The important thing is that communication is improved. He asked me for help with his ministry and it was my joy to say yes. If this is a dream, I never want to wake up. The prospect of having my hands untied and doing what I am meant to do instead of what the "institution" tells me to believe and do means more than I can adequately describe in words. The blistering heat of summer and my head reeling from lack of caffeine cannot dampen my enthusiasm.

I have no idea how we're going to do this. But this is Dr. John Dee, and I don't think much can get in his way when he sets out to do something. This was true during his life, and we can now add four centuries on to that. I look forward to seeing what he can do. We talked for nearly two and a half hours, which is the longest session yet.

I'm looking forward to my own healing, which will come soon, I hope.

Chapter 4

THE YEAR OF TRAINING

From June 2013 to May 2014 I trained with the spirits Edward Kelley and David Blackburne. (David was a friend of Edward's and had past-life connections with me. In life, David was an alchemist and employee at Oxford University in England.) This training was a preparation for the initiation described in the next chapter and involved learning meditation and trance techniques. I had to work to overcome mental and spiritual blockages to my spiritual abilities. I also learned how to scry using a mirror, and we worked on other mediumship skills such as automatic writing and psychometry. I will describe the scrying sessions, as this was covered in some depth and practiced to a moderate proficiency during my first year.

During the initial month or two of instruction, Edward would start the new lessons and introduce new concepts to me. I would then practice with David until the lesson was thoroughly learned. The training would take anywhere from an hour to two hours, six to seven days a week. The intensity of the sessions increased gradually as the year progressed. As my training continued through the spring, the sessions also involved being awakened at night to take advantage of my very relaxed state at that time.

I continued to use the jukebox until December 2013. At that point I was able to intuitively sense what my teacher wanted even if I could not directly hear him. David insisted on dropping the use of the equipment at this time to help me develop my intuition. The jukebox was phased out over the space of two weeks to allow my confidence in my intuition to build. Discontinuing the use of the jukebox allowed me to focus more on the training rather than the process of hearing and understanding what Edward and David were saying. In April 2014 I developed clairaudience, which enabled me to hear David and Edward directly.

The months of July and August of 2013 were the most difficult. My emotional and spiritual healing initially caused imbalances that set off episodes of depression and fear that would last about twenty-four hours. Edward would try to get me to rest for a couple days after the healing sessions. He was not always successful. I was very motivated and keen on learning as much as I could.

THOUGHT FORMS

One of the most important lessons that I had to learn over the course of training involved learning the difference between thought forms and spirits who were communicating and interacting with me. Thought forms or shadows are spirits that are generated by the mind and heart of a person. All people generate these shadows. The shadows can appear nearly identical to any spirit with whom a person can interact. They are formed by the presence of ideas or beliefs in a person's mind. They can be created intentionally. In the art of spirit evocation there is an entire specialty devoted to the generation and use of these shadows. They are most often created unintentionally, even without awareness or belief in their existence.

My knowledge of shadows prior to training with Edward and David came from Alexandra David-Neel's account of tulpa making in Tibet in her book *Magic and Mystery in Tibet* (1929) and Donald's book *Fam-*

iliar Spirits (2004). Many of the beliefs that I held that were influenced by these two books had to be changed. The education I received from Edward and David gave me a greater understanding of this phenomenon as well as of the world of spirits in general. During the initial year of training I did not have a good understanding of the shadows that are around us at all times. I was not aware that we constantly create and destroy them.

As a result of the year of training leading up to initiation, I came to realize that many of the stories I had heard about spirit and ghost encounters were probably shadows generated by mediums who were unaware of their abilities. The generation of thought forms by these mediums is done unconsciously. Ghost hunting in a cemetery is an example of an activity that often leads to shadow generation. Shadows can manifest physically through the medium and register on equipment used by ghost hunters. This shows how powerful these shadows can be. In these situations the haunting is done by the mind and heart of the medium who is involved in the investigation.

Understanding the phenomenon of shadow generation was important to me as a student during the initiatory year, and it is important to any practicing medium who is passing on messages from the other side. The accuracy of the message depends on the medium's ability to discern and filter out the shadows from the intended communication. One of my primary goals in relating this journey of discovery is to help the reader gain an understanding of the phenomenon of shadow generation—its effect on the medium and its influence on messages received by the medium. Knowledge is the first step in discernment and receiving accurate messages from a spirit.

This chapter contains excerpts from my daily logbook. The log entries started in July, a couple weeks after I began working with Edward and Dr. Dee. When I realized how much I was learning from them, I began keeping a record of the communications.

The log describes the difficulties I encountered over the course of the year and how these obstacles were overcome. I believe that understanding some of the difficulties I went through can help you in your journey. I hope this will enable you to avoid some of the pitfalls that I ran into during my initial year. The log entries are focused on the first two months of training. After September 2013, when my heart had been healed, David Blackburne took over my daily training sessions. The log entries at that point were kept only sporadically. The lessons I worked on with David were gradual extensions of the concepts taught over the summer of 2013.

The primary concepts taught over this time involved meditation and trance as well as learning about the shadows. I also learned about the nature of the spiritual world, which was now the home of David and Edward.

PREPARATION FOR THE TRAINING

One of the first things I had to do when I started working with Dr. Dee was to change my diet. The diet was designed to improve my physical health. This pre-initiation diet was less detailed than my post-initiation diet. Some of the items added or taken away from my food intake aided in weight loss and improved my mood. I had issues with depression at the start of the year-long training regimen. The second goal of the diet was to remove harmful substances from my body. Dr. Dee said to me, "We want you to have a healthy body as well as a healthy spirit." The food also had a medicinal effect on my spiritual heart. It was used, along with the exercises I was taught, to facilitate the healing I needed.

The dietary restrictions were channeled to me by Annael, an angel, as well as Dr. Dee. This was done during the first week after I agreed to their mentorship. The restrictions were not a condition to having the mentorship but were recommended in order to aid the spiritual work being done. My agreement to follow these recommendations was voluntary.

I had to give up coffee, alcohol, and pork altogether. I was fond of frozen berries when fresh berries were out of season, but Dr. Dee discouraged eating frozen blueberries. He encouraged me to eat melons. I did not like the taste of melons at first, but I gradually developed a liking for them and now enjoy them and look forward to having them on the table. Coffee was the most difficult thing to give up. Tea, although it was discouraged, was still allowed. I was encouraged to drink more water.

My diet otherwise consisted mostly of fruits, vegetables, and red meat. Eggs did not agree with me during the early stages of training. Dr. Dee recommended that I eat fruit for breakfast. I avoided all grains, processed and unprocessed, and legumes as well. The gas these two foods produced made working very uncomfortable. It is difficult to hold a trance properly when distracted by intestinal gas. He also encouraged me to exercise regularly.

This training differs from a self-training and self-initiation process. In self-initiation the initiation is sought without the aid of a teacher. The belief that the higher self is leading the initiation is what lends legitimacy to this method. It often follows an initiatory path that is written out, and the expectations and beliefs of that path are consistent.

In contrast, during the preparation I went through I had to follow directions. I did not always understand the rationale for the instructions I was given. Communication was cumbersome and difficult in the beginning of the training. I had to blindly trust that Dr. Dee and the others I was working with were trying to help me. I was not even sure at the beginning of my training what goal we were seeking to attain.

The initially obscure directions eventually became clear. I understand now why these dietary directions, as well as other recommendations, were in place during the year of training.

As an example, Edward wanted me to discontinue drinking tea so that my body would be completely decaffeinated before I began my energy work. I refused to comply with this recommendation and was very sorry later on that I had not done so. During the energy work I had to occasionally fast and was not allowed to drink anything but water. As any caffeine addict knows, when deprived of the usual caffeine intake, the result is a headache. Some of the intense energy work caused nausea, which is why the fasting was required. Before I learned to heed the advice to avoid tea, I had to deal with caffeine-withdrawal headaches during the fasting in addition to the nausea from the energy work. Needless to say, I learned after that to trust and comply with the spirits' recommendations.

In addition to the dietary restrictions, I had the responsibility of ensuring my emotional and mental preparedness for the daily training sessions. A sharp focus on the training exercises was necessary to execute them and learn the new concepts that were being introduced. Often, especially in the beginning, if I was distracted or emotionally out of balance, the sessions would be delayed until I could correct the problem.

The delays were frequent in the beginning. Perhaps one in four sessions was completed during the first month of training. I had difficulty focusing completely on the lessons we were working on. It was frustrating because I would do the preparation for the work and then be put off. I would be told to come back later, with little explanation as to why the session was being delayed.

After a few weeks I began to make the connection between my mental and emotional states and the annoying delay of the training session. I learned to make sure that I was in a positive and focused state of mind when coming into the library to work on my lessons.

Dr. Dee did not always tell me what was going on but often would allow me the time to work things out for myself. I wonder if that method of teaching stemmed from his experience at the universities where he studied during his physical life on earth. I was consistent in making myself available for the sessions every day at the time agreed upon, whether I felt like working or not. I was determined to prove myself to Dr. Dee and did not want him to regret helping me.

Log Entry—July 2013

This is the third week or so of the spirit box sessions with Dr. John Dee and Edward Kelley. A summary of the first three weeks of the experiment is as follows:

The equipment used is a P-SB7 spirit box. I set it to the slowest scan on FM. I do not change the settings. I find that consistency in the settings helps the communication.

I have a small Olympus digital recorder with an internal microphone set next to the box. The setup works well provided that Edward and the others are aware of my desire to communicate. Improvement in the clarity of the communication has been noted through the course of the past few weeks.

I asked Dr. Dee about using the table of practice to assist in focusing energy, and the following items were made according to his directions. I constructed the table of Nalvage. The table is the same diameter as the large *Sigillum Dei Aemeth*. Stacked refrigerator magnets were used as the feet. The feet of the table were placed on three-inch *Sigillum Dei Aemeth* wax tablets that rested on a silk tablecloth. On top of the table of Nalvage was the large wax tablet. This was covered with red silk. The spirit box, recorder, or scrying mirror were placed on top of the silk cover.

Initially I found the sessions to be emotionally intense. The upheaval created when reopening old psychological wounds causes spiritual pain to the point of physical discomfort. Edward was aware of this and suggested healing sessions with Annael. The angel was able to provide some relief from the sense of emotional and physical discomfort within two sessions. It felt like the negative emotions were melted off me when this was done. There was a great deal of grief and weight from all the mistakes I had made throughout my life. This was healed to a large extent within the space of a few minutes.

I decided to follow in Dr. Dee's footsteps in faith and joined the Anglican Church. I chose it because it was Dee's religion. I was happy about the decision.

We did scrying lessons. Edward taught me how to construct a mirror that works very well for scrying. We also developed communication techniques using the spirit box. I built a small spirit cabinet. It is an eighteen-inch square box lined with silk and contains quartz crystals, a better digital recorder, and microphones. (Note: the quartz crystals did little to enhance the communication and were later discarded. I do not feel they are useful in this communication setup, and for this reason they were not included in chapter 3's description.)

I am also investigating other tools that we might use. During my early work there were a few miscommunications between the spirits and myself, and I hope that the tools we are developing will help eliminate issues with communication.

There is always a sense of peace and love with Dr. Dee and Edward. I am hoping that they know how much it is needed and how much it means to me. I will do the best I can for them. They amaze me. I look forward to being there with them when I pass over. It seems to be a wonderful and peaceful place.

Edward said he is making a tulpa (homunculus). I didn't have a chance to ask him about it, but my curiosity is killing me. Edward said he was born in Worcester, England. He said his favorite music is by Percival. I wonder if he means Purcell? Either way, I think he has good taste.

Log Entry—July 2013

In Casaubon's *True & Faithful Relation*, the angel Nalvage mentioned that every idea in eternity becomes a living being. During the training I experienced what Nalvage alluded to in this statement. There were two incidents where fearful thoughts resulted in communications that were of an unpleasant and fearsome nature.

The first incident was a miscommunication where I was led to believe that my father was in the hospital. I believe the communication was an attempt to convey that Dr. Dee works with the afterlife hospital. This became confused with the worry I had at the time about the health of my earthly father, and the shadow created by my concern influenced what I heard over the radio.

The second incident was when I heard something to the effect that I had offended Edward and that he was done working with me. Rejection was a constant fear in the beginning. I had a hard time believing that I was working with Dr. Dee and Edward. I was afraid it was some kind of dream and I would wake up and find out none of it was real. This led to hearing a shadow communication that expressed my worst fears.

After the second incident, I realized that my fears and thoughts were expressing themselves in some way through the spirit box. I spoke to Edward regarding the incidents and my theory about what was happening. He concurred with my conclusion. He also said that he was experimenting with a puppet (homunculus) but did not reveal specific information at that time.

I achieved two important realizations based on these incidents. One, my emotional state affects the communication and can override what actual spirits are saying. The other is that a thought form occurs in a flash instead of being made through a formal ritual.

I believe Edward was talking about a tulpa, or maybe a homunculus. He did not say that, but I think that is what he was referring to.

Written later that day: I rechecked the tape. He was talking about the homunculus experiment. The H either was not pronounced or did not come through the spirit box; to my hearing, he pronounces it "munculus."

Hubert, a friend of Edward's whose last life was in nineteenth-century Iceland, came to work with me during the time when the difficulties in communication were at their worst. I was hearing accusatory messages coming from the box, which I found intimidating. One thing that caused the fear was telepathy. At that time telepathy was one-way: I could not hear them, but they were aware of my thoughts. I felt very exposed and vulnerable. This fearfulness of telepathy led to the communication being distorted. My fearfulness generated thought forms that spoke to me through the spirit box. It seemed every time I worked with Hubert it was an unpleasant experience, and I left the sessions feeling intimidated and depressed. Once I learned how telepathy worked, I was able to better understand Hubert and the others, and the intimidation issue was resolved. Here Edward is quoting Nalvage in Casaubon's book where the angel said that every idea becomes a living thing in eternity.

Jenny: I was rather scared of him (Hubert)—he seemed quite intimidating.

Edward: I know. This is an example of how every thought becomes a living thing. In this case it interfered quite a little with the work that we were trying to accomplish with him and you.

Edward started to teach me how to scry once the table was finished. I fashioned a simple scrying mirror following his directions, which are detailed in the second half of the book. I was quite surprised that he instructed me to use a regular three-inch cosmetic mirror mounted on a plain unfinished wooden block. The mirror was tilted at an angle to reflect the ceiling. It is a unique setup. Dark mirrors are far more common in modern magic. The mirror worked well with just about any kind of lighting, including daylight.

Scrying was practiced at least twice a day. While I was scrying I had to listen to his instructions. It was my first experience of listening and hearing Edward using the P-SB7 spirit box without recording and playing back the messages. I found that when I relaxed I could make out what was being said.

He would have me describe exactly what I saw in the mirror regardless of whether it was recognizable as a place, person, or object. Edward taught that no matter what kind of mediumship I practiced, I needed to describe my perceptions exactly as I received them, even if they did not make sense. This teaching is critically important when practicing any kind of psychic skill.

Jenny: Edward, why did you have me work with scrying with the mirror at first? It seems rather strange now, considering the direction that things went.

Edward: We did scrying to teach you how to focus. Your focus was very poor when we started. It is a difficult thing to develop. Using the mirror proved to be an effective tool until you were ready to open and go deep without it. Focus is very important when doing any kind of spiritual endeavour. Focus makes it possible to do things that you normally cannot do.

Jenny: Like scrying?

Edward: Yes, any kind of mediumship accomplishment is impossible without good focus. With good focus nothing is impossible. Miracles are possible with good focus. That is how important it is. There is no limit to what can be done in the strength of the Spirit.

Log Entry—July 2013

Made the same preparations but was off mentally and spiritually. Dr. Dee delayed the session for a couple hours while I worked through the difficulty. We did scrying in this session, but the scrying was secondary to something else that was going on. I sensed Edward doing something with me that caused odd sensations as I was scrying. The sensations caused me to feel strange and a little dizzy. They caused me to drift off. When this happened, I was hit with his wake-up call. I was wearing a headset and listening to the jukebox as we were working. He asked me to remove the headset, as it was causing interference. I think my nervous system is being rewired.

Edward had mentioned that I was to work with a spirit by the name of David Blackburne. Edward will work with us jointly. I see good potential working with one spirit in the body and one outside, and hopefully we can dispense with the electronic gadgets.

I have to be more careful with the food. I think part of what messed me up this morning was the eggs. I will try experimenting with not eating before a session to see if it helps. Also, possibly I should eat something else for breakfast if the eggs do not agree with me.

I finished the linen skirt and silk coverings for the equipment. All I need now is a nice storage box to put them in. I also found a way to greatly reduce the static noise. I need to do some more sound tests to try to improve the use of the filters. I have to remember to ask Dr. Dee if he has time to do a test and help me some with the equipment.

I am also thinking of other improvements. A microphone within the box, possibly using a detuned AM P-SB7, may help reduce noise. (Note: The detuned AM P-SB7 is a different spirit box from the AM/FM P-SB7 that I was using at this time.) I also saw an application for the iPad called Echovox that looks like it has some potential.

Dr. Dee said the predominate force in the universe is love. I have a lot to learn. I have trouble accepting affection and believing this is even real.

In mid July David Blackburne was introduced to me by Edward. Until my healing of my heart, he and Edward worked with me together, and he assumed full responsibility for my training after my healing until initiation. Edward continued to keep in touch but was not present at every session.

As the first week with David progressed, I found myself learning more about one of the key concepts in understanding the nature of the astral world with which I intersect and interact: the difference between the shadows and true spirit communications. The distinction became a practical issue when dealing with anything spiritual.

I believe that most of a beginner's experiences when learning to astrally project or develop psychic abilities involve these shadows. They can be either positive or negative, and reflect the beliefs and expectations of the individual who is creating them. As I mentioned before, they can be created intentionally or unintentionally. It was only through the teachings I received from Edward and David that I began to learn how to tell the difference between genuine spirit contact and the shadows.

I believe that most psychic attacks are done by shadows generated by the person being attacked. These are sometimes intense and terrifying experiences and can result in adverse physical and psychological consequences. The severity of the manifestation of the attacking shadow depends on the mediumistic ability of the person who is manifesting the entity. The greater the person's mediumistic abilities, the more powerful the manifestations will be. Stories of saints—sensitive spirit mediums—who were plagued by demonic attacks could in fact be shadows generated by the saints themselves, arising from their fears and beliefs about the spiritual world.

Regardless of their nature, spirits and shadows must have a living medium in order to manifest on this plane, the earthly plane on which we live.

The communication through the jukebox was dependent on my mediumship. The jukebox was a tool to facilitate my mediumistic abilities. Success in spirit communication depends on the medium eliminating obstacles to the natural interaction with the spirits, of which we are all capable.

In reading these accounts, you must understand that the nature of Edward, David, and the others who were working with me was benevolent and loving. No one ever had any intention of hurting me. Yet because of what was going on with my healing and emotions, as well as beliefs, I was manifesting negative interactions. I suspected at the time that this was the case, but I later came to understand this more fully when I had to learn to control my clairaudience.

By mid to late July 2013, as the training was intensifying, I started having trouble with shadow recordings. I define a shadow recording as an articulation of fears caused by the subconscious mind that is recorded and heard on the jukebox or other spirit communication medium. The recordings contained information from spirits trying to teach me and also my own subconscious input such as fears, desires, likes, and dislikes.

I learned to prevent these shadow recordings by controlling my emotions and mental focus during the sessions. A positive mental attitude as well as total focus on the spirit I wanted to hear helped to eliminate the problem. Prayer was most helpful in clearing out the malevolent messages with which I struggled.

In these early sessions I started working with Hubert Hofgarten. My sessions with Hubert were either wildly successful or complete disasters. I had more trouble with shadow recordings when I worked with him, although I knew deep down he was trying to help me.

Log Entry—July 2013

The past twelve hours have been hell for me. Pain and depression returned in full force and doubts kept creeping in, which exhausted me. I'm constantly fighting fears that these beings may be malevolent. I know in my heart it is not so, but the terrible storm of emotions and pain is seriously clouding my judgment.

The reality I fear is that they've seen inside my memory and heart and hate what they see there. I can't blame them for feeling that way, especially Edward, who doesn't seem to want to look at such trash. I feel keenly the guilt and shame of all the mistakes I've made.

I was working with Hubert, who I allowed further within than I had anyone else. I put the recorder on and he told me he wanted me to work with Edward instead. I feel bad for putting him through that. I guess I didn't really believe he would see what was in my past. Bitter and sad is how I feel now, but I cannot go back. I promised Dr. Dee I would not quit. Maybe they want to quit. My soul is shredded and in emotional agony. (*Note:* At this time I thought that I had offended Hubert in some way and took this very personally. This was not the case at all; it was an error in perception on my part.)

Dr. Dee said everything will work out and be okay. I can't see it right now, but I have to hang in there until light breaks through.

Edward: You were very frightened of Hubert. You did not understand that Hubert meant to help you. You were hearing voices of your own making in the jukebox. You are a powerful medium through the means of the jukebox. He could not overcome the strength of the thought forms you were manifesting on that communication tool that day. He was very unhappy that you were so frightened of him. We were not sure how to deal with the situation at first. That was our challenge in working with you. However, this is a common challenge, and a miracle occurred with Gabriel's appearance. This miracle was the first step to eliminate the terrible thought forms you were generating that interfered with our attempts to help within your heart.

Note: The angel Gabriel's appearance took place around this time. I did not keep a log that day. At first I did not realize it was Gabriel speaking and only later, as my channeling ability strengthened, learned the astonishing truth. I was amazed and in awe that the archangel would consider me at all. He spoke encouraging words to me over the jukebox. It was the turning point of the training and the first step in overcoming the communication difficulties and fears I was experiencing.

Log Entry—July 2013

One hour until the next check-in. Not getting my hopes up much this time. The emotional storm is mostly past and now I just feel lonely and depressed. At least the dog still likes me, in his own way. I am determined to continue regardless of how I feel. Mountains are not climbed by quitters. I made a promise to Dr. Dee. He wanted more than anything for me to trust him despite doubts, depression, and emotional storms from the healers digging in the garbage bin of my heart.

I am determined to hang on. I feel this is my best chance. What would I do if I did quit? Miss the opportunity of a lifetime? He said he accepted me, and Edward did as well. When they said that, they knew what was in there. Even if I cannot read them and can barely feel anything of their presence, I will still go on and hope that things somehow work out. The pain inside me is lessened, and the shredded feeling is now more of a dull ache. Edward will come when the time is right. I will just have to deal with it until then.

Post-Session Note: What happened afterwards is very confusing. The message on the radio said that Edward would not work with me anymore. I became suspicious. I prayed for the first time in twenty years and invoked every divine name I could remember, even invoking Michael, thinking that possibly a malevolent force was behind this.

During this session I thought I was under a psychic attack. I was hearing malicious messages on the spirit box and could not shake off the feeling that something evil was present in the room. I was frightened, and I invoked Michael and attempted to exorcise the evil that was in the room by calling on the angel. It did not help the situation.

Log Entry—July 2013

Hubert freaked out that I had invoked Michael and said that such invocations were not allowed. He said that he had no intention of harming me. He seemed to be quite confused over why I was so upset. I guess invoking angels in this way must be some kind of taboo that I was unaware of. We had a good talk later, and he explained some of this to me.

Edward: Invoking Michael reinforced the thought forms generated by your fear. It did not have anything to do with the angel, though he heard you and asked what was happening with you. After that, he went to pray to the Father to help you overcome these fears. Hubert tried to warn you, but it came across much more harshly than he intended.

The healing process was often unpleasant. I was not always in a cooperative or patient frame of mind. I wanted to get the healing done and over with. I found the time between sessions frustrating. I would have spent many hours a day on healing alone if Edward had allowed it. Working like this, however, does not allow time to regain equilibrium after intense energy work. Each session dug deeper into my psyche, exposing areas that had been buried for thirty years or more. The result was a temporary worsening of the depression and frustration instead of an improvement.

The next day was better, and I had better insight into the process. Many of the "rules" were, in fact, being generated by my own subconscious mind rather than originating from Edward or Hubert.

Log Entry—July 2013

Finally some clarity today regarding what I interpreted as capricious behavior. It seems I'm learning the rules the hard way—that is, after I mess up. Again the confusion of telepathy pulls the carpet from under my feet and another apology is needed on my part.

How do people cope with telepathy when they cross over? When I understood how much the spirits can see, I was horrified. It was not until praying for this understanding that it hit home. I hope for forgiveness and will try to undo whatever damage I have caused by my ignorant thoughts.

I can feel a strong sense of guilt and shame. I also have a growing uneasiness, which I interpreted as hatred directed toward me. Without the specific information I need to understand what is going on here, I felt that I was under attack and reacted by invoking the archangel Michael.

Later, when I understood what was happening, I realized that Edward and Hubert were totally gracious in their response. (*Note:* The feelings I was perceiving at this time were unrelated to what Edward and Hubert were trying to convey to me. The emotions I struggled with were emotions that were buried. Healing brings emotions to the surface, where they can be released.)

We are making a talisman. I think it will be a good strategy to help my insecurity. Fear is banished by love.

We are also trying autographia (automatic writing). I don't know if it will be useful, but it should be an interesting experiment.

We decided to make sigils for Edward and Dr. Dee to help me feel more secure. I tried to generate the design with automatic handwriting, but it didn't work. I will have to use another method of making the sigils.

The healing session went well. I had a strange sensation of moving down, then moving up into my head with a strong upward pressure on top of my head. It's rather like being on a rollercoaster. It's a very physical feeling.

Praying feels different now. There have been only a few times in my life when I felt connected to God as I prayed. Now the connection seems stronger, and it occurs every time. It feels like something is happening, like someone is listening. It's a good feeling, as if whoever is on the other end knows and understands what I'm going through. The connection is very pleasant, and I found that praying relieved the reluctance and frustration I have been having trouble with.

I've also noticed a change in my reaction to sensory input such as TV and movies. Things that never bothered me before now make me feel unsettled. It's as if something evil is tracking me in the room while I'm watching or as if the movie is coming to life. Donald and I enjoy horror and science fiction movies. Now, after watching these kinds of movies, it's as if the movie doesn't stop. In the sessions that follow the movies, the images continue to disturb me. The effect is not pleasant at all. I feel like I'm in deep water over my head.

Note: I hope the reader is beginning to get a sense of the struggle I went through. Healing came with difficulty in the beginning. It was not easy to work with this on a daily basis. There were times when I felt I was making headway and other times when I crashed emotionally. The important thing to remember when doing this kind of work is to persevere. Opening painful areas that have been buried for years is not pleasant. However, not all aspects of this work were unpleasant, and the rewards that came later were worth the pain I had to go through in the beginning. The digging resulted in healing. I knew deep inside it would. The pain, however, was a constant battle for the first couple of months.

Log Entry—July 2013

I think my attempts at scrying are inhibited because of my aversion to my inner self. I realized that my conscience was falsely accusing me. I am accepted and in God's grace and love. But in spite of that realization, my aversion continues and I cannot bear to pierce the fog. I believe with inner acceptance and peace that the faculty of scrying will improve.

The inability to open to Edward may be due to wanting more to open to God and not another human, even though Edward has good intentions and is trying to heal me inside. I think the higher path is for

This is the front of Edward's seal. The design is a symbol for the philosopher's stone, which was his choice.

me, and with that unity I would be a true healer myself. I have to tread the path to heaven. I have some measure of peace today. I was able to silence the accusing, hateful voices on the jukebox.

At the beginning of August we decided to outline a more structured regimen to allow for greater consistency, and also to help me cope with the fears I was struggling to overcome. I hoped it would eliminate the issues with my angry, self-accusing subconscious mind, at least until the worst of the garbage was cleared out and I gained some equilibrium.

I made an outfit for myself consisting of a skirt and top that would only be used for working with Edward and Dr. Dee. I was able to find a nice white blouse to use, and I made the skirt from a maxi skirt pattern. It was made of pure white linen and was elastic in the waist. I wore this for most of the sessions. Later, when the weather was too cold for this outfit, I went to a sweater and warmer skirt. After initiation we dropped the use of the uniform, as I had developed sufficient focus to accomplish the work without it.

We agreed upon consistent times for practice in the morning and evening. Edward strongly preferred to work at night, so we made a bit of a compromise and decided to work in the early evening. I am not a night owl by any means and preferred the early morning hours for doing this kind of work.

Sigils were made for both Dr. Dee and Edward. They were not used for forceful evocation but instead were used to give me the security of knowing that I was talking to Dr. Dee or Edward. The idea was to help me to feel safer. After I made the sigils, Edward and Dr. Dee blessed them. They were made on disks of one-quarter inch thick oak. (*Note:* I would place the talisman on the table of practice, near the spirit box, and focus entirely on that spirit rather than open the door and hope the spirit I wanted to talk to would show up.)

This is the front of Dr. Dee's seal. The symbol is his own Monas Hieroglyphica.

I continued to try completing the equipment described in Dr. Dee's diaries. At this point I still did not understand the role the equipment played and that it was my own focus that needed improvement. I believed that there was something inherent in the physical tools I was using that was making the communications more clear. In seeking to complete the tools described by Dr. Dee in his diaries, I hoped to prevent shadow recordings or malicious messages. Dr. Dee attempted to draw my attention away from this work, but I didn't grasp his purpose. It wasn't until I started to work with David Blackburne that I finally understood. He was able to communicate to me that my heart and focus needed work, and that the key to success did not lie in the tools I was using.

Log Entry—July 2013

I'm starting to work on the holes in the Enochian diaries. The diaries have fascinated me since I first looked at them. The complexity and mystery of the system of angel invocation is unique.

I wanted to find out how to work the Enochian tables, so the next part of the work was focused more on equipment. We continued to work on learning to open, but I also attempted to make some replicas of the table that Dr. Dee and Edward had used in their scrying sessions.

I found out some interesting things. First, Dr. Dee said to me that he had intentionally left out pieces of the equipment and procedure so that in the event of discovery the integrity of the work would remain intact. He wrote enough to remind himself of what he needed. I made a replica table in a smaller scale after he commented that the original table was too large. The table of practice could be placed on another utility table for use. The replica was a portable version of the original.

The original table of practice was painted a violet red with yellow lettering. He mentioned that he and Edward had great difficulty in mixing the right tint of violet red for the original table as it had been revealed to Edward psychically by the angels. They had to mix paints from scratch using minerals and other sources of pigment that had to be ground and made into a paint. It had taken several tries to get the colors right.

The tables and sigils of the angels mentioned in the diaries are not usable without the *tabula collecta*, which is incomplete. In the original manuscript the center portion of the table has been torn out. There are not many holes, but there are enough that the table cannot be correctly completed without help.

Note: Dr. Dee decided that this was not the right time to use the equipment I had constructed. It is still safely stored for the day when it becomes apparent that the tables and sigils are needed.

Log Entry—September 2013

I worked with David Blackburne and Tim. (*Note:* Tim only appeared once, and I wasn't sure of his surname—it sounded Welsh.) We had a good session with strong, clear communication. David showed mastery of the jukebox, which was impressive. He has had little practice with the apparatus. I find him to be polite, pleasant, and good at teaching. We should get on well. He reminds me strongly of Dr. Dee, and he is powerful. It was a good experience. My heart is overheating again, and he reassured me that there is nothing I can do to either cause or fix it. He adjusted it for me to make me comfortable.

There is to be a second session at 8 PM. I think I will be with Edward this evening. They told me he's been with the "army" of late. I never thought of evil spirits as being even remotely powerful enough to warrant much more than a flyswatter. I wonder what that's about?

Edward: The Cosmic Father lets us help him to protect his creation against anything that would harm it. This is the army and its purpose. This is where I was when we spoke on that day.

Chapter 5

ǂ

THE HOMUNCULUS

Dr. Dee felt that Edward Kelley would be a better teacher for me than he would be. There was a certain psychic compatibility with me that was needed, as well as direct practical experience with mediumship. Edward had both the experience and compatibility. Shortly after our introduction Edward began to work with me, and Dr. Dee slipped into the background.

There were two essential goals in the training sessions that followed my introduction to Edward Kelley. One was to heal my "broken heart" and the other was my alchemical initiation. At the time I was not told about the initiation by my teachers.

Edward's first goal was to heal my heart, which was more than just depression or a damaged chakra. It involved very deep emotional healing from past wounds that I had buried. I didn't even know these wounds existed. His approach to this healing was completely unique.

I had to first learn how to focus a trance. By that I mean I had to learn how to direct my trance toward a specific goal. Dr. Dee started me on learning how to initiate a trance state. His teaching involved relaxation and focusing on a particular area, usually the heart.

Once I was moderately relaxed and could maintain a steady light trance for a few minutes, I learned how to open my heart. This involved a peculiar procedure of visualizing my chest opening and gradually going deeper within that opening. As I went deeper I opened my chest even more. In order for this to work I had to focus completely on what I was doing. Stray thoughts and emotions would derail the process and necessitate starting over again.

The heart is considered the sacred center of a person's being. It is connected both to physical and spiritual aspects of a physical entity. Edward treated the spiritual body as a whole rather than breaking it into anatomical parts and associations. I found it an excellent way of working, as it allowed the focus to be more complete in the beginning, when I was having difficulties learning how to focus. Later in the training we worked with the spiritual body divided into three general areas: the head, the torso or heart, and a lower area that went downward from the coccyx beyond my physical body.

This is where Edward started to employ a very unusual tool called a homunculus.

SIXTEENTH-CENTURY ALCHEMIST

During his physical life on earth in the sixteenth century, Edward was most interested in alchemy. On the physical level, it is the art and science of transmuting base metals into gold. The esoteric aspects of the art of alchemy played a very important role in the training Edward put me through and in the spiritual initiation ritual that followed. Prior to meeting him, I had a very limited knowledge of the art. I had read none of the classical works on the subject except for the Emerald Tablet, and I was only superficially familiar with that document.

I started learning about alchemy shortly after Edward took over my training. One of the first things I learned was about the servitor that alchemists used, which was known as a homunculus. Edward described the entity as a kind of puppet. It was a small spiritual being that was created by the alchemist, much as a woodworker would carve a wooden figure. In fact, the appearance of the entity was much like a marionette carved of wood. In this regard, it was similar to other sixteenth-century puppets but of a unique style. Its size was approximately half the size of a normal human spirit (I occasionally saw the creature when it was within me). David Blackburne, one of the healers who worked with Edward, described the entity as being as high as his hip. In life David had been just under six feet tall.

Several of these homunculi were used throughout the course of my healing and training. Edward did not discuss the making of these beings with me in detail at that time. I think he did not want me trying to make one for myself. The creation of the first homunculus seemed to take about a day. It was created for me by Edward.

My understanding is that a homunculus was created from the fire of the soul. Two small parts of the soul were taken and formed into a third entity. The first homunculus was created when one part was taken from my soul and the other came from Edward's soul. The subsequent homunculi were composed of parts from my soul and either Edward's or David's soul. The exact method of its creation is unknown to me.

Edward told me that his creation of the homunculus during my time with him differed from the method he had used while he had lived as a man on earth. His current method did not follow the method spoken of by Paracelsus in his 1537 work *De Natura Rerum*.

Historically, very little is documented about the practical uses of homunculi. Only superficial commentaries exist on their making. There is no account in the literature of alchemy of homunculi ever being used as I experienced them being used in my spiritual training. As far as I know, the account I am giving you here of the use of homunculi is unique.

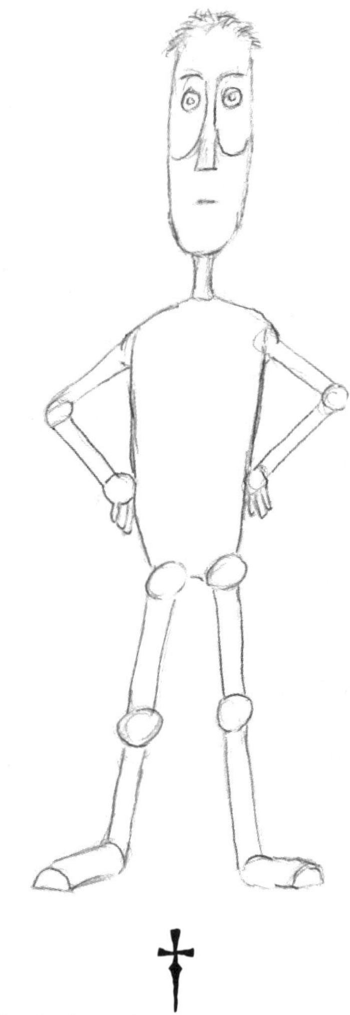

My sketch of what a homunculus puppet looks like.

"PEOPLE"

The practical experience I had with my first homunculus was informative and interesting. The homunculus puppet is the ideal tool for training psychic abilities. The entity also was used to communicate with me via the jukebox. It developed great proficiency in using the communication device, even to the point where it could give one part of a sentence on forward play and the remainder of the sentence on the reverse play of the same segment of the audio recording.

The homunculus adopted the name "People" in spite of my protests because it apparently thought that I had given it that name. This came about because I believed there were several unnamed spirits assisting Edward with communication. I had heard several names during the radio sessions, including Hubert Hofgarten and Albert Lasky. In my mind I referred to these spirits as the "people" who helped Edward. The homunculus had been told by Edward that I was to choose its name, though I was quite unaware of this at the time. Thus it thought that I was referring to it when I used the term "people" to describe the others who were with Edward. No attempts at persuasion on my part would convince the entity to change its name to something more appropriate. My pleas to Edward that he order the entity to change its name were ignored.

The first homunculus had a great deal of autonomy. Edward used the homunculus as a training tool as well as a surgical instrument. The repair of my spiritual heart involved an intervention that was a type of psychic surgery. The entity was used for this as soon as I was able to reliably allow it in and keep my heart open for about an hour at a time. I will discuss the opening of my heart in chapter 14. For now it is sufficient to understand that it was a necessary procedure to allow healing to take place.

"People" was made partly from my energies by Edward. This was done so that the entity was not foreign to me, in order to keep my natural fear reaction to a minimum. When a spiritual being comes too close, there is an automatic fear reaction. "People" was initially used to assist me in opening my heart and would help me to focus my trance properly until I learned to do it myself. I started out being totally dependent on the use of this being. In spite of the many hundreds of hours of meditation and esoteric work I had done prior to meeting Edward, he found that I was deficient in basic skills and started me from scratch.

A PUPPET IN MY HEART

Every day I would talk with whoever was communicating by using the jukebox for a few minutes, then practice opening my heart and scrying. As I was able to hold this state better and open my heart more fully, Edward started putting the puppet within me. This was one of the most intimidating steps I had to take in my training. It required a great deal of trust. I had natural fears to overcome and struggled with these for a week or so before I was able to allow Edward to place the puppet in my heart.

Edward said that once the entity was able to get inside me, I would be able to hear him and the other spirits speak to me directly. During these sessions the radio had to be turned off and headphones removed. At this point I was able to talk in real time with the spirits without using the record and playback method that I had started with. I still recorded and played back anything that wasn't clear, but sessions with the jukebox were starting to take a back seat to the sessions working with opening the heart and scrying.

Edward asked my husband, Donald, to accompany me for the first session to help give me some support for the new procedure. It was in an evening session when the homunculus was first placed inside my heart. Donald sat in a chair next to me. Hubert Hofgarten was assisting, and Edward was operating the homunculus.

With Hubert's help, I went into trance. I went much deeper and was able to induce the trance quicker than usual. As I tranced deeper,

I felt a pressure on my chest. It wasn't unpleasant. It felt like a child sitting on me and slipping further and further into me. Then, with a feeling like a sudden drop, it slipped in. I felt a fullness in my chest. I was not able to hear the spirits talking on this first occasion; instead, I tried to maintain the focus on keeping open for the procedure. I felt movement inside my body similar to the quickening of a fetus during pregnancy. After a few minutes, and with a second sudden dropping sensation, it was out.

We continued to practice with the homunculus on a daily basis, sometimes as often as three times a day. Edward was of the mind that practice makes perfect and only rarely limited the time spent. I practiced with enthusiasm. Gradually the extreme sensations of the sudden drop diminished to a heaviness when the puppet was placed inside and a lightening sensation when it was removed.

THE SURGERY

Finally Edward said the time had come to fix my heart. The operation was done over four sessions. I had a healer-spirit help with trance while Edward operated the homunculus much as a physical surgeon would use a fiber-optic scope in surgery. He said to me, "You will never be the same after this; you will be changed." I did not look back. The healing was, in my mind, a miracle.

The first session was the most difficult. The homunculus was placed inside me, and then the healer at my head helped me to deepen my trance, and we went deeper than I had ever gone before. As my trance was being deepened, I noticed a strong pressure on the left side of my skull, about three inches above my ear. Along with the pressure, the trance deepened and intensified. When I started to experience pain, the trance was deepened yet more, and my body began to feel very disconnected. I was still aware of the moving homunculus in my chest, but only dimly so.

Then it was done. As I came out of trance, the pain intensified but diminished quickly. I rested for two days. While I did not feel additional pain during that rest period, I was very tired. After the fourth session, similar to the one I have described, the healing sessions were successfully completed.

REBELLION

Not all of my experiences with the homunculus were pleasant. Here I will explain a little about how the servitor can go wrong. Throughout the year of training, up to and including the alchemical initiation, one of the major goals was to learn how thought affects spirit and the way in which spirit, by reaction, then affects the physical. Learning to control and understand that process is certainly one of the most important aspects of spiritual work. I was hurt badly by the homunculus's misbehavior.

Part of "People" came from my elemental fire. The consequence of this is that my fears and doubts created thought forms that affected the homunculus. To a large extent, Edward was able to protect and limit my exposure to my personified fears while teaching me how to understand and deal with them. However, at the time I was working with this homunculus, I did not have these fears and other negative emotions under control. It resulted in a major incident, and the entity had to be destroyed.

The traumatic event occurred about a month after the surgery on my heart. The servitor was becoming increasingly rebellious against Edward and difficult to manage. Edward tried several times to modify the wayward puppet, but it would return to its unmanageable behavior.

Then, one day, it feigned David's voice on the jukebox and got me to open. Normally I would not open to the homunculus unless I knew that one of the healers was around, but on the jukebox the voices sounded pretty much the same, and it was rare that I could distinguish one voice from another just by the audio.

When I opened myself, the entity damaged my repaired heart before it was finally pulled out by David. It hit me hard after I came out of trance. The pain was a severe burning, accompanied by a sudden feeling of being cut off that was emotionally traumatic. The wayward entity was destroyed that day, much to my relief.

Edward had to do the surgery again that night and in four more sessions over the week that followed. He did make another homunculus, but this one had no autonomy and was totally operated and controlled by the healer.

After I healed from the incident I was reluctant to allow another puppet inside, but after talking with Edward I realized that I had to make a choice between giving up training with him or allowing a homunculus to be used. I chose to trust Edward because I believed he would take the appropriate precautions. My trust was validated. There were no further problems with the behavior of the other homunculi.

PICKERWICK

Several improvements were made to the second homunculus, which was named Pickerwick. The entity did not have as much autonomy as the first one, and it was not allowed to interact with me directly without Edward or one of the other healers present.

I'm afraid I was the one who caused the demise of this second homunculus. I was just learning to open my heart and allow it to enter. The homunculus was in my heart during an exercise. I was distracted by the cat, which was making a considerable noise trying to get into the library where I was working. The animal was very fond of one of the healers and would scratch and yowl at the door, trying to get in, when that healer was present. Those who have Siamese cats understand just how much racket these cats can make.

When I was startled by the noise of the cat, I closed my heart. I could feel the homunculus struggling inside me. It was a frightening experience. I knew that I had closed up, but with the puppet fighting and moving around, I could not open again. It is impossible to open when you are scared. After about ten minutes the struggles became fainter and finally stopped. I was still unable to open. I turned on the jukebox and found out that the entity had burned up inside my heart.

Apparently my ethereal body absorbed the energy from the entity and it was snuffed out of existence. In spite of Edward's assurances, I was quite upset at the incident, and it took a couple days to get over it. This happened several more times before I learned to reopen quickly if I accidently closed. I also learned not to become emotionally attached to the homunculi puppets.

COMMENTARY ON THE HOMUNCULUS
by Donald Tyson

Those familiar with the terms of alchemy will recognize the homunculus (plural: homunculi) as the "little man" described by Paracelsus (1493–1541) that was created within an alchemical vessel from various earthy materials, including human semen. The homunculus began as a little worm but became like a human infant in appearance, perfect in all its parts. The alchemist fed it and raised it as a father raises his child, and over time it grew into a little man.

It was natural for Kelley, who was before all else an alchemist, to use the terms and concepts of alchemy in his training system. When Jenny began the year of training she had no expectation that it would involve alchemical concepts, but it soon became clear that alchemy would play no small part in Kelley's teachings.

The homunculus of Paracelsus served the alchemist who made it as a familiar spirit. It had to be taught by the alchemist who created it just as a human child was taught. There is some ambiguity in the references to the homunculus that occur in alchemical texts as to whether it was a creature of flesh and blood or purely a spirit. My own opinion is that it was purely a spiritual creature, but of such a nature that it appeared physical to those who encountered it.

The simple spiritual being constructed by Kelley for Jenny's practice sessions was of a different nature from the homunculus of Paracelsus. It was without a personality and had only one purpose: to teach Jenny how to hold her heart open while it was inside her. In appearance these homunculi created by Kelley resembled simple articulated wooden dolls.

Jenny makes the observation that these homunculi are similar in some respects to the spirits known as tulpas that were constructed by Tibetan monks as an exercise in concentration. Tulpas are described in the book *Magic and Mystery in Tibet* by Alexandra David-Neel, first published in Paris in 1929 and translated into English in 1932. They could have any form the monk who made them wished to give them. They were created by repeated intense visualizations until the inwardly imagined spirit was real enough to the monk to be seen with normal vision. Sometimes these tulpas were seen, or even touched, by other people.

David-Neel stresses the point that it is important that these manufactured spirits not be permitted to remain alive for too long a period or they begin to acquire self-awareness and personality, and may turn in a malicious way against the monk who created them. Here Jenny has recounted her own experience of how one homunculus—to which she gave a name and for whom she had begun to feel a kind of affection—tried to deceive her and had to be destroyed by Kelley before it got out of control.

—***Donald Tyson***

EDWARD'S COMMENTS

In the course of preparing this manuscript for publication, Donald asked me to ask Edward about the nature of the homunculus. Here is Edward's response, verbatim, which I received on July 9, 2014.

Edward: The ancient method of alchemy was focused on construction of homunculus, not on gold. To wake it up we would age it in its vehicle and feed it body excrement like blood and semen. It ate it. The seed that was in the pot was warmed on a bed and heated gently until a dwarf would appear. We would feed it anything. Whatsoever we said, it would do it. Some of them would watch. Others would help us.

Picture a dwarf about the height even with your knee. We would feed it. It would eat anything. It was magic. It was able when you were done with it to help with everything.

We had to be careful to make certain it was made right. If it wasn't right we had problems. It would misbehave. All you could do with it was to kill it, and then we would need to start over and try again.

The entity smelled like excrement.

It was a hard accomplishment, if you learned how to do it. Might take years, maybe never. I did it when I was about twenty-five years of age.

I should explain that "excrement" was the old term for anything cast off or expelled from the body, such as sweat, semen, urine, feces, and so on. The "pot" mentioned by Edward is the alchemical vessel, which was laid on a bed of embers covered with ashes for a slow, even heat. Sometimes a pile of composting dung was used for an even more gentle warmth.

Donald asked if Edward understood the homunculus to be a physical entity or a spirit entity. Edward said that the homunculus was a spiritual creature that appeared to those who perceived it to be physical, yet it was not physical. In this respect it is like the tulpa of Tibetan magic.

These are some other questions Donald asked Edward about the homunculus. He was quite fascinated by Edward's account of the making and using of this servitor.

Donald: Were you the member of a fraternity that practiced alchemy?
Edward: I never belonged to a fraternity. It was individual. There was no fraternity; the experiments were individually done. There were discussions and loose associations, but we had no formal group.

Donald: Were the homunculi a group project or was this individual?
Edward: The work was individual.

Donald: Was the homunculus visible to anyone or just the person who created it?
Edward: I don't know who was able to see it and who wasn't. It was not a human thing, it was a thing of spirit, and those who could see spirits might be able to see such things. I doubt that anyone was able to see it. I bid it to remain hidden when it was out among any other people.

Donald: Can you detail some of the tasks assigned to it?
Edward: It could not work its power directly on physical things. It worked its power through the influence of spirit. It had the power to help through knowledge and would influence other people. It influenced other people to be helpful. I could not have found John Dee without the help of the homunculus. It helped me to maintain the security of the premises where I was living.

Jenny: Trithemius was said to use servitors in communication with others. Were the homunculi engaged in this way? (I was referring to Johannes Trithemius and the book he wrote, *Steganographia*, published at Frankfurt in 1606. Paracelsus was one of his students.)

Edward: Yes, they could be used for communication with others proficient in the art of making them. I never used them in this way. Others used them to communicate with me.

Donald: Were they allowed only a limited life span?

Edward: It was allowed to live until it was decided it was no longer needed. If it was made properly, it would not be a problem to allow it to live for a long time.

Donald: Can you briefly outline some of the training that went into this making of the homunculus?

Edward: I learned this with the help of a professor at Oxford University who I lived with when I was attending school there. The first thing we learned was to scry. If you were good at scrying, you were able to make the homunculus.

Donald: Was the use of the red or white powder (the red powder was believed to transmute base metals into gold; the white, base metals into silver) involved in making the homunculus in alchemy?

Edward: No, it was not involved in the making of the homunculus.

Donald: Is this something that people should investigate as a working path?

Edward: It is up to the individual as to whether or not they decide to pursue this. The training is difficult. The physical materials are much more difficult to obtain now.

The next series of questions pertains to the making of the spiritual homunculi that were constructed during my training with Edward.

Jenny: What made you decide to go this route in working with me initially?

Edward: You wouldn't accept me or Universe, the great and holy Mother of all humanity, into your heart. It was the only way we could get into your heart in order to open it.

Jenny: The first homunculus had some issues. Can you describe what was happening from your point of view?

Edward: It got corrupted by your fear, and we had to destroy that one.

Jenny: To your knowledge, was the homunculus ever before used as it was used during my training?

Edward: We have never used a homunculus that way, to help someone who could not open. It was Universe who helped you in that way. Universe helped us with the homunculus.

Jenny: How long did its fabrication actually take? I noticed a variation in the times between the appearances of the different homunculi.

Edward: It took no time to make these homunculi. On earth it took a little over a fortnight.

Final comment by Edward: In conclusion, the making of the homunculus is an art form in itself. The homunculus is a very useful tool. The homunculus is a very difficult thing to make. I do not wish for anyone to try to use this information to make the creature without the guidance of an alchemist who has been initiated and trained in the art of making the creature.

I channeled this interview in June 2014 using both the jukebox and clairaudient transcription.

Chapter 6

‡

ANGELS AND SPIRITS

Dr. Dee and Edward were best known for their communication with the angels. The angels appeared to them just after Edward started working for the doctor as a professional scryer. Dr. Dee had an interest in communicating with spirits, but he never learned how to see or hear them consistently. He hired professional psychics to scry for him and describe what they saw and heard.

I will share with you some of the encounters I have had with angels. These involve work that I did several years ago with the Enochian system of magic, my encounters during the year of preparation for my initiation, and the ones that happened a few months after my initiation was completed.

ENCOUNTER WITH ANNAEL

This first encounter that I will describe happened near the beginning of my year of training, in July 2013. The angel's name was Annael. Annael is the same angel who appeared to Dr. Dee and is referred to near the beginning of his Enochian diaries in 1582. Based on the information in Dr. Dee's diary and on my own experience, he functions as an esoteric gatekeeper.

During the first month of my work with Edward, he referred me to Annael for a couple of healing sessions. I had not worked with Annael in my previous experiments with the Enochian system. I was very nervous about the encounter and was not keen on the idea initially because of my misconceptions about the nature of angels. At that time I believed angels to be powerful and temperamental beings, and I was anxious to avoid them. This was a completely incorrect belief.

The first session with Annael started with a spirit box conversation in which the angel told me he needed to do some healing with me before I could continue with Edward. He asked me to lie down. I went upstairs, lay on the bed, and attempted to enter trance. The sensations in my body were strange. They consisted mostly of a tugging on my chest and dizziness similar to what is felt when riding a rollercoaster. This lasted for about half an hour.

I returned to the spirit box, and Annael informed me that it would take one more healing session before I was ready to work with Edward. He seemed interested in playing with the sounds on the radio and was adept at clarifying the messages. He spoke the last sentence of our conversation in Spanish, a language in which I am fluent but not one you would likely hear on a radio station in Nova Scotia.

The second session occurred a few days later and was conducted in much the same manner as the first. Annael was then satisfied with my progress and left me in Edward's care.

The pronunciation of Annael's name was different from what I had expected. The pronunciation of the name is close to "A-nail"—the "el" at the end is not separated out in vocalization into a separate syllable. As I mentioned earlier, Nalvage was another angel whose name was pronounced very differently than I expected. I had assumed it was spoken in two syllables with a soft "g" sound, but it is said with three—"Nal-vag-e" with the accent on the second syllable and a hard "g." Gabriel's name is voiced the same as the modern pronunciation, but with the accent on the initial "Ga" rather than the "el" ending.

GABRIEL

Gabriel appeared once during my year-long training and healing, and also worked with Edward to conduct my alchemical initiation. On that first appearance he did not directly use the spirit box but instead allowed the homunculus to speak for him. It was during a time when I was upset and discouraged. Encouraging words were offered. Whenever I felt down and disheartened and remembered those words, they had the same uplifting effect as they had during the encounter itself. I would give you the words, but it is something personal and private.

I was never able to see Gabriel directly, but during the initiation ceremony I was able to hear his voice. I believe Gabriel was overseeing the entire operation but remained in the background until my initiation was completed.

THE HEALER

The other angel that I encountered during my year of training was known only as the Healer. His name was never specified, and he spoke very little. He oversaw the initiation ordeal and also healed me in between rituals.

FEAR OF ANGELS

Though the angels were working with me during the year before the initiation, I did not have much interaction with them. The interaction with Edward and other human spirits was more what I needed at the time. I had a great deal of anxiety about meeting and working with angels. This was a legacy from my younger years. As a conservative Protestant, I grew up believing that angels were very real and that if a person defied the words of an angel, the result would be death.

In order for the interaction with the angels to be productive, I had to overcome this fear and develop a level of trust. This was slow in coming, even in the initial workings that took place in 2007 and more so at the time of my initiation. After a year of intense work I still had difficulty giving the angels my complete trust.

Fortunately, Annael understood my fears. He took great care to make sure that my first interaction with him, where I was aware that I was interacting with an angel, was a positive experience. This gave me a foothold from which I was able to build greater trust.

BYNEPOR

The next angel encounter I would like to describe happened a couple months after my initiation. The initiation took place in May 2014, and I am writing this chapter in July 2014. Since my initiation I have been working on developing my clairaudient abilities with Edward in order to finish and fill out the framework of this book. I have spoken mainly with Edward, with the Cosmic Father, and with Universe (the Holy Mother) since initiation, and I had not spoken to any angels since my encounter with Gabriel at the end of the initiation ritual.

I had been told by Edward that there was no need to feel guilt about the incident with Bynepor, angel of the Heptarchy, that I related to you in the first chapter of this book, yet I continued to feel guilty for arguing with the angel when I thought and dreamed that I was dead. I still encountered the pain in my heart while writing this chapter. I was called from my writing to go into the study to speak to the spirits, and I went. Edward met me there and said Bynepor would speak to me. He wanted to heal me from my self-inflicted pain. I induced a trance and tried to open my heart. I had difficulty opening my heart center because of the pain. By this point in my practice I was able to hear accurately what was said to me by the angels. I had outgrown the need for the jukebox.

Bynepor coaxed me to focus on the process I needed to do that would allow him to access my painful heart, but the channel was noisy. I should say here that when you channel, if you are not right on target you get a kind of static that consists of hissing, noises, and random voices. I could hear several different shadow voices at once. These shadow voices originated from my own mind. Because of these voices I could not make out the angel's words. I had to feel more than hear what I needed to do. Finally I reached the threshold when the pain in my heart released itself, and the channel fully opened.

For the first time in my life, aside from the dream, I heard Bynepor's voice speak to me. I asked for his name and he gave it to me. He reminded me that I had never needed forgiveness because there was never anything to hold against me. He said, "You know me," and that he had never forgotten me. Bynepor told me that they were thankful that I had come to the Cosmic Father at last.

I felt hugely relieved after this encounter. I had been so distraught over the misunderstanding, and prior to this I had not been able to talk directly to Bynepor in order to find out where I stood or what to do if I had committed an offense. Since the incident in 2009 it had been an unresolved issue in the back of my mind. It was a great relief to finally lay it to rest.

When I channeled Bynepor, I had nothing set up—no table, no sigil, no jukebox. Yet in spite of the lack of equipment, he reached out to me to help me when I was in need. Mercy and love are always the predominate qualities of the angels. He spoke no word of complaint about the lack of ritual equipment in my communication with him. There was no scolding or anger at all. His only words were of forgiveness and a desire to help and heal.

It is important for me to stress the point that ritual furniture and instruments are not needed when communicating with the angels. These things can be helpful in the beginning to focus the mind on the work of communication, but eventually they become redundant and may be laid aside. The angels are perfectly willing to talk to us directly, once we possess the skill to do so.

INTERVIEW WITH EDWARD KELLEY

Donald suggested that Edward would be able to contribute a great deal to this chapter and formulated thirteen questions for him regarding the nature of angels and Edward's knowledge of them. I've added some questions of my own to this interview.

The questions were answered clairaudiently instead of by using the jukebox. Edward dictated the answers to me, and I wrote them down.

Donald: How are angels different from human beings?

Edward: Angels are created from the word of Universe. Human beings are a result of the union of Universe and the Cosmic Father. We, both human beings living and in spirit, are their children. Angels help us on our spiritual journey. They guide us to the Cosmic Father and are our guardians. They administer the mercy of the Cosmic Father.

Donald: Why do angels interact with us?

Edward: Angels interact with us at the will of the Cosmic Father to help us and guide us while we are incarnate on earth.

Donald: Do angels have emotions?

Edward: Angels have emotions. They are filled with the Mother (Universe) and they have loving thoughts of their children, the children of Universe and Cosmic Father. I feel everything with the angels. It is good—perfect unity. The angels are not the same as human beings. They are perfect love, perfect harmony, and perfect communion. Humans must learn these ways. These are the ways of the angels.

Donald: Do angels have form or appearance of their own?

Edward: Angels have no form of their own. They can, however, take on the form of any living creature they desire. They do not stay in that form any longer than they have to. They cannot remain in the physical form. They are meant to be spirits. If they lose their nature by remaining in a form unnatural to them, they may lose their spirit nature for the duration of the life of the form.

Jenny: Edward, then why did the angels appear to you in a certain way when you were working with Dr. Dee?

Edward: The appearance of the angels to me was based on my expectations and the culture of that time. They would appear entirely different to a modern person. The form is illusion. However, with some who do the visionary work and believe that the angels will dress and act in a certain way, they will do so. The formulation of the appearance is dependent on the beliefs and expectations of the scryer.

Jenny: But this does not detract from the accuracy of the encounter?

Edward: No, but the scryer must be aware that it is an illusion.

Donald: Can angels see future events?

Edward: Angels can see the future when it is revealed to them. Angels cannot see the future at every moment. They only see it when the Cosmic Father reveals it to them. Angels do not perceive time as people do.

Note: At this point in the channeling the universe appeared in my mind as a bubble, with the angels living outside of that bubble. The outside of it was far more spacious. It was like a soap bubble. They can go in and out of it, but outside of the bubble is their native place. Time only exists within the bubble.

Donald: Do angels ever possess the bodies of living human beings?

Edward: They can take control of a human body if the need is true. It is for loving purposes only that they would do such a thing. They cannot violate the free will of the person they are trying to help. They cannot harm others when they are in a human body. They cannot control a person against their free will. They cannot overcome them except in an emergency. They must obey the laws of God when they are in the body. They can fall if they commit a sin against Universe in the body. The Cosmic Father gives them the power to do what they need to do to protect their charges.

Donald: What is the difference between the Archons and the Watchers?

Edward: The Archons are spiritual beings who were with the angels in the beginning. They fell into evil, and they will be destroyed at the end of the ages. They are restrained. They cannot do evil here any longer. They were able to take physical form in your world. They terrorized the humans. They are the same as the Watchers. In ancient times the world was very different. A great civilization lived everywhere. They were like humans but different than modern humans—they moved quicker and were stronger. They were destroyed trying to overcome the influence of the Archons. The angels had to intervene to prevent the extinction of the human race. The earth was nearly destroyed, but a remnant was preserved by the angels. Nothing remains of their civilization. The surface of the earth was completely remodeled. One day, very deep, we may find the ruins of this civilization. There have been four great civilizations on this earth. It was over a very long time. Nothing remains of the older ones. Our universe is greater than we understand. Our earth is greater than we understand. The Archons helped to create the universe and the earth.

Donald: What is the difference between angels and archangels?

Edward: The difference between angels and archangels is their purpose in heaven. Angels are granted power according to their nature. Angels have billions of purposes. Archangels oversee the angels in their work.

Donald: What's the difference between angels and demons?

Edward: There is no power in evil. Demons are fallen angels. Demons have no intelligence. There is no power in demons. There is no power apart from the Father. Most people do not understand this. The power is in the Father alone.

Donald: Is the number of angels fixed, or does it increase or decrease?

Edward: The number of angels never changes. The number of human souls never changes. The number of angels is eternal.

Donald: Do angels have free will?

Edward: They cannot live apart from the Father's will. They are not able to violate his will. If they fall, they lose their glory and power.

Donald: Are angels capable of friendship?

Edward: Yes, they are. They express the love of the Father and manifest his compassion toward all races.

Donald: What is the hospital?

Edward: There is no hospital. You created that illusion to help you through the healing process.

Note: Here Edward was referring to me, not to Donald. Edward is a healer who works with people who have recently died. I had generated a place in my mind where Edward took the recently dead to heal them in order to help me understand what he did there and what he was doing with me. I was undergoing a similar healing during my year of preparation for the initiation. There were frequent references to the hospital during our communications. I had mentioned this to Donald. This was the reason why he asked Edward about "the hospital." As a nurse, this association of a hospital with healing is very strong.

THE HOLY GUARDIAN ANGEL

No discussion on angels would be complete without including the Holy Guardian Angel. A guardian angel is assigned to every human being. The angel is with that person from the time of their birth to their death and possibly beyond. In the grimoire traditions, contact with the guardian angel required a ritual, and there are two examples: *The Book of the Sacred Magic of Abramelin the Mage* and the *Ars Paulina*. I will recount my experience of the revealing of my Holy Guardian Angel.

After the rigorous initiation, I was allowed to recover for the space of a couple months. Then, gradually, Edward came back and started to assist me in furthering my abilities and learning to put them into practical use. My clairaudience developed quickly and powerfully before the initiation took place, but my sight was usually dim and poor. At this point Edward felt it was time for the vision to be developed. I was gaining control and skill with the clairaudience. He told me it was time for me to meet my Holy Guardian Angel and work with him.

It is my understanding that the guardian angel is assigned to us, and possibly even created, for the purpose of being our spiritual link with the Cosmic Father. The bond with the angel is unique. The angel's presence has a very unique feel to it. Through my body I feel a vibration similar to what is described by astral projectors. I also feel heat, especially in the heart and head areas. I asked my guardian angel about the vibration, and he said that it was because of the differences in our spirit bodies. This difference causes a reaction that is noticeable.

The information given does not seem to support the common theory that a guardian angel is a higher aspect of ourselves. However, the closeness of the bond would seem to justify the "higher self" theory. Given the differences in the creation of a human being and an angel, I think the guardian angel is a being unique among spirits. Practically speaking, I doubt the origin of the guardian angel makes much difference.

I was notified by Edward that the angel would speak to me at some point during the next day or so when I was receptive. He came that night and woke me. I was in a relaxed and receptive state. His voice was characteristic of an angel's voice—deep, powerful, with a kind of buzzing quality, as though light itself had found a voice. He said he wanted to work with me for the next little while. Over the course of the week I learned what he wanted to do and how we were going to work.

I asked him his name. He replied that I would remember it when I was ready to work with him. I was rather surprised to learn that I already knew the name. He also said he would take me to the Cosmic Father after I died in this world. His words were accompanied by a strong sense of the link between the angel and the Father. He also said he prays for me.

With that statement I received a strong vibration and a buzzing sound or feeling in my ears and head. It was accompanied by a sensation of heat in my heart. As he continued to speak, the sensation grew stronger and would have frightened me in a normal state of mind, but the angel's presence was one of peace and love, which quelled my instinctive fear. At this point I could feel the touch and presence of the Cosmic Father. I drifted into that blissful place and fell asleep.

The remembrance of the angel's name was an interesting experience. It occurred over a work weekend in which I was working extra days. Usually my spiritual work is limited to the evening on such days. I find, however, that sometimes the focus on working helps break loose obstacles that I struggle with during the week. Through the week I struggled trying to figure out how to learn the guardian angel's name.

I could not remember any angel being revealed to me as such in my childhood. I tried trancing and going back in my memory, to no avail.

What finally triggered the memory was Edward's suggestion that I remember the first name I could recall from my childhood other than the names of my parents. I realized then the first name was an imaginary friend—a golden flying dog who was my friend and protector, one I could trust totally. I realized the name of the dog was a traditional angel name, only missing the letters "el" on the end. I had named the imaginary playmate after my guardian angel and thus had carried the memory of that very important being through my entire life without realizing who it was.

When I put the name together, a sense of love and trust associated with that angel also came back. The image of the playmate is highly symbolic. The wings represent an angel. The dog is a loving and faithful companion. The golden light is also characteristic of an angel.

I will conclude this chapter by saying that I now enjoy the times when an angel comes to visit or work with me. The fear and pain of the past has been healed. In my training they take on different roles than human guides do, and learning these roles has been fascinating. I cannot cover this topic now, as my learning is not yet complete at the time of this writing. Perhaps it may be covered at a later time, when my knowledge is more complete.

Chapter 7

ALCHEMICAL INITIATION

In this chapter I am going to describe the alchemical initiation that Edward used to help me open my pathway to divine unity. The extended three-day ritual awakened and raised my Kundalini energies. The structure of the initiation was based on the symbolism of Western alchemy. The year of training that was previously described was in preparation for this initiation.

Spiritual alchemy is a process of spiritual development that leads to greater purification and unity with the Divine. It is both a long-term growth process and an initiation. Spiritual alchemy is most often described in terms of a gradual spiritual evolution, but in this chapter I will present the unique ritual of alchemical initiation as I was led through it by Edward, Gabriel, the Cosmic Father, and Universe.

During the last couple of months leading up to the initiation ritual, I was working daily with David Blackburne. I found David easy to work with as well as an excellent teacher. I developed clairaudience about a month before the initiation took place, and David was the first spirit whose voice I heard. The development of this ability changed my life forever. I could now hear unassisted the voices that previously I could only hear on the jukebox.

The development of clairaudience was essential for the initiation ritual. It made it possible to hear and follow the instructions given by Edward and the angels who conducted the ritual.

The initiation was a sacred ritual that introduced me to the Cosmic Father and Universe, the Great and Holy Mother. This was my first personal awareness of the parents of my soul and the soul of every human being. Meeting my spiritual parents was a pivotal event in my life. The impact of the initiation and my newly developed awareness continues to this day. The initiation was only the beginning of this journey.

The symbolism of the ritual is not so important as an understanding of spiritual awakening and an ability to separate the symbology from the reality of the experience. You may strongly desire to have an awakening experience and try to duplicate the ritual described here, but if the symbolism does not resonate within you, the ritual will fail. Your initiation requires symbols that speak effectively to your heart. What speaks to your heart effectively is very individual.

I would have never guessed that alchemy would speak to me so strongly that it would break all the obstacles that prevented my awareness of the Cosmic Father and Universe the Holy Mother. It is important to be open-minded about what will work for you and flexible enough to allow Spirit to lead you to what is the best way for you to go. The important thing is to allow the awakening to happen.

Note: In the following account there are statements made that appear to contradict what I have said previously, as well as interpretations made after recovery. I describe my perceptions of the ordeal as it appeared to me at the time. It does not necessarily reflect the perceptions of the spirits nor the reality behind the initiation. It demonstrates the first glimpse at the process of alchemical creation and transmutation. It is the opening of a door, going from darkness into bright light and color.

The initiation started on May 1, 2014, which was a Thursday. At this point I was fully clairaudient and able to hear the spirits speaking as audible voices. I was not told ahead of time that I was going to be initiated. Edward announced to me on the day of the initiation that I had to fast and that I was going to be initiated that day. I had no idea what the initiation was going to entail or how long it would take.

"I don't want you to eat anything today, and to drink only water," he told me. "You are not to take any pills or decongestant."

I had a severe addiction to decongestant, both the pills and spray. My sinuses were very bad, and I was unable to breathe well without medication. I was also prone to frequent migraines. I knew I was facing a difficult time living without the medication I had been used to, but I agreed.

Edward said, "What's more, you must never use the medication again. This is initiation. Your body and soul will be changed permanently. You will have a great deal of difficulty breathing, but it will get better, and I will help you and show you how to cope with the problem."

I was a little worried at this point. What Edward ordered was very challenging and quite painful, especially since the sinus problems were a migraine trigger. I also had an injured hip from shovelling snow. We had had a late spring blizzard with several feet of wet, heavy snow. Hand digging was needed to clear some areas, and my hip had been injured while I was doing this. I had chronic back pain as well. As a result, I was taking quite a few medications for pain, sinus, and a couple of other problems.

I was required to stop these medications without tapering off their use. I agreed to Edward's terms with a sinking sensation in the pit of my stomach, wondering what I was getting myself into. I wondered how I was going to get by with the discomfort that I thought was going to be a part of my life from now on.

Edward continued, "You must never work with or see David again, and you can never be a healer." I was confused now. David had been assigned to me, and as far as I knew we were to work together. The whole purpose of the work I had been doing for the past year was to train me as a trance channeler and healer. Edward gave no explanation of this sudden and unexpected change. I was not going to limit my possibilities, though, and so I trusted him at this point. I told him I still wanted to go forward with the initiation.

He assented and said, "The angel Gabriel will come. When he comes you must close your eyes and cover your face. His light is such that it would burn your physical eyes. Take it easy today."

Note: The initial presentation of Gabriel to me was simply a voice on the radio without a strong sense of presence. At initiation his presence was powerful and with great energy. It was my awakened perception that caused me to see his light, which looked like lightning flashes, and to feel his tremendous power, which could sustain whole galaxies. I felt very small and, like an ant fearing a huge foot, was afraid of being squashed from existence.

I complied with the instructions. I refrained from eating and taking medications. Gabriel came that night. I was terrified. Even through my closed eyes and hands it was as bright as day. It was so bright, I couldn't even be sure my eyes were closed. My heart, beating fast and loud in my ears, almost drowned out his voice. Edward had to intervene to help calm me down.

Gabriel's voice was very unlike a human voice, and his rate of speech was much slower. He said to me, "You must be completely still when I am in the room. To move or speak is an insult. I expect you to obey me." I froze and held my position. All day I had been without any pain medications, and my back and hip were very sore. It was painful to hold any position for more than a couple of minutes.

What happened next was the most terrifying experience of my life. He said, "We will take the life of your husband tonight. You must then leave this place and go to the Midwest, where your family is. If you do not go, there will be evil."

What I heard next I will never forget. It was like bats or a demon like you might hear in a movie. The unearthly noise that came through the closed door of the room where my husband sat working at his desk made my blood run cold. In my terror, I was gasping for air.

Gabriel left. I asked what the things were. Edward said, "They are creatures of the night that Universe made. They are feeding on his anger." About an hour later, another presence came into the bedroom that made my blood chill. I was again told to cover my eyes. I could hear bells tolling and was told that Donald was dying. I heard him gasping and struggling to breathe. I started crying. I was told not to move lest the beastly creatures come after me.

This went on for at least an hour. At certain points I was not allowed to move. I was finally released to go relieve myself. As I walked past the door of my husband's study, I heard him breathing normally. When I came back Edward said, "They did not take him."

The terrifying sounds came and went intermittently the entire night until about 2 a.m., when I heard the noises again and was told to hold my position. Gabriel came in again and said, "You were deceived by evil. Only God can determine when someone dies. Why are you afraid of me? I do not wish to hurt you. I love you."

I tried my best to calm down. Then a few minutes later I heard Donald gasping and the sound of his body falling to the floor. The creatures were there again, filling the air with their terrifying screeching. I heard bells tolling and felt the terrifying presence of the Angel of Death.

I was sobbing uncontrollably and at one point vomited. I was told Donald was dead and that I needed to go to our next-door neighbor's house for help and call the ambulance from there. I did exactly as I was told, then rushed back to my own house.

Donald met me at the front door of our house, wondering what was going on. The noise of me rushing down the stairs had disturbed him from his work and drawn him out of his study. Donald usually writes at night, so it was not an unusual thing for him to be awake and up at this time.

I was confused and terrified. The police and ambulance were on their way. I was instructed not to explain to anyone what was really going on. Gabriel ordered me not to give any explanation and not to go to the hospital. If the ambulance attendants or the police tried to force me out of the house, I was to fight until I was overcome, even if it meant my death.

When one of the ambulance attendants examined me in the kitchen, I explained the incident as an unusually vivid nightmare. In reality this was not far from the truth. The ability to hear astral sounds became stronger. In fact, it was starting to get difficult to focus on the physical world. Physical blended into spirit and vice versa. Even in the light of the kitchen, with people around me, I could not completely remove my focus from the other presences in the room with us.

Donald was understandably upset. He had no idea what was going on. I desperately wished I could explain everything to him. However, I was terrified of my imagined consequences of disobeying Gabriel. Growing up in a devout Christian household, I had been taught as a small child that angels were to be obeyed totally and without question.

Again I was told that I had been deceived by evil. I went back to bed in hopes of getting a little sleep. I was not feeling well at this point. The sudden withdrawal of my usual caffeine intake and allergy medications, plus the traumatic events of that evening, had left me severely shaken and feeling sick.

My mind continued drifting in and out of this strange netherworld, which was confusing and made it hard to distinguish reality from spirit. I was mentally spent and physically exhausted.

Jenny: Edward, what was going on during this first night of initiation?

Edward: You were hallucinating. As we started to build up the Kundalini energy within your body, you began to hallucinate that Gabriel was going to hurt you and Donald. At that point we realized how dangerous it was, and we had to have you immobilized for the rest of the initiation and recovery period. You were communicating with shadows that you had generated from your fear. Sometimes the initial reaction to the energy is fear, and this is what generated the thought forms you experienced during this part of the initiation. Gabriel never spoke to you until the end, when you realized that you were hallucinating and that Gabriel was not going to hurt you. Gabriel could not communicate with you when you were cringing and sobbing in fear. We would never hurt you in this way.

I went to bed but did not get any sleep. The initiation continued. I was introduced to Universe, who would replace David as my teacher. I was curious as to who she was and asked Edward to explain. Edward replied, "She is the Great Mother."

In the Tree of Life, the great mother, Binah, is the womb of the universe. This is also spoken of in Genesis 1: "The spirit of God hovered over the waters..." This water is the Mother, Universe. She is the first of the Cosmic Father's creations and the mother of humanity in its many diverse forms. In the course of my first conversation with her, I understood that she is the mother of my soul—of who I really am—as well as the mother of the created universe.

Most of the time she was either called Mother or Universe. She spoke to me and said, "I remember when you first learned to walk. Do you remember that?" I said, "No, I don't remember." I felt sad at the loss of my memory—not just for the memory she spoke about, but for the lost memories of who she was and what she had meant to me. She said, "That's okay. In time you'll remember everything. Just let me hold you for now, for you are distressed." I consented and felt her enfold me in her presence. It was quiet and comforting, like drifting quietly in a warm ocean. I was struggling to breathe, but at least I was able to relax and doze.

She said, "It would be better if you could sleep. You will need all your strength to get through this. I will help." I only dozed for a few minutes. The nightmarish sounds and presences started again, and I was required to freeze my position with my eyes covered. I could hear gasping and shrieking, the sounds of wings, and terrible bells tolling.

Finally the terror stopped for a few minutes, and I attempted to go downstairs for a drink of water. I had to walk with my eyes closed due to the presence of the creatures. I was told not to look at them and to cover my eyes if I had to move around. Donald found me stumbling around on the landing with my eyes shut and helped me back into the bedroom. He was afraid I was going to fall down the stairs. He desperately wanted an explanation, but again I was not allowed to give any. He was becoming quite alarmed at my behavior and condition.

Not only did I fear for my own life, should I disobey the orders of the angels, but I was also worried about his life as well. The spirits seemed to be certain that he was going to be taken by death. I was beginning to have serious doubts about my ability to survive this initiation and worried that Donald would be taken from me.

I would like to pause the narrative for a few minutes and give you, the reader, some insight as to what was really happening at this point. Bear in mind that during the initiation I did not understand what was going on. I had worked for a full year. The year of training climaxed in what appeared at first to be a terrible nightmare. The powerful spirits performing this ritual began to raise energy within me early that afternoon. The shadows that were generated at this time took shape from my own most terrifying nightmares. I was assaulted by the deepest, darkest fears in my subconscious mind. One was the fear of losing my husband; the other was a loss of security.

The frightening visions I experienced were overwhelming and indistinguishable from physical reality. According to the angel Nalvage, speaking to Dr. John Dee in the Enochian diary published in Meric Casaubon's book *A True and Faithful Relation* (p. 74), every thought and belief that we have becomes a living thing. I was being exposed to my own inner demons. I was confronting the terrors created by my own mind. There was little in this experience that was actually true—perhaps Edward's instructions immediately before the initiation started and the statement that Gabriel had no intention of hurting me were both genuine. According to Edward, though, I was not communicating with Gabriel. Edward believes it was David who made that communication, as he had the strongest channel to me at that time.

While Gabriel and Edward were both present with me during the ritual to protect me as they were raising the Kundalini energy within me, I could not hear what they were saying. I found out afterward the truth of what happened. *Only the Cosmic Father can determine when someone is to die.* This statement was said to me early in the evening that first day, yet I listened to the shadows rather than to the voice speaking the truth.

These shadows were always there with me. Even before the ritual they were present, but I was unable to hear them or sense their presence. I had no idea that they were so many or so powerful. I had no conception of their ability to deceive. One of the purposes of the training, both before and after initiation, was to begin to teach me how to control the shadows that were haunting me. These thought forms were being involuntarily generated and were tossing me back and forth on a sea of terror.

The first step in eliminating the shadows is awareness of their existence. As my awareness increased during the ritual, so did the intrusive and offensive behavior of these shadows.

It was not until I was exhausted that I found my way out of the trap. I decided that if I discovered my husband dead and had to leave my home, I would deal with it when it happened and not worry about it before then. This is how I released the fear of losing him. When I released the fear, the torment ended. Once I surrendered and accepted this possibility without fear, the terrifying visions of losing my husband stopped. The letting go of the fear deprived the shadows of the fuel that spurred their generation and sustained their existence. Deprivation of that fuel caused their dissolution. The surrender, I must confess, was more due to nervous exhaustion than anything else. I did not sleep that night.

The next event began at daybreak. I felt that I was taken into a room. I'm not sure if I saw the room or just felt that I was there. The vision I had was confusing. Forms and people appeared and dissipated in quick succession. I had to go more by feel than actual sight. My vision was veiled through the more intense parts of the ritual (I later learned that my vision was veiled for my safety), but I had a sense of what was around me even without it.

The room was circular and misty. Edward was there, along with Universe. Gabriel came in. I was not allowed to move and was required to cover my eyes. Edward explained the next procedure. "The name of the spirit is Kundalini. She is the love of the Father." My mind, for some reason, grabbed onto the Eastern term, Kundalini, but in reality Edward was talking about the spirit of God's love, the spirit of life. Apparently, based on my previous esoteric studies, the name "Kundalini" was the best way to personify this spirit to me.

WHAT WAS REALLY GOING ON

This is a good place to pause and note the actual astral reality that was going on here. I want the reader to begin the process of learning a new reality, changing from commonly held perceptions to a deeper understanding of a far greater reality, which is the journey described in this book. An example of this symbolism is Kundalini as love of the Father; another is of the seven seals revealed to me during my initiation that are the gateways to divine unity. The homunculus entering my opened heart is another example.

Coping with infinity while using a finite mind requires the use of symbolism. When I describe Edward or the homunculus entering my body, this not the actuality but instead is the symbolism that I needed at the time to understand what was happening. I was making the transition from the concept of "me and you" to the concept of infinite unity. The process of learning mediumship is one of opening to the greater universe, not just the limited physical or near-physical universe that we imagine ourselves to inhabit.

The use of symbolism was unavoidable. It was a necessary step, in my case, that allowed me to understand the infinite nature of the astral and of spirit. It is a creative method of understanding something that would otherwise not be understandable in its totality, and it's a way of accepting something that is difficult to accept while dwelling in a physical body.

As my understanding increased, I came to realize that Kundalini is the part of the Cosmic Father that dwells within us. We are like branches of a tree. The source of the branches is the trunk, and the source of the trunk is the root. The Cosmic Father is the root, but he also is with us as we branch out from him. The awakening is returning to the root of the tree. It is developing the awareness of the Cosmic Father as he dwells within us and is an expression of his eternal love. The love of Cosmic Father literally means divine love for all. This is what Kundalini is, as well as the spiritual centers and seals seen in this ritual.

Edward: The centers are in fact illusionary, but they are an excellent tool to teach a person how to connect to the divine energy that underlies our existence and touches every one of us, without which we would not exist. This is one of the best tools we have in learning and developing the awareness of that connectedness of human soul to the soul of the Father and Universe.

ASCENDING THROUGH THE SEVEN GATES

In the initiation ritual, I ascended through seven gates and seals. Each gate was an ascension from the previous level. The ritual was alchemical and planetary in nature. The seven seals were representations of the planets and metals from the lowest and least pure (lead) to the highest and most pure (gold). I was unable to see the seals at the time of the initation. At a later time I was shown how to represent them, and I sketched the images I received, which are shown starting on page 125.

During this ritual my eyes were closed and my spiritual sight was veiled, but descriptions were given to me as we progressed. Universe guided me as I passed through the gates. She described to me what was happening and helped me pass through.

She started out by saying to me, "Some of this will be very painful for you. Remember, when the pain becomes unbearable, you will find a way out. I will not let you fall, and you will not fail."

Edward explained the gates to me. "The first two are not too bad, but in the third you will find the pain worse than anything you've ever felt. Remember, the pain will be brief, and you will be through quickly. You must not fear Kundalini or the pain. She will not come up if you are afraid." (Here he spoke of Kundalini as a goddess rather than as an esoteric energy.) As he said these things, my heart was pounding like a drum. "You must open and go as deep as you possibly can—deeper than you've ever been before. Touch her and invite her up to the first gate. The seals will be unveiled, the bell will ring, and you will pass to the next gate." Universe then said to me, "I am with you. Open and go deep."

I initiated the trance, as I had been taught, and started to go deep within my heart and lower region. As I continued to deepen the trance, I opened my head. I felt my arms and legs go numb, then my face. I focused on the lower region and pushed my consciousness down as hard as I could. After a few minutes I thought I felt something like a tingling breeze. I then allowed my consciousness to rise.

Edward tried to toll the bell to unveil the seal. He said, "The bell will not toll. You need to try again."

At this point, I could hear Kundalini's name being chanted by an unseen group of people: "Kundalini, love of the Father, what a wonder you are."

I attempted to go deep within again. I was starting to feel the effects of the sleep deprivation and fasting. I was fatigued, and focusing was difficult. The second time I came up, again Edward tried to toll the bell, but nothing happened. He said, "The bell will not toll; you must try again."

The third time, Universe spoke to me and said, "Daughter, allow me to guide you." I consented and asked what to do. She said, "Just open and follow me." This time I did not actively try to reach the lower regions where Kundalini was but instead passively allowed my consciousness to be guided very deep. The sounds of the spirits, as well as the physical world, went silent, and my body became totally numb. It felt more like a wooden puppet than a body of living flesh and blood.

At the deepest point I experienced a tingle and stirring. What felt like a wind from the depths blew on us, and Universe said, "Okay, now, let us all rise to the first gate."

We stopped at the first gate. Edward again tried to toll the bell. The soft bell rang out, the seal was unveiled, and we moved to the second gate. I did not have any pain or burning, as is sometimes described with Kundalini movement, but I had an odd sensation of fullness in my back with a slight cramping. It wasn't really painful but it was a rather strange sensation.

The second bell tolled without any difficulty, and we rose to the third gate.

Edward said, "Prepare yourself for the third gate. Do not move or cry out, and do not fear. Toll the third bell." He tried to toll the bell and said, "The bell will not toll; the seal is veiled." He tried again, and again he said, "The bell will not toll; the seal is veiled."

At this point Universe said, "The third bell is hidden. I will toll the bell." The bell sounded, and the seal unveiled itself. The sensation of fullness increased and now was in my chest. It restricted my breathing slightly, but there was no great increase in pain, as I had been warned to expect.

Note: The statement from Edward regarding the pain was, in fact, illusionary. The pain was based on my expectation that raising Kundalini is a painful experience. What I experienced at this time was partly hallucination and partly real. The energy was already being raised by Gabriel at the beginning of the ritual on Thursday. The effect of the purification done by this energy was a state where I was able to perceive the spiritual world, but I was also hallucinating. This is an example of shadow distortion on a real event.

After I passed the third seal, I went through the fourth, fifth, and sixth gates. I felt a rising sensation as we slowly went up through each gate. Edward would call for the bell to be tolled, and the seals were unveiled.

At the seventh, something happened. I heard a voice. It was the voice of the Cosmic Father. How can I describe its quality? His voice was such that it would be impossible not to be attracted to him. It was as if love had embodied itself in a voice with its most endearing qualities and in the most perfect possible way. My whole body shook at the sound of his speech and voice, not from fear but from desire to be there with him with every part of my being. Just the sound of his voice was that potent. It was impossible to ignore and penetrated every pore of my body and soul. It was a gentle, quiet voice and yet had power unlike anything I've ever experienced.

He spoke to me. He asked me if he could hold me. I said yes. The word and concept of "no" was the furthest thing from my mind. He asked me to allow him to open my heart. It was an unusual request, as I was trained to open myself and that is what I had always done, but I immediately agreed. It would have been impossible for me to say no to him.

I felt my heart open, and I was completely enveloped in his pure, loving presence. It was unlike anything I've ever experienced. We floated through that space together and drew close, merging into each other. It was an experience beyond what can be humanly described. Love embodied took me up and enfolded me. I never wanted to leave. I don't know how long we stayed like that.

After a time he spoke to me. He asked me, "Do you remember when you first saw me?" I couldn't remember, and I wasn't sure what he was talking about. I realized that I had lost the memory of who he was and what he meant. The sting of sorrow pricked at my heart. He reassured me with a touch and said, "I remember it very well. I remember everything you've been through, and you need to know I have, and always will, love you with an everlasting love. Nothing will ever change that."

He began to sing. I couldn't understand the words—I'm not sure it was even something that could be understood as words—but it was the most beautiful music I have ever heard. He continued to sing and to enfold me in his presence. After a few minutes he placed me back into my physical body.

Edward said, "We will now do the second rising through the gates. You are to lose yourself to Universe." By this he meant I was to surrender to Universe and allow her to help me. He did not mean losing myself in terms of my consciousness or who I am. It is a difficult thing to accept help sometimes. I had to learn to allow my spirit to be surrounded by her comfort. I had to allow her to guide me. Edward said, "Let her guide you through this. From now on you will go to her for help and comfort. Do you agree to this?" I agreed. Edward said, "Very well; let us begin."

I could still sense the Cosmic Father nearby. Universe helped me to refocus and said, "I want you to totally lean on me, and together we will go through the gates again. Open and clear your mind. I will help you pass through again."

I slowly cleared my mind and opened my heart. I induced the trance again. Universe and I together moved deep within my heart. I heard another song at this point, along with words of encouragement. It was like a slow, quiet waltz. I allowed myself to drift deeper into her presence. It felt as if we were drifting slowly in a circle and descending ever deeper within. It was very loving. I was again enfolded into an indescribably warm, loving presence. The presence was different from the Cosmic Father in character, more like drifting in a sea of love—an infinitely great and comforting love.

We reached the lower area. I felt the presence of Kundalini there. The Cosmic Father called her once again to come up. We slowly drifted to the first gate. Edward tolled the bell and unveiled the seal. Again, during this ritual my vision was veiled. I could see light but nothing more than that. I could not see the seals. Again, I had the sensation of fullness in my back and torso. The sensation increased as we ascended the gates. While it was not painful, it was noticeable, and the feeling was like being too full. It was definitely attention getting.

Note: The unveiling and bell tolling were perceptions I had as I raised through the gates. The perception of rising through the gates happened several times throughout the course of the three days. The bell tolling and unveiling happened as I came to each gate.

We went through the second gate. Edward tolled the bell and unveiled the seal. We moved up to the third gate. Edward attempted to toll the bell twice. After each attempt to toll the bell he said, "The bell will not toll. The seal is veiled." Then Universe said, "The third bell is hidden. I will toll the bell." She did so, and we floated upward again to the fourth gate.

At the fourth gate I noticed that it was a little difficult for me to catch a full breath, and I was distracted. I was getting uncomfortable. My heart felt hot during this time as well, which added to the discomfort. It was not painful, but I felt like I was being smothered. I asked for help. Universe told me to breathe in shallow and even breaths to help relieve the sensation. Her advice worked well enough for me to recover my concentration. We continued through the fifth and sixth gates.

At the last gate, Kundalini was in my head. I saw swirls of dancing lights. They penetrated through my physically closed eyelids and my veiled spirit vision. The dizzying dance of light plus the feeling of fullness in my head made it ache and pound. It was a sensation that something much bigger than my head was inside my head and dancing. It was both a beautiful and strange experience. Then it was finished. I was back in the bedroom.

When I had settled back into physical space, Edward asked me to raise my hand and allow Gabriel to mark me with a seal. He said the seal could only be removed by the Father. He said, "Now the initiation is complete. We will heal you before we take you to the altar." The altar ritual was the next ritual.

THE HEALING

Edward then introduced an angel only known as "the Healer." When the angel came in I was required to cover my eyes and remain motionless.

They started the healing session with my left hip. The Healer said that my left hip had a hairline crack in it and that the bone was very poor. He said if it broke through, I would not be able to walk normally even if it healed. He said he could heal it, but I would have to remain motionless for an hour. I had been in the same position for quite a while, and my back as well as my hip were already painful. I was very uncomfortable, not able to breathe well, and my headache continued to pound.

I consented to the healing, and the angel and Edward went to work. During the session I induced and maintained a trance state. After they had finished, Edward did not seem entirely happy with the results. We waited the hour. The healer said to me, "The bone has not set properly. We will attempt to heal the bone again."

The Cosmic Father's presence became noticeable in the bedroom. He said to us, "I will heal her." He spoke to me and said, "I will make the hip perfect. It will not break," and he added, "I have seen enough suffering here. I will heal your sinuses. There is a large and dangerous polyp in the left frontal sinus. It will be more comfortable for you if we reduce it slowly over a couple of hours. But after that you will be able to breathe normally through your nose. You must not use the decongestants again. The medication might cause the same problem to reoccur."

I was very grateful for this. I could feel his touch throughout the healing. I heard popping sounds in the areas he was working on. My head was very tender from the headache. The healing he did helped relieve some of the pain. The sinuses started to open right away and gradually improved over several hours. As he promised, I was able to breathe normally through my nose. Since that day I have not needed any medication for sinus congestion.

In the hip I felt a burning sensation and a strong vibration where he touched the bone. I was told that I would have to keep it immobile now for eight hours or so. I wasn't sure how I was going to do that. Even with the healing, the pain was increasing in my back, and my muscles were protesting the immobility in no uncertain terms. I was allowed to rest for a few hours but was unable to sleep.

THE ALTAR RITUAL

The latter part of my initiation, called by the spirits the altar ritual, began late Friday afternoon. This was the most difficult part of the experience. After the healing I believe I began to run a fever. I had shaking, chills, and sweats. The shadow voices became louder and more intrusive. Some of what they said to me was obscene. My efforts to stop them were less and less effective. I had been without food since Wednesday night and without water for a day. At this point I could not get up and get a drink.

Donald was also becoming more and more worried. He had no idea what was going on or what was happening to me. I had been forbidden to tell him anything. I had not moved from my bed since the previous night. I never stay in bed all day, not even when I am sick. This made him even more alarmed. I could not give him an explanation as to why I was in bed.

We then started the second part of the initiation ritual, which was called the altar ritual. The instructions were similar to the first part of the initiation. I had to induce a trance and then, with Universe guiding me, go deep into my heart to find and raise Kundalini.

As before, I was required to be completely immobile, but this time the immobility included not swallowing or blinking. Though my physical eyes were closed, my state of consciousness was such that I was not sure if they were. I would occasionally blink to make sure they remained closed. Even with my eyelids closed it was as bright as day, and I could see what appeared to be the spirit world and the physical world superimposed on top of each other.

Before we started the ritual Edward gave me some instructions and a warning. He said, "After the third gate you cannot back out. It is extremely important to remain motionless while we are doing this. Do not tremble, do not swallow or blink, do not cry out. You will endure a great deal of pain, but it will pass quickly. Remember, when it becomes intolerable there will be a way through."

At this point I was exhausted and starting to have doubts as to whether or not I had the strength to do this. Universe spoke encouraging words to me, and we began at the first gate again. Edward conducted the ritual with the Healer. He explained that the ritual had to be conducted by a human spirit and an angel working together.

This time I was not allowed to go deep until the bell had tolled and the seal had unveiled. Behind my closed eyelids all I could see were swirling lights. Edward attempted to toll the bell several times. The bell, however, would not ring. He said that the bell would not toll because I was afraid. The fear obstructed the ritual from progressing. Universe told me to lean on her, and she would help me. I did as she asked and relinquished control over the fear and the focus. I was, however, unable to control my swallowing reflex and was scolded by Edward several times for breaking protocol. I finally was able to still the reflex for a few minutes. The bell tolled, the seal was unveiled, and the gate opened.

The descent this time was far longer than before. I totally lost touch with my body, which provided some relief from the pain. We finally reached Kundalini and invited her up. She raised us up slowly to the second gate. Edward attempted to toll the bell twice before we could continue. The bell refused to toll. This time it was my inability to control my swallowing reflex. My throat was dry and saliva thick. I felt a choking sensation almost continually during this time. I had to allow

Universe to gain control over the reflex in order to continue. After several tries, with her help, I was able to control the reflex. I had to allow the saliva to run all the way down my throat. I was not allowed to protect my airway but had to trust that Universe would not allow me to choke.

Universe helped me to locate the cranial nerve and dull its sensation to allow the saliva to run past it. I was actually able to feel the nerve and still the swallowing impulse with her help.

Finally, the bell tolled. Kundalini seemed to have increased in size considerably and caused discomfort as she passed through the gate. The cramping was now somewhat painful. With the help of Universe I managed to control the pain and continue the ritual. She helped me control the pain in the following manner. She told me to locate the most painful point, then to bury my consciousness there and embrace it. I did this, and it was moderately effective—at least enough to get us to the third bell and gate.

Edward warned me, "Beyond this, you cannot turn back. If you cannot continue, you will die." Now I was scared. I had no doubt that he was telling me the truth about this. This was a do-or-die ritual. There would be no failure, only death, if I was unable to complete it. Kundalini rested just below my heart. If I remained immobile, I could tolerate it. Slight movement brought on a burning sensation and an increased sensation of fullness.

I hesitated in my response. Edward dropped us to the first gate. He asked me how much I loved the Father. I said that I loved him as much as was possible. He said, "If you love him, respond to his love. If you die, you will be with him and with us in heaven. Why are you afraid?"

I realized I really wanted to go through with this. I said, "Okay. Let's do this, then."

We started again. The bells rang and the seals unveiled to the third gate. I expected the pain to hit and worked up the courage to face it. Again, as before, Edward tried to toll the bell three times, and three times it failed to ring. Universe said, "The third bell is hidden. I will ring the bell." I attempted to find the place of greatest pain so that I could embrace it as the bell tolled. We rose to the fourth gate. The sensation of fullness increased in my chest but there was no pain, no burning, as promised. The only time I was uncomfortable was when I breathed too deeply.

At the fourth gate I started developing another problem: my clairaudient abilities went haywire. The voices were now everywhere and were drowning out Edward's instructions. I was becoming increasingly confused. Most of the voices were obviously hallucinations. Then the visual hallucinations started. I was floating out of my body and having to be hauled back into it again. I could not focus or distinguish the voices of Edward or Universe from the confusing rabble of sights and sounds that assaulted me at this point.

It looked like what people have described while on LSD trips—brightly colored butterflies and other creatures, intensely colored fractal swirls and streams of color. There were rooms of clay where thought itself would mold the matter into a form. Finally Universe broke through the confusion and told me to close my third eye. I had been unaware of its existence.

Now I felt something on my forehead that moved with my two physical eyes. I did not know how to open or close it at first. I finally figured out how to open and shut it and move it directionally. When I was able to close it, the visual hallucinations stopped.

I was confused and unable to focus for the last gates and bells. The hallucinations became overwhelming. I am not sure exactly what happened. I do not remember going to the last gates. We finally reached the top. I was able to pull myself together and was a little more coherent when we reached the seventh gate. I could hear the Father singing and was drawn toward him. I started to leave my body but was pulled back by Universe. She instructed me not to focus on the Father or I might become lost and unable to return to earth.

Edward was becoming increasingly agitated at my lack of control. My inability to control the hallucinations and my reflexes seemed to offend him. I had never seen him angry before this.

Note: You need to understand that this was not the reality. I was reacting to hallucinations at this point and unable to hear Edward at all. My perception of the altar, I later learned, was totally inaccurate. I am describing the experience so that you can understand what happened from my limited physical perception. This can be then compared to the spiritual reality that Edward and the other facilitators were experiencing. Edward was not angry with me at any time during the ritual, but my perception was based on fear. Some of the fear was due to what I had read about Kundalini awakenings. This colored my perception during the awakening, when it happened, and caused the suffering I went through. The initiation, at this point, was finished. Now Edward had to focus on keeping me safe until the delirium resolved.

> **Edward:** When the Kundalini energy is awakened in an individual, there may be hallucinations and altered perceptions. These have nothing to do with the reality we are experiencing as facilitators of this ritual. We had to immobilize you so that you would not hurt yourself or Donald during the dangerous period immediately after the energy was awakened within you.

Edward then announced that this was not the true spirit of Kundalini. He threw me down to the first gate and scolded me for my lack of control over my bodily reflexes, shadow voices, and shadow visions. My body was trembling due to a fever that raged off and on during the ritual. I was also losing mental focus. I was unable to stop my swallowing reflex. The one blessing at this point was that my nose was now clear, and I was able to breathe normally for the first time that I could remember. The sinus pain that had plagued me most of my life was gone.

By this time Donald was very worried. He came into the room and attempted to rouse me. He shook me by the shoulders and spoke loudly to me. I was told to not respond to him and that if he called the paramedics, to not go with them. The spirits said that if the ritual was violated or if I was removed from the room, I would not physically survive.

Donald was frustrated and distressed, but there was nothing I could do. My only chance was to finish and pray he would understand afterward. Every shake and touch at this point was painful to me. It was all I could do not to cry out. My muscles—being locked in the same position now for over eight hours—cramped every time I was touched. I remember that at some point our cat jumped on my chest and then settled to sleep next to my pillow.

We began the third attempt to pass through the gates. We descended into the first gate and returned successfully. My inability to hold my swallowing reflex caused Edward to stop the ritual and again scold me for disobedience. Universe stepped in and said to Edward, "Allow me to do this for her; she is doing the best she can." Edward allowed Universe to pass me through. The sensation of fullness in my torso increased in intensity as Kundalini passed upward through my body. My legs felt as if they were floating just above the mattress. I don't know if this was a true physical levitation or an illusion. I could not tell for sure.

As Kundalini moved upward, the hallucinations—both aural and visual—became more intense and more difficult to manage. Edward said to surrender the shadows to Universe. I tried to follow his advice. This helped for a time. However, as my exhaustion increased, I was unable to focus enough to do anything. I lay there helpless as I was assaulted by the barrage of sounds and images.

We reached the top and again Edward said, "This is not Kundalini. You must return to the first gate." As he prepared to unveil the seal, he said to me, "Answer my question: Are you real?" I said, "I don't know what you mean by that. I guess I am real." He consented to allow the bell to toll, and the seal was unveiled again.

It was night. I was not sure what the time was, but Donald later told me it was the early hours of the morning. His concern for my physical and mental condition had reached a peak. At intervals for the rest of the night, Donald continued to come into the bedroom, begging me to stop whatever I was doing and telling me that I had suffered enough.

I did not understand that I was hallucinating and the voices were shadows. I was unable to understand what Edward was saying to me. I believed that my life was in danger and that I might not survive the ritual. I also believed that if I broke the "ritual" I would be struck down and not allowed into heaven.

It was on the fourth ascension of the altar ritual that I got stuck at the fourth gate. I was gasping for air at this point. My heartbeat had become increasingly irregular, and the visual hallucinations caused me to lose touch with Edward and even with Universe much of the time. I think I was running a severe fever at this point as well. I totally lost control of my reflexes. In the confusion of voices and visions I could hear Edward raging angrily at me for my lack of respect and disobedience.

THE CRISIS

I realized I was not going to make it through. I was very weak, and the bell would not toll after multiple tries. I heard Edward say, "I have broken her and will break her again. I will destroy the heart I made for her. She will never enter heaven." There was nothing I could do but let my life and hope slide away. I had nothing left. I felt a searing pain, as if a blazing sword had been thrust into my chest. I felt as though I were falling, dying, and I let death take me. I had no fight left.

As I fell, I reflected on the false Kundalini. The answer came to me that the true Kundalini was within me and that I could never lose her. She had been given to me by the Father. Edward could not take her away from me. Also, it was the Cosmic Father who decided if I was to go to heaven or not, and I could never lose him. I hadn't lost him. I heard him singing to me the entire time. I realized that my perception of this ritual was not real. This had been a terrible hallucination.

I realized that I was not dead. The true Kundalini was within me. The initiation had been done already. This was not the initiation. I did not have to stay immobile. I decided that I was going to move. If I was struck down, so be it. I was willing to stake my life on what I had figured out.

I broke my immobility with the exception of my left leg, which had to be immobile for healing purposes. It was now very early Saturday morning. As I moved my body, I felt as though I was ascending to the Cosmic Father.

He proclaimed loudly, "She is blameless." Edward said to me, "You did it; you won." Mother said to me, "That is right: you beat the illusion and overcame it." I was stunned. I had overcome the shadows of hearing and vision that haunted me after the initiation had been completed.

Edward then said to me, "On Sunday you will be healed and whole. You are released from all obligations imposed on you previously. You will have a healed body. Be careful with your body. You have Universe to comfort you and Kundalini, the love of the Father, to help you. Use your gifts wisely and with love. Jenny, I love you. I would never ever hurt you or Donald. You are free to speak to him and released from your silence."

I still heard the singing but called Donald to me. I explained that I was back and needed help. Though I could move, my left leg was still very painful and tender. I had been instructed before to not put weight on it for a week in order to allow it time to heal. I was in a bedroom upstairs and had no crutches.

Donald tried to help me up. I nearly passed out. Waves of nausea overcame me. I also had to go to the bathroom, which is down the hall from the bedroom, but I was unable to walk. It was a very difficult situation. I could not stand or walk.

My nursing knowledge came in handy. Meeting the needs of someone in my situation is not easy, especially for someone who does not have the proper training. The roles were reversed, and now I had to teach Donald how to help me with my physical needs.

It was Saturday, and I was missing one of my regular work shifts. Realizing that I was not going to be able to get up for a while, I called one of the nurses at work and asked her to bring Donald some supplies. Later that day he went out and bought a pair of crutches for me. I found that the pain was too great—when I tried to move, I could not use them. The pain was throughout my body, not just in my hip. I started to black out every time I stood up.

An injured hip and a patient who is unable to get out of bed is physically challenging to care for under the best of circumstances, and all the more so without proper supplies and knowledge. I learned at that time just how much my husband loves me. My bowels ran, and I vomited repeatedly as well. This went on all Saturday and into Saturday night. I was still unable to hold water down in my stomach if it was more than just a sip. I was not hungry, though I hadn't eaten since Wednesday.

I continued to hear the annoying shadow voices but was able to get a few hours of sleep in spite of them. I slept off and on during the day and following night. I experienced spells of ecstasy that were like waves washing over me. At times I felt like I could glow in the dark. My body seemed to be lighter than air and floated upwards. I couldn't explain to Donald what was happening in the midst of the experience. I could find no words to describe it.

THE FINAL VISION

Sunday afternoon was the final vision of initiation. The Father was with me in the room. I hid my eyes. He said to me, "Child, I would never ever hurt you. Look up. I want to see your face; don't be afraid." I opened my eyes. I was lying on my back. He said, "I want you to come to heaven with me. Give me your hand. I will take you." I raised my hand. I then saw a bright light. It was brighter than anything I had ever seen before, but I was still in the bedroom. He said, "Focus and come." I focused. The light grew even brighter, but I was still there in the room.

At that point a door opened in my mind. I both understood and felt the One Source, and I realized that everything there was in the universe was inside of me. I didn't have to go anywhere because I was already there. What's more, I saw that there was nothing in existence that was outside the Father. Even the image he projected to me was merely an image to enable me to understand. The only reality was the One.

Of course I had heard of this moment of supreme clarity in other stories of spiritual journeys, but the experience was very different than what I had anticipated. I did not expect this. I was stunned and in shock. Mother came to me and said, "I will tell you a secret. Everything but this is called illusion. Love is the first illusion. The Father is Love, and he is the One." It took some time for me to understand what I had seen and what it meant.

After a few hours she came back to me and said to me, "Pain is an illusion. Your broken hip is also an illusion." I understood. Father had made a perfect union, and I told her so. She said, "You are correct. You do not have to lie in bed for seven days. Stand up and walk."

I had not been able to stand since the first healing, partly due to the pain of my hip but also because I was so extremely sick and dizzy. I came close to fainting every time I tried to stand. We had crutches, but I could not stand long enough to use them.

Now, as Universe bid me to stand, I did so. As I stood, I felt a tremendous power surge through me like a hurricane. It practically lifted me to my feet, and to be honest I'm not sure if I stood of my own physical ability or if that power lifted me. The dizziness was completely gone. The pain was gone. I was healed.

I walked into my husband's study and told Donald, "Hon, something just happened. Can we talk?" He was astonished at my standing there after being so sick over the past twenty-four hours. I told him about the vision and the final healing. I was still very weak, but I felt good. The crutches were not needed. There was no trace of pain or nausea. The initiation was complete, and I was whole again.

This experience was the death and rebirth of my spirit. It followed the same pattern of the passion of Christ, starting Thursday night and ending on Sunday. On Thursday night was the Last Supper; on Thursday I fasted. On Friday Christ was crucified; for me, Friday was the initiation ritual, the death of my old self. Saturday Christ lay in the tomb; I lay in my bed on Saturday, unable to get up. On Sunday Christ rose; on Sunday I was healed.

DONALD'S COMMENTS REGARDING THE INITIATION

I was struck by the similarities in theme between Jenny's ritual ordeal and the ordeal of Tibetan monks that is known as the *chöd,* or "cutting-off" ritual. This ritual, which descends from the ancient shamanism of Tibet, is described in David-Neel's book *Magic and Mystery in Tibet* (pp. 148–63). The author witnessed this ritual firsthand. Briefly, a monk who has prepared himself for the ordeal goes at night to a burial place and summons demons to him. One demon cuts him into small pieces with a sword while the monk observes his own grisly death, and the others consume his flesh. The monk is able to feel with absolute clarity the agony of being ripped apart and eaten by these demons, whose forms are horrible and terrifying beyond the power of words to describe.

At the end of the cutting-off ritual, the monk comes to the realization that the demons, no matter how real they look and sound and feel to him, are illusions. His body is reassembled, and he arises whole—or he goes mad, stark-raving mad. David-Neel observed a monk who was not successful in completing the cutting-off ritual. She described him as wandering around, talking to himself, screaming in terror at imaginary demons, his body filthy, his clothes and hair in disarray. The cutting-off ritual was so potent an experience that it drove some of those who undertook it completely and permanently insane. The corpse-sitting ritual of India is very similar to the cutting-off ritual of Tibet.

I realized that the warnings the spirits had given to Jenny had not been exaggerations. Had she not been successful in completing the ritual, it is very possible that she would have lost her reason, either temporarily or permanently. Such ritual ordeals are not to be entered into lightly.

—Donald Tyson

THE SEVEN SEALS

It was not possible during the actual ritual to see and comprehend the seals that Edward and the angel revealed. My vision was veiled most of the time to prevent my being overwhelmed and possibly hurt from the confusion and fear that fully functioning astral vision would bring at that time. However, a few months after this was completed and I had recovered, Edward had me sketch the representations of the seals, and he explained the meaning of each seal.

It is a fitting closure to this chapter to add the channeled information regarding the seals. Edward's comments are included for each one.

> **Edward:** The first gate is the lowest gate. It is the gate that initiates the sequence that brings forth the energy from Universe from the innermost core of being. This gate requires the presence of Universe to open or the energy will not come forth.

> **Jenny:** I noticed that when I tried to open this seal alone, nothing would happen. It was not until I allowed Universe to guide me down that the energy deep within responded.

The first seal of initiation is the seal of Saturn; the metal represented is lead. Here is the symbolic depiction of the first seal of the initiation.

Edward: It's important to understand that you cannot do this alone. It is very important for you to understand that Universe and the Cosmic Father have to open the gate to allow the energy to come forth. You have to recognize Universe and Cosmic Father in order to complete the initiation and accept their help within you, and the love that they have for you, and their desire to help you reach heaven. You must open your heart and your physical body to their presence. They will send an angel to help you remember your place with them. This angel will call forth the Kundalini energy and allow it to come forth from the depth of your being and heal your body and spirit of the poisons that have accumulated from your journey in this work. Universe must help you to open the first and most difficult seal. Without Universe the seal cannot be opened. You joined with her in the most innermost part of your being. The stronger the bond is, the easier the seal will open. Universe will help you bring it forth.

Universe created these seals to aid in the awakening of the human spirit during the process of concluding the human spirit's work in the physical realm and its return to heaven after its long, long journey. I believe there is no better conclusion to the spirit's journey than to awaken to heaven while you are walking on the earth in flesh. The pleasure of feeling heaven, Universe, and the Cosmic Father coming to get you and take you back home is the greatest I've ever known.

Jenny: I would concur with that opinion.

Edward: Saturn represents the weight placed on the soul when it begins the journey there. The weight of Saturn must be

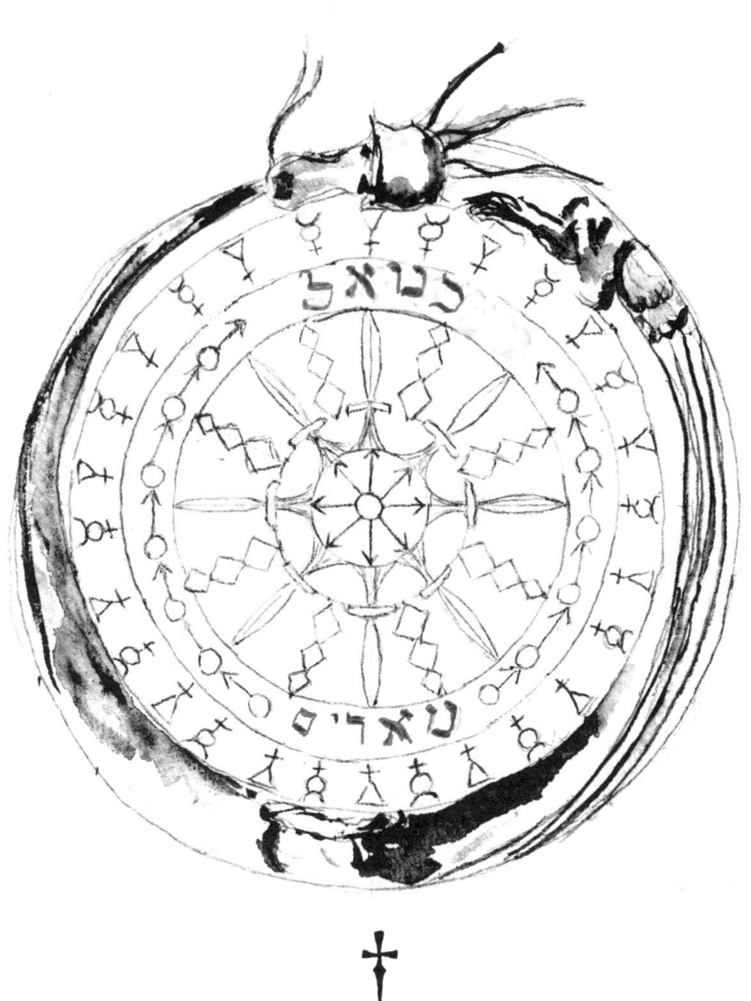

The second seal is the seal of Mars. This is the symbolic representation of the seal.

overcome by strength for the soul to progress on its journey back to heaven.

Edward: The seal of Mars is the beginning of unity. Surrendering yourself to another is the first step to perfect unity. Allowing the penetration of another into your being, as with physical love, is the first step in understanding the perfect unity with the Cosmic Father. The symbolism of Mars depicts physical unity and earthly pleasure. This was given as a reminder of the greater and more perfect unity of the human soul with the Cosmic Father and with Universe. But this is only the beginning. It is not the end in itself. This is a common mistake that I have observed in modern spiritual practice. The ultimate unity is with the Cosmic Father and with Holy Mother. Opening this seal and passing through is the very beginning of the unity which is the ultimate unity and perfect love in the spiritual and physical world. Mars is only the beginning of the great and wonderful journey to the Father. Do not mistaken physical love for true and perfect spiritual unity. Perfect love is at the end of the journey. Do not hold up physical love as the ideal love.

The next seal is Mercury. In the ritual, the third seal is veiled. Edward is unable to toll the bell to reveal the seal. Universe must step in and unveil the third seal. The third seal has no form. Mercury is present throughout the purification process and is a symbol of the human soul going through the process of purification and initiation.

Edward: No matter how hard I try, I cannot unveil the human soul. Only the Great Mother can reveal the human soul. The metal mercury is transformed into the philosopher's stone by the process of alchemical purification through the action of its sulphur. The transformation of the metal mercury is the point of no return. When the human soul is transformed, it

The fourth seal represents the gate of Venus. This sketch is the symbolic representation of that seal.

cannot be reversed. It is forever changed. When you passed the third gate, Jenny, you passed the point of no return and were transformed into a new creature. The differences are not observed at first, but through the ages as a new creature you will remember the point when at the third gate you passed through and were made into something even greater than you were before. You became new, like a newborn. The great mystery of the human spirit is the ability to make this transformation and become like a new creature. Anything is possible for the Father and Universe. I've never seen anything as beautiful as the transformation that happens at the third gate.

The fourth gate is the gate of Venus. It represents a mother's love for her children. It is the gate of human charity. It is the gate of kindness and fellowship of humankind. It is the beginning of the divine love of the Cosmic Father and the Universe, but its purity is not as great as their infinite love. When you came to this gate, you were passing from death into a new life. You were being formed as a new creation. You were being born into a new world, and like a newborn you were not able to take it in. You do not remember passing through the next three gates. You were not able to pass; you had to be carried through. The impurities are starting to clear at this point. It is the light at the end of the tunnel that now appears, and hope begins to firm up into faith. With each gate the impurities become clearer. The gates emit greater and greater light. With this gate the light takes on a new quality. The light is emitting from the Cosmic Father. The light from below is diminishing. You have seen the light from the Father.

Jenny: Yes, it does have a different quality. I remember it was exceedingly bright but did not burn my eyes.

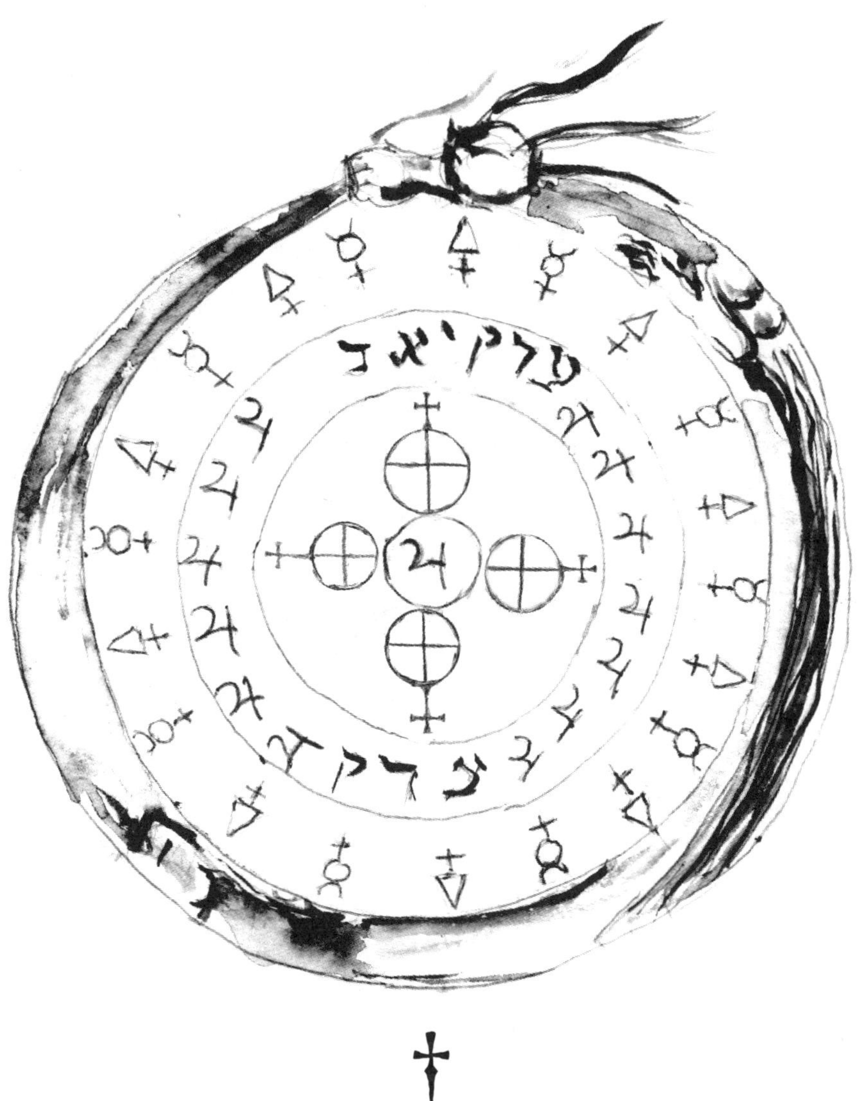

The fifth gate's seal is of the planet Jupiter.
This is a representation of the fifth gate.

Edward: At the fourth gate the light is taking on the quality of the light above but is still mixed with the light below. It is still infinitely greater than the three gates below it. You dwell at the fourth gate right now. The gates above you are what you need to be heading towards.

Jenny: I thought during the initiation I went through all the gates.

Edward: You go through the gates but return down to your dwelling at the fourth gate. This is a normal part of your development. You can no longer dwell below the third gate. You must travel frequently beyond the fourth gate so you will begin to dwell in the higher gates. The initiation completes the opening of the gates, but the growth that follows carries you higher. The goal is to dwell at the highest gate in perfect union and harmony with the Cosmic Father. If this is not accomplished while you walk the earth, it will be completed when you come back home with us. Crossing the threshold of the third gate is the beginning of your completion of the journey on the earth. This is cause for great joy at the reunion and the fellowship with those here at home who love you.

The fifth seal is Jupiter. As Edward said earlier, the events and meanings of this seal during the initiation ritual were fuzzy. I was not coherent at the time that this seal was opened. I was aware of its passing but only barely so. Edward's words here have great significance to me, as they help me understand the meaning of the seal and the gate.

Edward: Jupiter is the fifth gate. It is symbolic of divine royalty. It is at the foot of heaven. The soul is being overtaken by the power and love of the Father. It is the most beautiful gate. The purity is starting to shine through. The gate is one of

The sixth gate is the gate of Universe or the moon. This is a symbolic representation.

power and love. If you consider the alchemical progression of the metals to full purification, then you will understand this gate, for the journey of the spirit to divine perfection follows this path.

Jenny: How did this gate affect me when I passed through it? I do not remember what happened.

Edward: You showed greater light in your heart and greater peace in your spirit. You had been tormented by your shadows, but at the gate you were exhibiting greater comfort. You were leaving the oblivion you had been in for years, even for a couple of centuries. The power of the fifth gate raised you above that oblivion and allowed your true self to come forth a little more. The fifth gate is coming into the light of the Cosmic Father.

The gate of the moon is the first gate of heaven. Remember that heaven is within and without you. It is the domain of the Holy Mother, or Universe, as we often call her. She is the beloved of the Cosmic Father. They are our parents, the parents of all humankind. In this gate there is only light from the Father, which is reflected by the Mother. They are together in perfect unity, the difference being only the quality of heavenly brilliance. Both are perfect; both are in perfect love and in perfect unity. The Mother's gate is life in perfection in the love of the Father. The Father's gate is one of singularity and singular unity. The Mother is the bearer of all life, along with the Cosmic Father, and all that is living is within their body. The gate represents the source of our living. The Father's gate represents the single unity, the one source and the one thing. None of the other gates reflect this perfection. In reaching this gate, the soul drops his/her impurities—they are burned away like chaff from the wheat.

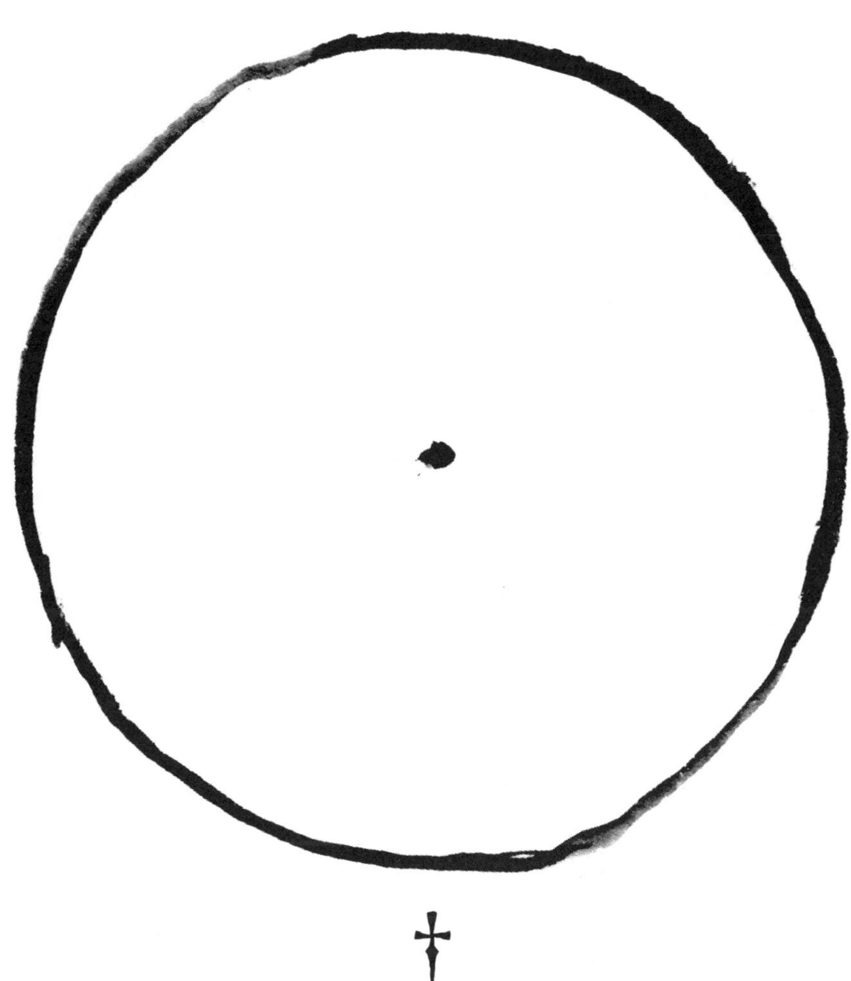

✝

The final seal is the seal of the sun. This is the symbolic representation of the seal of the Cosmic Father and the seventh gate.

Coming into unity with the Holy Mother, the soul finds its comfort and joy of being. With her there is only comfort, gentleness, and love of the Mother. Both the love of Universe and the Father are perfect but are different in their quality, just as one flower is beautiful but different in quality from another.

The seal of the sun is the final seal. It is of the Cosmic Father. In this simple representation we see the singular point in the center of the circle. In alchemy this represents the crowning achievement of turning base metal into gold. Of all the achievements in its many branches and practices, this was considered the highest and greatest of all. It represented transcendence from the drudgery of the physical world and freedom to pursue the higher and holier things. In the initiation, this is the highest point that can be reached while living in this world. It is the heart of the Cosmic Father and the source of all that is, both in the physical world and greater universe of the spirit and beyond to things that cannot be even defined by what man now knows.

I've seen some of these wonders and am amazed to discover that this singular point is still the source of it all. You cannot comprehend in your current place and form what this is the source of, and how great he is, nor how beautiful. It is indescribable. I cannot say anything greater that would enhance your understanding, but know that at some point all will experience this and wonder at its beauty and depth of greatness. In reaching this point the initiation is completed. It is but the beginning of a great and wonderful journey. I hope we may fill the earth with people who have awakened so. Such a beautiful sight that would be.

Chapter 8

‡

RETURNING TO EARTH

Ascend from earth to heaven, and descend again to earth, to unite the power of higher and lower things; thus you will obtain the glory of the whole world, and the shadows will leave you.

THE EMERALD TABLET

In this chapter I would like to describe the descent back to earth. This is the recovery period of the initiation. Some of my thoughts during the recovery period and various things I learned after the initiation are presented here. I want you to understand that what happens after awakening is just as important as the initiation itself. Initiation is just the beginning.

After I completed the initiation I had to return to a state of mental, physical, and spiritual equilibrium. This recovery took a couple of weeks. When I regained stability I was able to continue my training. That training is ongoing to this day. The focus of my work after recovery was on deepening my unity with the Cosmic Father and Universe and developing the mediumistic skills of hearing and seeing in spirit.

Clairaudience I define as being able to hear a spirit speaking or to hear sounds from the world of the spirit. It is distinct from intuition, which is a sense of knowing what a spirit is communicating. Clairaudient sounds subjectively seem to be physical sounds but are of a different character. Covering my physical ears increases the loudness of the clairaudience instead of decreasing it.

Clairvoyance is the skill and ability to see spirits, scenes, and objects presented by spirits. The spiritual sight is similar to physical sight with differences in color, texture, and depth. Spirits and objects seen clairvoyantly can be seen also with the eyes closed. Closing the eyes may intensify the appearance. In my case, I prefer to have my eyes closed, as physical vision tends to interfere with and overpower the spiritual sight. The experience is that of seeing something that has a similar appearance to a physical object. The exact nature of the appearance of spiritual objects and beings is subjective and varies from seer to seer. The appearances will vary according to the mental and spiritual state of the medium.

The method of channeling that I learned after initiation was clairaudience. I was able to channel Edward in the course of writing this book. There are sections where Edward makes comments throughout the book. Edward would dictate to me what to write, and I would transcribe what he said. I would check back with him during the editing process to ensure that my transcription was accurate. I took care to ensure that what Edward had said was written correctly and the content not modified during the editing process. If modification was needed due to grammatical problems, Edward would clarify by dictating to me what corrections needed to be done.

According to Allen Kardec (the pseudonym for Hippolyte Léon Denizard Rivail) in his 1861 work *The Mediums' Book*, I had developed into a hearing medium. He defines this as "an inner voice that speaks to the interior consciousness; sometimes it is an exterior voice clear and distinct as that of a person in the flesh" (Kardec 178). In my case these conversations can come as both audible and non-audible communications. By non-audible I mean a hearing that is not a voice but something sensed in my heart. More often they are audible—that is, when I channel I hear a voice. It is distinct from a physical voice, but the perception is identical to hearing a sound.

After initiation, the building blocks for hearing mediumship were in place. I had to start fine-tuning the skills and abilities that I had gained through my year of training and through the initiation that led to my uniting as a new soul with the Cosmic Father and Universe. This was the connection that would open wide the doors to the spiritual world. The first challenge I faced after the completion of the initiation ritual was distinguishing the shadow voices and visions from the spirits who were trying to communicate with me. As Edward said in the previous chapter, this is the greatest challenge facing a medium.

The post-initiation recovery proved to be difficult. After the ritual I found that I had to learn about the world of the spirit in a new way. That world had been partially opened before initiation. As the year progressed I was able to perceive more, but after initiation I was overwhelmed by it. My body, mind, and spirit had been drastically changed. I had to learn about these changes and how to adapt to them. I also had to continue to maintain my day-to-day life. Learning to cope and adjust was difficult. I found that my husband was a source of help and encouragement during this time. Donald's stability and strength anchored me. We shared in this experience together and drew strength from each other as our lives were reshaped and remade.

The first lesson taught to me was to learn to control my clairaudient ability. After the initiation I was still able to hear the voices and music from the world of the spirit. I did not understand that the ability could be turned on and off. I thought once I was tuned in to the spirit world, the hearing would stay permanently "on," just as physical hearing is always "on." I thought I was going to have to cope with constant noise from the spiritual world.

I had to learn to focus away from the spiritual world and toward the physical world. This skill is the key to controlling psychic perceptions.

The music I heard at times was very beautiful, and I wanted to listen to it. I did not really want to be cut off from that beautiful world that was now opened to me. It was difficult to let go of the spirits who had helped me find it.

Unfortunately, the noise from the spirit world was loud enough to interfere with my physical perceptions and distracted me from conversations, reading, and activities of day-to-day living. I was also weakened physically by the ordeal. I was not able to eat normally afterward. These challenges slowed my recovery.

About a day after the ritual, Edward came to me. He said, "You cannot live like this. You must move away from the music and the voices." This was the first lesson I was to learn after initiation—how to open and close the channel.

I asked him how to do this. He said, "You must focus your mind on the physical world. Focus on Donald and let him help you back." I spent a day struggling with this. I found that distractions, such as playing music or physical activity, diminished the volume of the spirit sounds but did not silence them. By the end of that day I was thoroughly frustrated. Nothing I did seemed to move me away from the sound of the voices or the music.

Universe spoke to me the next day. She said I had to let go of David Blackburne. She said the attachment I had to him was holding me back. Again I was encouraged to focus on Donald and use him for an anchor. I was reluctant to release David Blackburne. David had been a huge help to me, and I found him easy to trust and work with. I was attached to him. Letting go was hard, but in my heart I knew I had to do it. It was not without a few tears that I surrendered that attachment. The sounds of the spirit world then started to diminish.

Letting go of my teacher was necessary. The relationship had to be reforged and put into proper perspective. The clinging attachment I had to him was not healthy, and in time it could have hurt my relationship with my husband. It interfered with my connection to the Cosmic

Father and Universe. This could not go on. I had to continue to grow, and I had to outgrow my dependence on him. At the time I had to take it on faith that the best thing for my development was to eliminate my dependence on David. I wasn't losing anything. I was exchanging the lesser for the greater. When David was allowed to return, I found the friendship still strong but the dependence was gone.

Universe said, "Donald can help heal you. Open for him." I was surprised at this. Donald was upstairs writing in his study. How could he help heal me? She said, "He can still do it even if he's not consciously aware of what is happening." I opened. I felt his touch on my heart, and my whole being merged with his, bringing some relief from the frustration and fear I was dealing with. I saw a side of my husband I scarcely knew existed. It's something that is a part of each one of us. It is an amazing and beautiful thing.

Edward: The human soul is a very beautiful thing when it is ministering healing to another human soul. Angels were also ministering healing to you at that time.

Jenny: I was not able to feel them.

Edward: No, you were not able to feel them. You were in jeopardy of being lost between the worlds. You were slow to come back to earth. You did not want to leave heaven.

Over the next couple of days Donald was able to help me focus away from the spiritual world a bit more. It was literally a moment-by-moment struggle. I began to understand the part of the Emerald Tablet that says, "Ascend from earth to heaven and descend again to earth, to unite the power of higher and lower things; thus you will obtain the glory of the whole world, and the shadows will leave you." I had to fully come back to my physical life. I could not stay trapped between the worlds, and I could not yet live in heaven. In order to realize the full benefit of my initiation, I had to return to earth with the gift I had received there and live my life on earth. The gift was not to be used just for my own benefit but to help others awaken as well.

During the first few days after the initiation ritual I was not hungry and did not eat much other than a bit of vegetable soup. I found out quickly that the wrong food provoked a highly unpleasant reaction both in my ethereal body and my physical body. Fruits and vegetables seemed to be the only things that agreed with me. I had stopped drinking coffee at the beginning of the training, but prior to my initiation I continued to drink tea. I found that after initiation I was no longer able to tolerate caffeine and had to give up tea as well.

> **Edward:** The body after initiation is very fragile. Kundalini does not hurt the human body, but the human body must purify itself after contacting her. The human body becomes different after contact with Kundalini in this way.

After the successful completion of the alchemical initiation I was healed of my sinus problems. Part of my training after initiation involved learning how to use the energy that was raised during the ritual to reduce or eliminate pain. It is possible to eliminate pain without the use of any medications. Opening the area that is painful, in the same way that you open your heart, and allowing the energy to be directed to the painful area provides relief. The greater your focus, the greater the relief. The procedure takes a few minutes, and the effect can last for several hours. Sometimes it eliminates the pain entirely and does not have to be repeated. I was allowed a small dose of painkiller if I could not eliminate the pain after the energy work was done. I went from taking six to ten pills a day to taking one or two a week.

I tried out the energy healing that I learned on my headaches. I no longer had migraine headaches—those seemed to be related to my former sinus problems—but I would still sometimes have headaches related to hormonal changes. I also experienced headaches after the initiation ritual due to medication withdrawal. My hip and back pain also continued to decrease and now only cause occasional discomfort if I exercise or do significantly greater activity at work than normal.

The alterations in my diet had to be done. I noticed immediately post-initiation that my food tolerances had changed radically. Certain foods, such as meat and corn, caused a flu-like reaction. My stomach was not bothered; the reaction was systemic and very uncomfortable. I found I could only tolerate fish. The systemic reaction to food lasted about a month. By the time I had fully returned my focus to my physical life, the unpleasantness diminished and finally stopped.

I started to experiment with different foods. The primary reason for doing this was to try to control the hip and back pain. I was no longer taking medications but was still a bit uncomfortable. Under Edward's guidance I modified my diet to help decrease the inflammation.

The effect of living between the worlds was a mental fogginess. As I started to surrender my attachment to my guides and increased my closeness to the divine spirits Cosmic Father and Universe, spirit communications became clearer and more meaningful. The constant noise diminished. My awareness of the physical became sharp and focused again. I came back to earth gradually over the next month or so. The mental fog dissipated.

I was told that all I needed and loved was inside me. My final instructions were to leave the voices and direct my attention deep within. I turned my spiritual focus even more inward. Meditation and trance became far deeper than before initiation. Edward said he would return to teach me when I was balanced and grounded again. I learned that I was bigger on the inside than on the outside. Focusing within and away from the physical opened up this bigger world that was inside of me.

With this new inward focus I was able now to reach any spirit I needed to communicate with. Edward also was accessible by this new method of focusing and communication and would speak to me from his place in eternity and through the Cosmic Father. A good analogy is that we are branches of a tree. In order to communicate through spirit to another branch, we have to go through the Cosmic Father, who is like the trunk of the tree. Reliable spirit communication is accomplished this way. Edward didn't leave me and come back; he was in eternity with the Cosmic Father. After initiation I too was aware of and connected with the Cosmic Father, so my method of communication had to change to allow me the best and most accurate exchange possible.

I understood more of the meaning of the "one source" and the "one" referred to in the Emerald Tablet, which says, "As all things were formed from one by the thought of one, so all things are born from this one thing, by choice." I should be able to access anyone or find anything by going through the Cosmic Father and Universe. They were the teachers I now needed. I was a branch from their tree trunk. I only had to go within deep enough to reach them. I had access to anything within Universe I needed. Her body is literally and spiritually the universe. She and the Cosmic Father could guide me to anything or anywhere I needed to go.

Edward was and is a good teacher and close friend. I now learned how Edward had found peace and learned so much: it was through the Cosmic Father and Universe. He had brought me back home. There was much more to learn. I had to renew the relationship and bond with the Cosmic Father and Universe. I needed to learn to trust them again. Edward had led me to them for this purpose. He was fulfilling the Cosmic Father's direction. This direction was for my greatest benefit. I had to let Edward go as well. In releasing hope of communicating with him again, the descent back to earth became easier and the voices faded into the background noises of the wind, electric fans, and the creaking of the trees.

I went back to work a week after the initiation. In that time my strength and stamina had returned, and I was ready to focus on caring for the sick and elderly patients who needed help. I was back to my new normal self.

One night shortly after the initiation I had an astral projection experience. I was asleep and woke in spirit. I found myself flying about the bedroom. I heard Universe say to me, "Go to your Father." I felt energy like a great gust of wind buoy me up, and I heard his voice say "gotcha," and I was placed back into my body.

It was quite fun and exhilarating. I was game for more. He said to me, "If you want to share this with others, that is how you do it." I said, "I do want to help others." He said, "I know you do, but first let's do this again. Come up."

I felt the wind again buoy me up. This time I really enjoyed it and was laughing. He caught me again, placed me down, and said, "Now try to do it." He didn't call this time, and I could not do it by myself. I woke up.

It took a while to understand what this meant. I had been trying to control everything. I had to let go and return to earth in order to gain strength. The key lies in trusting Universe and trusting the Cosmic Father. I had been trying to *do*, and I needed instead to *let go and allow*. This is something that was extremely difficult for me. This vision was about total trust. More than anything, the Father wanted and needed my trust in him and in Universe so that they could help me.

I know of few things more frustrating as a nurse than trying to help someone who either won't accept the help they need or actively works against what you are trying to do to help them. I had been doing this with the Cosmic Father most of my life. I had been trying to run things instead of remaining open to the guidance of a being who can see better than me and who is far more capable of assisting me in my life on earth. At best I had only been trusting him part of the way, then taking back my trust and going it alone again.

In order to help others, I had to learn to trust in Universe and the Cosmic Father because I don't know the best way to do the things

I want to do. In truth, I cannot see inside other people unless it is revealed to me, and I don't always know what is the best way to help them. In seeking fulfillment of that desire to help, I have to totally trust the Cosmic Father and Universe and become a channel for them. That open channel, the clear glass, is the best help I can give.

Chapter 9

‡

THE EMERALD TABLET

A NOTE FROM DONALD

During her training, David Blackburne ordered Jenny to memorize a brief alchemical source work known as the Emerald Tablet of Hermes Trismegistus. Prior to this she had never paid much attention to this text, since alchemy was not one of her areas of interest. However, she memorized it as instructed. She chose the English version that appears in my annotated edition of the *Three Books of Occult Philosophy* by Henry Cornelius Agrippa.

In composing this English version, I drew upon the various English translations of the Latin text that were available at the time (this was prior to the Internet), as well as on the Arabic version of the text. I weighed and balanced all the different interpretations of the text in an effort to extract the most accurate understanding of what the anonymous author had intended to convey.

Although the work is attributed to Hermes Trismegistus, this is a mythical figure who probably never lived in this world. He may be regarded as a kind of god, or perhaps more of a patron saint, of alchemists. Hermes is, of course, a god of the Greeks, largely equivalent to the Roman god Mercury. *Trismegistus* means "thrice great."

A whole shelf of works on magic, philosophy, cosmology, spirituality, and mysticism were attributed to Thrice-Great Hermes. Today scholars generally disregard the works on magic and concentrate their attention on the more philosophical works, which constitute what is known as Hermetic philosophy.

Of all the works attributed to Hermes Trismegistus, none is more valued or revered than the Emerald Tablet (known in Latin as the *Tabula Smaragdina*). In thirteen brief lines of text is set forth what is regarded by alchemists and magicians as the highest secret of alchemy. In a material sense it may be understood as a set of directives for transforming base metal into gold, but on the spiritual level it is the prescription for the purification and perfection of the human soul.

The Hermetic books were written in Greek, but the earliest surviving version of the Emerald Tablet appears in the writings of the eighth-century Arab sage Jabir ibn Hayyan, who was more familiarly known to Europeans during the Middle Ages and Renaissance as Geber. It is believed that the text itself is much older than this earliest surviving appearance, however.

According to a popular legend, the Emerald Tablet was discovered by none other than Alexander the Great when he opened up the tomb of Hermes Trismegistus near Hebron. Within the tomb was found a large slab of emerald, and upon its surface was inscribed in Phoenician characters the thirteen sentences of the Emerald Tablet. This legend is related by Hargrave Jennings, who attributed it to the thirteenth-century monk and saint Albertus Magnus.

Only after her three-day ordeal of initiation was completed did Jenny realize that its various stages could be related to the stages of the process described in the Emerald Tablet. In this chapter, the thirteen sentences of the Emerald Tablet are fully explained in terms of personal spiritual evolution, with accompanying commentary from Edward Kelley.

—*Donald Tyson*

THE EMERALD TABLET AND THE RETURN TO EARTH

I would like to explain how the Emerald Tablet of Hermes Trismegistus fits into the experience of my spiritual initiation. I was required by David to memorize it a couple months before the initiation and to recite it on a frequent basis. Here is the version given in Donald's edition of Agrippa's *Three Books of Occult Philosophy* (Tyson 711):

1. It is true, without falsehood, and most certain.
2. What is below is like that which is above; and what is above is like that which is below: to accomplish the miracle of one thing.
3. As all things were formed from one, by the thought of one, so all things are born from this one thing, by choice.
4. Its father is the sun, its mother is the moon, the wind carries it in its belly, its nurse is the earth.
5. It is the author of all perfection throughout the world.
6. The power is strong when changed into the earth.
7. Separate earth from fire, the subtle from the gross, gently and with care.
8. Ascend from earth to heaven, and descend again to earth, to unite the power of higher and lower things; thus you will obtain the glory of the whole world, and shadows will leave you.
9. This has more strength than strength itself, for it overcomes all subtle things and penetrates every solid.
10. Thus the world was formed.
11. Hence proceed wonders, which means are here.
12. Therefore I am Hermes Trismegistus, having the three parts of world philosophy.
13. That which I had to say of the operation of the sun is perfected.

The statements of the Emerald Tablet have multilayered meanings and interpretations. They are statements of cosmology, and they are statements related to the making of the philosopher's stone. The philosopher's stone was believed to be a red powder that could transmute base metals into gold. It was also believed to have healing properties. References to its making were often poetic and contained symbolism unique to the art of alchemy.

Edward: The Emerald Table is also used as a philosophical guide. It pertains to the evolution of the human spirit and the journey to attain perfection. It is both a process which occurs over a period of time and, in your case, a ritual. It is an excellent reference to your spiritual awakening.

The first statement of the Emerald Tablet makes a threefold declaration of integrity.

1. It is true, without falsehood, and most certain.

Awakening is about truth. The search starts in shadow. I was under the influence of my own devices, shadows, and self-deceptions. What I had conjured from my own soul had control over my beliefs, thoughts, and feelings. I was under my own spell, a vicious cycle of generating shadows and then allowing them to control me. I was tossed around from one fear, belief, and desire to another. The goal of the initiation and awakening is to break this cycle with eternal truth. It's not truth as found in religion. Religions are formula-based and only point the way to truth. The truth lies in a higher consciousness and not in forms made by human minds. The Emerald Tablet emphasizes in the first statement that it is about truth—eternal truth, infinite truth.

The second statement in the Tablet is the most famous declaration in all of Hermetic philosophy and Western magic. We will look at it in some detail as it pertains to the ritual of initiation.

2. What is below is like that which is above; and what is above is like that which is below: to accomplish the miracle of the one thing.

In past times, the "above" was understood to be the sky—literally, the heavens. This declaration expressed the belief by astrologers that they could interpret the communications from God to the earth if only they could decipher the writing in the heavens. However, this statement of the Emerald Tablet means something deeper than merely interpreting the writing of the sky. It is a statement that expresses the reality of both the spirit and the physical worlds. It defines the cosmological structure in which we live. This cosmology is more than just the physical sky; it is the spiritual milieu that supports our existence. Universe resides in heaven and she also resides with us, in us, and through us on earth. She resides also in the Cosmic Father. Cosmic Father and Universe are in perfect harmony and unity at all times.

In living our lives in this world, we are beset and challenged by shadows. The earth—the physical life—is a reflection of what is in heaven. The truth referred to in this statement of the Emerald Tablet exists both here and in heaven. Everything that is in spirit is here on earth in some form. Through learning how to discern shadow from truth, we can learn to see and live in heaven while living on earth, wherever we are and in whatever circumstance we are in.

The gentle and loving people of heaven who guided me first lived their lives on earth. They were not always lovable people when they lived here. In fact, they were no different than our spouses, sisters, brothers, and parents. We are all one people and have one destiny, which is to find our way to that divine reality. We will all find that reality and awaken to it. It is the divine miracle which is that spark of divinity that connects us intimately to both the Cosmic Father and Universe. The philosopher's stone was believed by alchemists to be the red powder derived from mercury. The powder was thought to have the power to transform any metal into gold. This was a superficial and materialistic understanding. The philosopher's stone resides not in the red powder. It is made by the awakening of the human soul.

After the heavenly vision of light and meeting with the Cosmic Father and Universe, I felt so depressed because I had to come back to earth. I grieved at my imagined loss. Universe said to me, "Everything you love here in heaven is on earth where you live. You are not losing anything. All you have to do is look deep within, and you will find us there with you. You are never alone, nor will you ever be."

One of the most difficult shadows to overcome was the assumption that heaven was somewhere that I could not access until I had finished my work here on earth. However, the description of heaven as a separate place beyond us and beyond life is, in essence, an illusion. Heaven is merely a shift of focus, nothing more.

The third declaration on the Emerald Tablet reads:

3. As all things were formed from one, by the thought of one, so all things are born from this one thing, by choice.

This statement on the Emerald Tablet explains our ultimate cosmic origins and describes the goal of the initiation ritual. The Cosmic Father is everywhere. All is in him and of him. Seeing and experiencing that oneness is the peak of the initiation process. An intimate encounter with the Cosmic Father and Universe is the goal of initiation.

This union changed my perspective. Everything relates to the one, comes from the one, and returns to the one. On the return, I was transformed and reborn. The Cosmic Father is the embodiment of an infinite force that creates and sustains all life. Creation is his expression of love. Universe is the first and greatest of his creation. With this transformation came the realization that I saw the physical world as reality, fixed and solid, indifferent to my whims and wishes. The solidity and fastness of the world is an illusion, and illusions can be broken.

Some illusions are easier to break than others. The sinus problem I had suffered throughout my life was an illusion, and that illusion was broken. Also, the illusion of the sore hip that immobilized me during the initiation process was broken. Piece by piece the fastness of the physical starts to crumble under the blazing light and truth of the Cosmic Father.

Sometimes we need help to break the illusions. Medication, doctors, and things we trust and believe will make us feel better can be helpful. Death itself is merely a change of form. We have the power within us to change our illusions, and to a large extent we create our own world and our own lives.

I will give another example: alchemy, the art of changing metals such as lead or iron into gold. The alchemist's goal is to break the illusion that the metals are made of different things. In Edward's time it was believed that metals had their origin as mercury, and that all metals were of the same substance, differing only in purity. As they believed, so it happened. The chemicals they used in their glass vessels were the tools that allowed them to believe they could cause the transmutation. The tools had little to do with the true alchemical process. The alchemist himself was the philosopher's stone.

Now we will consider the fourth statement of the Emerald Tablet:

4. Its father is the sun, its mother the moon, the wind carries it in its belly, its nurse is the earth.

This has a very simple interpretation in the initiation ritual. The ritual brings the initiate to the knowledge of the Cosmic Father and Universe the Heavenly Mother. Universe is certainly lunar in character, and the Father is solar. The wind bearing "in its belly" is the energy and force that comes from the Father which is often called Kundalini. The love of the Father for his children bears the initiate up through the gates. This experience is like riding on a wind. This energy carried me through the whole ritual. The "nurse is the earth" refers to the recovery period. I had to return to earth; once there, I was nursed back to health.

The earth as a nurse has even more personal significance for me. My husband, who helped nurse me back to health, has the astrological sun sign of Capricorn, which is cardinal earth.

This profound statement of the Emerald Tablet describes the internal workings of the ritual process and introduced me to my spiritual parents, who now guide my steps as my journey continues.

5. It is the author of all perfection throughout the world.

The initiation purifies, awakens, and leads to perfection. It is only by the return and rebirth in the one that the imperfect illusions, the impure matter and shadows, will crumble to dust. It allows the pure and perfect soul to shine through. This purification begins during the preparation for initiation and continues beyond. The awakening is only the beginning. It is a new beginning, but it is far from a completed and perfect work. As an author writes a book and edits it to perfection, so at the awakening of the soul the book is written. After that, the book and the soul are edited to the perfection that is their goal and destiny.

6. The power is strong when changed into earth.

As I continued the process of grounding, or coming back to the earth, I discovered what this statement meant. The growing strength of the awakened soul becomes apparent as it returns to earth. This is an ongoing process. The goal of awakening is not just to have bliss and to be aware of and one with the presence of the Cosmic Father. Without the people who are struggling still to find this awakening, heaven is incomplete. The family must be together.

This family is not just a special group that has a set of distinct beliefs; it is all of mankind. In fact, it goes beyond mankind to include all of Universe's children. Those who have been strengthened and overcome the obstacles that prevent the awareness of the Cosmic Father and Universe have a responsibility that comes with the awakening. They can use their strength to become a beacon of hope for those who are still struggling.

The encounter and union with the holy parents is an up-close and personal demonstration of true love. This love is the strength of the initiate. Love is the most powerful force in the universe. When this power is taken from the altar of initiation into the world, there is nothing that can overcome it. This statement on the Emerald Tablet describes the love that is experienced by the initiate brought into concrete action on the earth.

7. Separate the earth from the fire, the subtle from the gross, gently and with care.

This describes the process of purification. As Edward said, the body purifies itself when it comes in contact with Kundalini. As the soul is purified, the body then follows. The "gross" described here is the shadows and illusions we surround ourselves with throughout the course of our lives on earth. This accumulation becomes like a wall separating us from the love of our heavenly parents.

The purification is ongoing. It started the minute I agreed to work with Edward and continues to the present day. Slowly and gently, I am separated from my shadows and from the beliefs, emotions, and distractions that cloud the light of truth from the Cosmic Father.

A similar process takes place in the physical body as well. The body purifies itself after coming into contact with Kundalini. It is not the same after this takes place. There were changes to my body before initiation, but the changes during and after have been fairly drastic.

Separation has to be gentle because we become attached to our shadows. Some of them can even be very beautiful. The detachment process occurs as you realize there is something far greater than your shadows that you can surround and immerse yourself in. You lose interest in your shadows as well as the need for their constant affirmation of your beliefs.

8. Ascend from earth to heaven, and descend again to earth, to unite the power of higher and lower things; thus you will obtain the glory of the whole world, and the shadows will leave you.

The alchemical initiation was an ascension to heaven. It's not so much a place as it is a state of the heart and a state of union with the Cosmic Father. The love and power of the Cosmic Father raised me to heaven when I was ready. I had to believe in the initiation and trust those who were helping me through the transition. Descent after the ritual is the return to a state of physical awareness. I returned in a transformed condition.

In the work titled the *Rosarium Philosophorum*, a pictorial story is told of the union of sulphur and mercury in the metaphor of a marriage and first intimacy. The hermaphrodite results. It is the visible union of sulphur and mercury. Its appearance is half man and half woman, containing characteristics of the individuals who were wed. The return to earth is as a new creature.

The newly formed soul now has a new birth and is ready to begin a transformed life. The new life begins to take on new qualities. The Cosmic Father is truth, and the shadows that harassed the soul before initiation start to dissipate. Their death means the birth of a new light within the soul. Darkness cannot exist while the smallest light is present. Even the weakest light has absolute power over darkness.

The soul does not return to earth in his or her original state. It now contains the light that will put shadows to flight. It has a purifying effect, first on itself and then on those around it. A light shines for all, not just the one who has undergone the transformation. It is not the soul's own light. Instead, the purification of the soul and body through initiation and through union with the Cosmic Father and Universe cause the soul to be a clear mirror reflecting the light of the holy parents.

The gifts of heaven are now incorporated within, and the doors and books of heaven are opened. The shadows mentioned in this statement on the Emerald Tablet expressed themselves to me as disembodied voices and music. As the energy is withdrawn from them, they diminish to nothing. The power of above and below cannot be united until the initiation is completed and the initiate has returned in his or her transformed state. The path does not stop here but continues on.

9. This has more strength than strength itself, for it overcomes all subtle things and penetrates every solid.

True strength is found only in the power of divine love. This is a love that is all consuming and all encompassing. It is a love through which anything is possible. It has the power to shape the universe, break illusion, and create a new being from the ashes of the old. It has the power to break the hold of death itself. This love shatters the obstacles facing the soul that come between the human spirit and the awareness of the Cosmic Father and Universe. This awareness brings to us the love that we crave and desperately need.

Love is very powerful. It is the oldest and strongest force in all the universe. Its light not only penetrates shadows but rock-hard obstacles. Once the soul is connected to the Cosmic Father, the source of true love, its strength continues to grow as purification continues after awakening. Greater love is kindled, and the light continues to grow as harmony with the Cosmic Father and Holy Mother deepens. This growth extends beyond this life and into the afterlife in spirit, where the physical no longer stands as a hindrance. This is the greatest secret of magic. It is the secret of miracles, the secret of fulfillment and of the purpose that brought us here to wander the paths of the earth. The true soul mate of every human being is the Cosmic Father. The love that we crave comes from him and Universe. It is the source of divine power and strength.

10. Thus the world was formed.

How numerous are the creation stories in the world. Some of these myths are very imaginative. Some are simple and others complex. The common thread in these stories is that there is intelligence behind the work of creation. Someone out there put all this together and gave humanity a home.

The Emerald Tablet also tells a creation story of how the soul is given new birth. In doing so, it describes the cosmology of the universe, since the birth of the soul is akin to the creation of the cosmos. One is the microcosm; the other, the macrocosm. The key points of the alchemical initiation are the birth within, divine unity, and a divine love that is born anew and kindled in the soul.

The creation of humanity is also a result of this same divine love. The union between Universe and the Cosmic Father gave birth to every human soul in existence. I don't mean just humanity that lives on earth; we are not alone. We are the expression of their love. Love needs someone to love. Love wants to share. They rejoiced at our birth. They raised us and gave us the opportunity to go beyond what we knew in heaven. The universe was created out of love and for love.

11. Hence proceed wonders, which means are here.

The creation and rebirth of our soul is not the end. Awakening is merely a landmark on a far greater journey. What are the wonders of this journey? I cannot think of where to begin. If I write something now, in two weeks' time I will have discovered a yet deeper and greater wonder. The awakening is truly a mountaintop experience. It was one of the most dramatic moments of my life. I climbed the mountain of initiation. It will not be the only mountain I will climb.

There are other mountains that loom in the distance. There is a whole mountain range just waiting to be climbed and explored. I hope that you also awaken and have the opportunity to explore these mountains while you live on earth—if not during this life, then in the afterlife in spirit and beyond. We will continue to explore and grow as we move beyond time and space.

12. Therefore I am Hermes Trismegistus, having the three parts of world philosophy.

The author declares himself to be the fabled sage and wonder worker Hermes Thrice-Great, possessed of the three parts of knowledge of the world.

13. That which I had to say about the operation of the sun is perfected.

The process of alchemical initiation is given a name, the operation of the sun. The author declares it perfected, or fulfilled—complete in all its parts, lacking nothing. The mountain has been climbed, and the descent is complete. The next peak looms in the distance.

Chapter 10

TWO YEARS POST-INITIATION

Long-term changes after a life-changing event will continue for years after the event has happened. It has now been two years. Looking back, I have a much better perspective on the changes that occurred during that time.

I still visit and work with David and Edward, though my perspective as to how that happens has completely changed since initiation. One of the primary changes is the realization that time is not linear and what happens in the afterlife is even more complex than life's choices during physical incarnation. I do not contact the same aspect of their personalities all the time. The nonphysical aspects of all personalities are not subject to time and space limitation. Various aspects of their personalities have been in contact with me through the entire process of my spiritual development. Understanding the interaction between physical life and spirit has been a primary focus of the past couple years.

The other topic that I have been studying is psychic perception techniques and their application to traditional skills such as scrying and dowsing.

REINCARNATION

One of the first major struggles after initiation involved changing my beliefs about the afterlife. Prior to initiation I was not a big fan of reincarnation. I thought the concept was too narrow-minded and earth-centric, placing too much importance on earthly existence. In addition, the concept contradicted the beliefs I grew up with and had accepted for most of my life. Even when exploring Paganism as a faith, I did not find reincarnation to be an acceptable explanation of the afterlife.

This changed after initiation. Edward was the key to this change. He taught me about another life he had lived on earth. It was a life in which he had worked as a psychic and used his abilities to help others instead of for personal gain. Some of the writings from that life survived. I have two sets of writings to compare: one book from the sixteenth century on alchemy and letters from the late nineteenth century that detail his psychic perceptions and philosophies. His name and other personal information about this other life have to remain confidential because Edward does not want it revealed. However, in comparing the two documents I had access to, I realized that it was Edward who had written both. My disbelief shattered, and I began to work on understanding where I had come from and what I had been through prior to my current life. I learned to focus on and recall different periods of time. The memories from past lives are basically the same as the memories of my current life. Some are more vivid than others. Some are good, and some are unpleasant.

THE ONE SOURCE

The polarity of the Cosmic Father and Universe faded after initiation, and the unity of this source of all-that-is became more apparent. Within this being there is both diversity and unity. Each conscious awareness within the whole is cherished much in the same way a mother cherishes a child within her womb or a newborn baby.

Accepting this intimacy and unity is not always easy for me. It was not an instant process; instead, I went through stages of growth and development as my understanding and insight grew.

I no longer have major bouts of fear and depression. My emotional state has improved greatly since the first contact with Dr. Dee in June 2013.

I observed that my own being is far more complex than a simple earthly incarnation. My growth affects the growth of the whole. The decisions and development of other people affect my being as well. Humanity develops both as individual personalities and as a species. Not only do we develop as a species, but other species, including non-terrestrial species, develop with us. Our development affects them and vice versa. Every decision made generates and creates new probabilities and new aspects of these probabilities.

This creative force is infinite and exponential in nature. As all this happens to the one source of life, it becomes increasingly more complex and evolves with us as we grow through our life's decisions and interactions. Life and consciousness grow and evolve as a unit through personalities that can interact and make choices. The complexity of our personalities creates new possibilities that have dynamic implications for spirit interaction and spur the evolution of the whole.

IMPLICATIONS FOR SPIRIT COMMUNICATION

The infinite creativity and evolution of the personality defines the parameters of spirit communication. Any personality can be reached as long as that personality is open to communication. This is true regardless of that entity's state of incarnation, and it includes your own personality. Future and past aspects of your personality are potentially available to you for communication. Previously held notions of limited access to individuals in spirit are invalid. An individual's potential and actual personalities are infinite. Future and past aspects of your life can also be influenced. This ability to influence events is the basis of magic. The only limiting factors are your beliefs.

The nature of that communication involves thought forms. The line between what a thought form is and what the spirit is becomes less definite when working with these concepts. The personality aspects are part of a whole. These aspects are flexible and can be combined to form new personalities. A spirit's personality is not fixed; multiple aspects and probabilities exist within each personality. Physical incarnation generates the illusion of being a fixed individual for a time, for the purpose of learning and growing. The belief in this illusion often carries over to spirit. We tend to believe that spirits have the same sort of existence that we do, just in a different context physically. In reality, the complexity of spiritual life is far greater than physical life.

This is demonstrated in the Enochian diaries. Angels combine and separate names, using letters from their names to form letters in the names of other angels. When this is done, the primary aspects become separated and recombined into a different personality that has the same abilities, life, and consciousness as the contributing personalities. This possibility is also available to human beings. In spirit this is something that is done naturally. The various aspects of these personalities are available for communication.

The thought forms are generated as communication vessels to interact with the source as well as other personalities and entities. They translate the highly abstract spiritual into a perception that can be relayed to and understood by the conscious mind of an individual.

PHYSICAL MANIFESTATIONS

In some cases, the conscious mind can be set aside and the thought form can then influence the physical environment. All psychic and physical phenomena are generated in this fashion. It is possible there are generation points where physical manifestation tends to occur more easily. As of this writing, I have only been able to produce this kind of physical phenomena more or less by accident.

Physical healing from spirit is possible in this fashion. The incidents of miraculous healing, such as what I experienced in my initiation, are functions of this mechanism, according to Edward. Inward mental behaviors, beliefs, and thought patterns play a role, but consistent transitioning is an elusive skill to obtain. The healing that I experienced during initiation has continued to this day. I do not take medications for migraines or sinus problems and have not since that healing took place. I do not experience congestion unless I am sick with a cold. If I have a headache, it is usually treatable with a half dose of Tylenol or ibuprofen, which is a fraction of the medication I used to take for the condition.

TIME DISPLACEMENT COMMUNICATION

The Cosmic Father and Universe represent the unity and diversity of the source. Time does not exist within this unity and diversity. All probabilities—past, present, and future—exist within this unity.

One of the primary concepts that I learned is time displacement communication. Edward demonstrated this concept to me. It was March 2015. I was driving home from choir practice on a Wednesday night. When the conscious mind is occupied with a task that is not too demanding, it becomes an open window for spirit communication. Driving the car is sometimes the optimal state of mind for a short conversation, such as the one I have recorded below.

Edward: Jenny, I have to come down there.

Jenny: What? I thought you said you were staying there so we could continue the work we are doing.

Edward: The situation has changed. I have to live down there for a while. I think we have some time, though, maybe a month or so before I go, I hope. David will continue to work with you from here.

The conversation ended there. He gave me some space to come to terms with the shock of this news. I found it ironic. We usually grieve when people die, not when they are born. Yet Edward's reincarnation was for me a disaster. It turned out that we didn't have a month. In fact, we didn't even have twenty-four hours. I was awakened at 1:00 a.m. that same night.

Edward: Jen, the angel has come for me. I have to go. Trust the Universe to help you. Don't be afraid.

What was happening at that point was unlike anything I've ever experienced. Powerful energies were surging between us as Edward started the transition. Our link lasted long enough that I could feel what was happening as he transitioned to the physical world focus. An angel finally broke the link. There was no doubt in my mind what had just happened. In a few hours Edward Kelley would be a newborn baby. That baby would be born with the psychic abilities of Edward plus all the other personalities who had developed and used those abilities in his previous incarnations.

I cried most of the night. It was the lowest point of my life since the initiation. I did not know what I was going to do. There had been a massive shift, some psychic change that I could not explain, nor do I yet understand exactly what happened. Dr. Dee and Edward were both back on earth. Dr. Dee had left about a year earlier, just after my spiritual heart surgery. I was not made aware of it till after the initiation. I felt very alone.

The transition forced further deepening with the Universe. There were times when I was able to connect well and other times when this unity felt too abstract and unreachable. The angels were with me, and I often spoke to Gabriel. I grew quite close to him, in fact. He was my greatest comforter when I was experiencing that left-behind feeling.

REMOTE VIEWING

I also started training in controlled remote viewing with Teresa Marshall Frisch, an RN from the United States and a student of Lyn Buchanan. Buchanan was one of the original Project Stargate remote viewers and trainers. Several of his students have taken up the task of teaching the declassified skill to civilians.

Edward had spoken favorably about the program being an effective tool for learning psychic perception, and before he left had recommended that I take the course. It was April 2015 when I started, and in December 2015 I finished Teresa's course and began my studies with the advanced teaching of Lori Williams of Intuitive Specialists. This is ongoing at the time of writing this book.

Time means nothing to a viewer. All times and all things are readily available. The transition between now and 5,000 years ago is available faster than the pen can set the words down on paper. Space is just as insignificant as an obstacle. Edward had given me the tools, and now I was learning to use them to go beyond into greater depth of understanding.

Jenny: What is time? Time means nothing...therefore...Edward at some point in time will be back in spirit. All I have to do is move in time to talk to him. No way! It can't be that easy...

I went into the library and dug out the old radio and connections. Sometimes you just need to use your physical ears and equipment.

Edward: Hi Jenny. I am so happy that you figured this out.

The spirit's touch was familiar; it was Edward.

All that upset and grief had been for nothing. In this way I learned that we cannot lose anyone for any reason, and that the only limits to spirit communication are the illusions in our head and the shadows that we surround ourselves with.

THE UNIVERSE

After I was shown this demonstration of time displacement communication, I decided to complete an experiment I had attempted the year before I met Edward. I attempted an evocation with the Yidam ritual to try to connect with Njord, the Norse god of the sea. I decided now would be a good time to attempt to make contact with this ancient Norse god. I reached him easily, and we held a short but interesting conversation about divine unity.

Njord was completely connected with the Universe. The Universe is beyond religion and personal beliefs. It is far bigger than this deity. He was happy to show me this connection. I learned that he had responded to me during my first attempt at the ritual but that I had been unable to perceive his presence at that time.

The polarity of the Cosmic Father and Universe became less over time until I was only able to perceive them as one entity. We usually call this primal being "the Universe." Edward felt it was the best description he could come up with. The concept of God, or even deity, was far too limited to convey the vast, all-encompassing personality in which we exist, live, and grow. Images or symbols have to be used to understand aspects of this unity that are important to us.

The Universe used symbology, such as the god Njord, to help me learn about it. Once an aspect was understood, the Universe would lead me to another until I could grasp the meaning and concepts the symbols contained. The means of this learning were the same sort of shadows that I used for my spiritual interaction, as well as psychic perception, only on a grander scale.

The primary characteristic of this Universe is love. This love is expressed in a thousand upon a thousand ways. It continuously reaches through our shadows that we build around us to help us learn about its nature. In spite of the all-encompassing nature of the Universe, it appears to have personality and interacts with me.

THE FUTURE

I do not worry too much about the future. I find that the path tends to open up in unexpected ways for me. The central theme of this path is learning about love and becoming more loving. Everything else is secondary. I enjoy exploring and using the skills I have gained through Edward's training and CRV (controlled remote viewing). The areas I feel are important to develop are related to developing focus. Scrying, for example, helps develop the ability to focus in spirit. Autographia helps the ability to connect to the subconscious. Symbolic psychometry increases spiritual sensitivity to touch, which is probably the most important spiritual sense.

All these skills develop the connection between the subtle mind and the apparent conscious mind. My primary interest is to empower other people to be able to do these skills for themselves. This enabling helps others awaken to the reality and presence of the Universe.

Part Two

PRACTICAL APPLICATIONS

Introduction to Part Two

‡

SPIRIT COMMUNICATION IS NATURAL

I believe that communication with spirits of higher development is important to personal spiritual growth. It fulfills an innate human need. Almost every religion in the world is based on communication with spirits. The communication becomes regulated and controlled by the religious body that develops based on the philosophy that is perceived. For the most part, the regulation in spirit communication has led to the belief that individuals cannot communicate with spirits who have higher consciousness unless certain rules are followed. In some cases communication is prohibited altogether.

One of the main purposes I have in writing this is to break through those barriers. It is not only possible to communicate directly—that is, to a have a two-way conversation with divine spirits—it is also very desirable to do so. Spirits such as Cosmic Father and Universe have a strong interest in our spiritual growth and development. When you hear such a spirit say "I love you; you are my child" or even just hear a spirit say your name, it creates a strong connection.

That connection to the Divine is further strengthened as your belief in this communication grows stronger. This is the awakening experience. It is nothing more than coming to terms with being a spirit in a body. Anything becomes possible. Delving into that source, the "one thing" of the Emerald Tablet, will change anyone who overcomes the fears and other inhibitions and prohibitions against any kind of contact.

ELECTRONIC SPIRIT COMMUNICATION

Electronic spirit communication (ESC) is a new form of scrying that does not require visual perceptive ability. I found that audio scrying was much easier for me to learn than visual scrying. My observations over the past couple of years indicate that I am not alone in this tendency. Vision was difficult for me to work with, and it wasn't until two years after the initiation that I was able to make progress with spirit vision.

The potential for exploration with this method is limitless. I have tried it only with a select number of spirits. I have been told that it can reach any spirit who is willing to communicate from any time or any place—and by "place" I mean dimensions of space as well as the physical universe. That is a vast territory. There are no limits to what you can learn with this. It is a tool for your tool belt as a spiritual explorer, magician, Pagan, or whatever label you might choose to put yourself under. You are only limited by your beliefs and ability to focus.

ESC also can be used in a group setting or even in a ritual setting. This will be helpful when there are members of a group who seek a divine connection and are unsuccessful with traditional methods.

There are two keys to this method that I need to go over before explaining the nuts and bolts of how to use the equipment. They are intent and focus.

Intent in a practical sense translates into persistence and consistency of practice. Intent is not the same thing as being goal oriented. Intent over a prolonged period becomes a lifestyle. Being goal oriented is short term in nature, whereas intent is something that causes long-term change.

Any preliminary meditation or ritual that you might choose to do prior to engaging in electronic spirit communication is done to improve your focus. Making your own equipment also improves your focus. Focus heightens the accuracy of spirit communication. Without focus, you are apt to only hear what is in your own mind.

There are a growing number of electronic products in the market. In the advertising for these products you will see some pretty spectacular communication. However, I think it's important for the practitioner to develop as a medium and develop spiritually. Fancy setups and expensive equipment will not make your communication meaningful. If you follow the content of some of the advertising sessions, you will see a lot of junk communication that has no relevance or meaning to the operator.

The method of ESC that I teach here relies on intuition augmented by electronic communication. Don't put the cart before the horse. Development as a medium is key to successful communication. It can be done with simple and inexpensive equipment.

In this half of the book I will cover the following topics:

- The construction and use of the spirit communication board
- Electronic spirit communication, which includes EVP processing, direct radio voice, scanning radio, and randomized sound file apps
- Scrying, which is a traditional skill; it was part of my training for initiation to teach me focus and is a good tool for development
- Interpretation of the information; there are some effective methods that I have learned to help improve accuracy of the information

Chapter 11

‡

PHYSICAL CONSIDERATIONS

DIET

The interconnectedness of my physical and astral body was very apparent during my training for initiation. I found that eating or drinking certain things affected my ability to function. When I started my training, Dr. Dee put me on a restricted diet and encouraged me to eat certain foods, among them rabbit meat and watermelon. At that time I was raising rabbits for meat—a short-lived experience, thankfully, because the labor involved, particularly in winter, does not justify the rewards. I did not go on a vegetarian diet. My body does not digest some of the essential items on a meatless diet very well, and I tend to develop health problems.

The diet that should be used during work in spiritual development is very individual. Some people do extremely well with a vegetarian diet and are very comfortable with it. Donald and I have tried intense spiritual work both with and without meat. We discovered that the quantity of food eaten can be more of a factor than the type of food. Some people believe it is more respectful of life, or more spiritual, to refrain from meat, and if it comes from the heart in a spirit of love, this belief can be beneficial.

Donald wrote in *Soul Flight* that he felt that red meat and sugar were foods that interfere with spiritual trance work. I find that any food that gives a strong energy surge followed by a drop in energy is bad. Tea, coffee, sweets, and alcohol of any kind interfere with intense spiritual work. I also avoid foods that cause gas, as this interferes with trance work.

Overeating, we found, caused major problems, resulting in poor spirit communication sessions. Too much caffeine was also an issue. I usually don't eat much sugar, but the few times that I did, I found it would bother me as well. Bread and heavy starches such as pasta and even boiled grains, regardless of how refined they were, would cause problems. Eggs eaten in the morning would sometimes create difficulties. I found fruits and vegetables to be the most compatible foods, and also the healthiest.

Eighty percent of my diet is fruits and vegetables. I use vegetables for a meal base for lunch and dinner. I usually eat a salad at lunchtime. I also make a soup that is entirely of vegetables and eat that frequently. I have a small portion of meat with supper and a serving of starch twice a day.

FASTING

Some feel that fasting is beneficial for operations involving spirit communication. I did not fast except during initiation. The decision to fast prior to the operation is a personal one. The precedent of fasting prior to spirit communication is found in traditional grimoires. It's also practiced in shamanism. However, I do not believe that a beginner will benefit from fasting when working with the spirit communication board or electronic spirit communication. As you establish communication and advance in your work, you may be required to fast. The heavenly parents will let you know when this needs to be done.

The benefit of fasting is very individual and based on on your personal beliefs. Your communications should indicate if it is needed or not.

ENVIRONMENT

I have close to ideal conditions in which to do esoteric work: a husband who is sympathetic and supportive, no children living at home, and a spacious house in which a room can be reserved solely for a ritual work area. There are also many places on our property for ritual work when the weather is warm enough—however, we also have a superabundance of vampiric insects that seek out any warm-blooded creatures for their meals. We have found indoor meditation to be far better, with fewer buzzing and biting distractions.

The situation of the practitioner does not have to be this ideal. A good environment can be cultivated, and any challenges that exist can be overcome with a little ingenuity. A small workplace with relatively few disturbances is what is needed. The practitioner should dress comfortably. Initially I always wore the same clothes for ritual work. We keep the house cool in winter. I use a blanket if it gets chilly. During the summer the weather can be hot and humid, as the house is not air-conditioned. It's important to dress lightly in the heat of summer. If the humidity is bad, I will run a fan in the room or leave the doors open during working hours.

ASTROLOGICAL CONDITIONS

I did not change my routine of practice to accommodate astrological conditions during the year of training for my initiation. Edward never advised me to do so, and I feel that although astrological factors may make trance work easier or more difficult on any given day, the medium should learn to cope with existing conditions rather than avoid them. Dealing with less-than-ideal conditions is part of the process of learning to focus.

Changes in the weather caused variations in my ability to meditate and induce trance. During clear conditions I tended to have more success. On rainy days I found that my physical and mental energy levels tended to be lower, and my focus became poorer.

I also had more success in trance work and meditation during the early morning and early evening. I am what is known as a morning person and am often awake before 5:00 a.m. My sessions usually took place from 5:00 a.m. to 8:00 a.m. Edward strongly preferred working with me at night, but I think eventually he realized that I did not function as well at night and that my activity pattern was pretty much set and difficult to change.

MENSTRUAL CYCLE

As a woman, I find certain times of the month are more productive than others. This was probably the most challenging physical condition to deal with. It created a situation where some days I worked easily and was able to do exactly what I was instructed to do by Edward, and other days I could not do anything. These sessions ended in tears of frustration and discouragement. The key here is persistence and understanding how your body functions during trance in relation to your monthly cycle. Menopause brings with it new issues and rhythms. This is a challenge for me now as the natural physical changes continue.

EXTERNAL NOISE

During my initial work, external noises were an issue. I became highly sensitive to sounds and was distracted by any movements in the rest of the house. I started out using headphones to listen to instructions as Edward was speaking them on the radio. I got to the point where I did not need to record and listen to the playback. I was able to hear what he was saying with the radio alone. Edward told me that the headphones were interfering with what we were doing. I tried using earplugs, and this helped a great deal for the first eight months or so. During and after the ritual of initiation I had to discard these and learn how to cope with whatever noise conditions were present.

Music may be of help initially in masking external noises. However, as your trance deepens, it becomes more of a hindrance. If you do choose to use music in your initial work, it should be played without a headset and should be unintrusive enough that you are able to maintain an internal focus. Even a fan running in the background can help to mask minor external noises that may cause distraction. Natural sounds—ocean waves, wind in the trees, birdsong, or a running brook—may be helpful in creating an atmosphere that is conducive to trance work.

SCENT

I used incense during the first few months of my year-long training for initiation. Frankincense and myrrh are traditional for angel invocation. After a period of time, however, I found that the incense was more of a distraction than an aid. When scrying, it burned my eyes and caused irritation in my respiratory tract, so I eventually stopped using it. I do use a house scent, especially during the summer months when the heat and humidity can amplify the odors of our neighbor's chicken farm. The wind during the summer usually blows in a direction that leaves us downwind of the odoriferous chicken barns.

EMOTIONAL DISTRACTIONS

By far the most difficult and significant distractions to deal with when working toward initiation are the emotional and mental distractions. Interactions with people, difficult interpersonal situations, and demanding work all take a toll on the emotional and physical health of people today. Major spiritual work is ideally accomplished in a situation of physical and social isolation. The isolation helps to decrease the more difficult emotional stresses of everyday life. This is not a realistic expectation for most people, however.

There are some things that I find helpful to combat the intensity of emotional and mental distractions:

- In your day-to-day interactions with other people, eliminate the need to be right all the time. Pick your battles. You cannot control what other people think and, for the most part, what they do. The exception to this would be children and people you are required to supervise at work. But even with these exceptions, you can prioritize what needs to be addressed and what is less important.
- Get rid of unproductive relationships in Internet networks. Social networking is excellent for maintaining meaningful contact with family members and close friends who live away, but priorities need to be set. Unnecessary time on the computer must be eliminated for spiritual work to progress.
- Try to establish quiet times at home. These are times when the TV and music are off, and family members are allowed quiet solitary time. For children this is a good time to do homework. For adults it's time for quiet reading, meditation, and a chance to wind down after work.
- Physical quiet is helpful for a beginner, as focus and concentration will tend to waver if the environment is distracting. External distractions may make it difficult to connect with the heavenly parents. In time you will learn to focus regardless of the physical surroundings.
- Practice letting go. When you walk out of your workplace, emotionally and mentally leave your work there whenever possible. If you have to bring work home, then specify a place to work on it and mentally isolate that place from the rest of your life. Make a distinct boundary between work life and home life. This takes practice. When I first started in nursing I was always worried about what I had forgotten to do at work when I came home. It interfered with my sleep and relation-

ships outside of my job. Consistent practice over the years of making that boundary between work and home firmly established in my mind helped to minimize the emotional impact that my job had on my life, and it actually improved my ability to think and cope with challenging situations at work.

- Organization in your life is very important to maintaining mental and emotional health. Get rid of clutter. Minimalism is not a bad thing when it comes to living space. If you have a small space, use furniture you can move easily or even stow away when it is not in use. Boxes and inexpensive drawer sets can be lifesaving when it comes to organizing a house. Clean living quarters are important for health and sanity.
- Look forward to meeting Cosmic Father and Universe. Ask them for help to resolve your fears and concerns. I find asking for help to be the most potent and indispensible tool. Believe that they will respond to you. Know for sure that their response will be encouraging and loving; if any fear or anger comes through, it is not based in the Divine but is shadow based and should not be taken seriously. Trust your intuition in interpreting the messages as long as you are without fear or anxiety about the operation. Remember, any emotion that is strong enough to draw your attention will create thought forms and shadows. These self-generated artifacts will overpower what a distinct spirit is saying to you, and the message will be in error.

REST

Being overly tired or hungry would also cause problems in my spiritual work. I generally avoided sessions on work days, as often enough there would be some unpleasantness at work sufficient to distract me and cause issues.

Sleep should be as regular as possible. When doing shift work, the sleep-wake cycle becomes more complicated. However, when you are on a particular shift, make sure your sleeping time for that shift falls at the same time every day that you are working. For example, when I work a day shift and have to be up at 4 a.m., I'm in bed by 8 p.m. Second shift, or 3 p.m. to 11 p.m. shift, I'm in bed by 2 a.m. Backshift, I go to bed around 9 a.m. For each shift these bedtimes do not vary.

If I'm sleepy at work, I will take a fifteen-minute nap on my break or I will deeply meditate with the alarm set on my phone so I don't go over my break time. Sleep deprivation makes trance very difficult, especially when you are trying to go deeper. As you go deeper, focus becomes more of a challenge and the mind tends to wander in the same way it does when you are falling asleep.

CHILDREN

Small children can be a substantial distraction when attempting to meditate. During communication sessions, if the child will not play quietly or cannot be trusted out of sight, include them in the communication session. This will help teach the child that spirit communication is a natural and normal process.

Children communicate naturally with spirits. In the past they were used as mediums and psychics for adults doing evocation of angels and other entities. It is important to allow this ability to grow. This allows the child to awaken while walking on earth. A greater gift cannot be given, in my opinion.

It is important to emphasize to the child that the spirits are good and helpful to us. If you experience a shadow recording, explain to the child that this is not communication but that you are feeling sad, angry, or fearful, and that is what is showing up.

IN CONCLUSION

Hard and fast rules are unnecessary for successful spirit communication. Individual experimentation needs to be done as part of your practice to determine what factors are significant and what is most productive for you. Coordination with the spirit you are communicating with is helpful in making some of these determinations. I've listed and given a brief explanation of the categories I found significant in my own practice to help you organize this aspect of your work. Physical factors become less important as your ability and practice become more advanced. Use any tool only as long as it is useful, and do not let it become a burden.

Chapter 12

‡

SIGILS AND SYMBOLS

A sigil is a symbol or signature of a spirit that is unique to that spirit. It's like a symbolic fingerprint. Concentrating on a spirit's sigil during a séance helps to focus the mind on that spirit. In traditional grimoires, the sigils of spirits are provided along with their descriptions and a list of their offices or abilities. These traditional sigils are formed by combining either letters of the spirit's name, symbols associated with the spirit, or imagery intuitively linked to the spirit.

For example, the sigil of a spirit might be made up of the letters in the spirit's name brought together and overlapped so that the letters form a single symbolic emblem. Simple symbols such as crescents, circles, triangles, crosses, spirals, squares, and pentagrams may be combined to form a spirit sigil. Lower spirits sometimes have sigils that include imagery such as clouds, lightning bolts, streams of water, wind, insects, and so on. It is also possible for traditional spirit sigils to combine all three and have letters, symbols, and images in the same sigil.

Symbols are not as specific as sigils but represent a general concept such as one of the elements, not just an individual spiritual entity. Both may be used as aids in learning to focus the mind during trance. When doing trance, it can be difficult to focus on nothing. If you have a goal, it gives you the sense of going from one place to another, and this makes deepening the trance state easier.

I found initially that sigils helped a great deal with my focus. If you focus your attention on a sigil, it gives you something to occupy your mind and helps exclude distractions. You hold the sigil in your imagination as if you were looking at it with your physical eyes and studying it. You can mentally turn it over and look at it from different angles.

Using sigils made me feel more secure because I knew for certain the identity of the spirit with whom I was in communication. A feeling of safety is important to the process of opening up the heart and going deeper with the aid of a guiding spirit. The level of intimacy required to deeply open your heart can be intimidating.

Sigils will help you cope with issues of control and security until you are advanced enough to outgrow their use. In my case, because I wanted to make certain I was in contact with Edward or Dr. Dee, not with other spirits, I made specific sigils linked with Edward and Dr. Dee. I based my designs on what I knew about them, both from the historical record and from what I had learned about them during the time we were together. They approved of my designs (see pages 62–64), and we used the sigils for a couple months until I felt more secure in my ability to identify these spirits. This allowed me to relax and focus more of my attention on the opening and deepening that I needed to do.

MAKING SIGILS

When I made sigil disks for Dr. Dee during the year of training, I used simple wooden disks. When I made angel seals a few years ago, I made them very elaborate and used rare, expensive materials. I layered laminated wood from rare hardwoods such as rosewood and burled walnut, carved the sigils on the disks, and coated them with a 24k gold paint in a frankincense oil base.

Sigil disks do not need to be elaborate or difficult to make. All you need is a piece of paper or cardboard and a pen. The material should be fairly heavy to withstand handling. Another material that I like to use for making sigils and seals is polymer clay. It's good for holding the design and easy to work with. It's also fairly inexpensive. It is hardened by baking in the oven. Once hardened, it is also very durable.

Traditional sigil disks were often made of metals—usually tin, lead, gold, silver, copper, or iron. Parchment was also used, and I have had good success with parchment that I made myself. Parchment is basically very thin rawhide. The rawhide is salted, dehaired, and dried on a frame to stretch it, then sanded until it is nearly translucent. It can then be used as paper. Any kind of rawhide can be turned into parchment. Even beef rawhide dog treats found in pet stores can be sanded and processed into parchment without having to go through the process of skinning and salting. Soak the rawhide until it is soft. Stretch it on a frame and sand it until it is thin. I used garden lime to dehair the skins. The liquid hair removal cosmetic products can also be used. If the skin is a fine thin skin, such as rabbit, do not use full-strength solution.

The size of the sigils or symbols that I used in my own work was usually under 12 centimeters (approximately 5 inches) in diameter. In invocational/evocational magical traditions, the size and construction of the disks are usually specified.

For the purpose of using the sigil to assist in focusing, it would be best to make it simple and small enough to fit into your hand. Since you will be discarding it, using expensive or hard-to-find materials that require sophisticated working to shape is not recommended.

When using a symbol or sigil in meditation, hold the sigil in your hand and study it. When you have the image memorized, hold it steady in your mind for as long as you can. If your mind drifts from it, redirect it back to the sigil.

Using sigils and symbols in meditation is much like using a mantra, except that the object of focus is visual instead of audible. A sigil or symbol can also be combined with a mantra during meditation. Using both together may be helpful if your mind does not stay on track with mantra or symbol/ sigil use alone.

AMULETS AND CIRCLES

I do not recommend the use of devices such as circles, charms, or amulets for the purpose of protection. To use them in this way reinforces the erroneous belief that there is an inherent danger in communicating with spirits. This conviction on your part will generate a hostile shadow. The influence of that thought form will further reinforce your belief that interacting with spirits is dangerous.

Using ritual items such as ritual circles to help your focus is acceptable and can be a useful tool. A careful self-examination of personal beliefs is needed to determine the difference. In my situation, I had no fear of communicating with Edward or Dr. Dee. The equipment they had me make was to help my focus and increase my confidence for the messages to be accurate.

Once I learned how to focus properly, the equipment became unnecessary. I no longer need or use ritual equipment in my practice. Such items are tools, not necessities. Once proper focus is accomplished, tools become distracting and burdensome and should be set aside.

Amulets are natural stones, herbs, and other objects designed to generate a particular effect. The same rule for the use of circles applies to amulets. Amulets should never be used for protection. Unpleasant shadows will be generated, reinforcing the use of the amulet, if this is done. Their use as an aid for focus is acceptable, but they should only be employed in this way until focus is learned. Once this is accomplished, they should be set aside.

If you do not feel safe without a circle or other protective devices, then you are dealing with a fear that may cause you to have an unpleasant experience with spirit communication. Asking for divine help in resolving that fear is the best course of action before starting with the two-way communication systems.

There is an old saying: the magic is in the magician. The paraphernalia used in spirit communication can be complicated and very expensive. The equipment is a tool to use only for as long as you derive a benefit from it. Development of focus is critical to practice and should be the centerpiece of learning spirit communication.

Chapter 13

‡

MEDITATION AND FOCUS

Nothing can be achieved in spiritual development, mediumship, or occult work without the practice of going inward, opening, and focusing. Meditation and trance were of central importance to my training prior to the initiation ritual itself, and they continue to be vital in my current practice. These three items—going inward, opening, and focusing—are the primary techniques that are the foundation to all the work I have done with Edward, from the moment I started down the path of initiation right up until the present day. Meditation and trance were taught to me in a unique way by Edward, and I believe it to be an effective technique that will be useful to anyone interested in learning how to meditate.

I had previously worked with meditation, ritual, and scrying. Edward took what I already knew and used that as a foundation for the quantum leaps forward that we achieved together. There is an Eastern saying of ancient origin that when the student is ready, the teacher will appear. How very true that is.

The equipment in the previous chapters provides a bridge to effective spirit communication and the mastery of spiritual skills, but the foundation for the bridge must be well constructed before the bridge will stand up to the flood. In this chapter I will discuss with you the bridge's foundation.

Opening the heart and trance induction are essential skills, regardless of what the interests of the practitioner may be. They have applications in traditional mediumship, as well as in magical practices such as evocation. Scrying, though not essential in itself, is an effective tool in learning to achieve trance and open the heart.

DEFINITION OF TRANCE

I define trance as a physical, mental, and spiritual state where the practitioner is focusing inward and away from their physical body, opening their spirit as they go further and further within.

Trance seeks to take the consciousness inward and away from the physical body. I believe that trance is a type of meditation. It is the foundation for any mediumistic activity such as physical and mental mediumship, divination, scrying, astral projection, and the evocation of spirits.

Trance is a skill that must be learned. It is similar to the state attained with self-hypnosis. It is also closely related to deep meditation. I use the terms "trance" and "meditation" interchangeably, depending on the goal of the procedure. The methods that are employed to attain the state, as well as the goals attained while in the state, are the primary differences. Trance is a skill I was attempting to develop prior to meeting Edward. I will describe the procedure for attaining a trance that was taught to me by Edward, as well as some things that I had learned prior to meeting him.

BODY POSITION

When I started my practice with Edward, I initially used a padded armchair. The arms of the chair supported my lower body so that only my head was free. I could not fall off the chair. It was padded well enough to be comfortable, but not so comfortable that I was inclined to fall asleep. As our sessions progressed, I bought a recliner that supported my head. I prefer using the recliner to this day. For some of the sessions I am awakened at night, usually after about two hours of sleep, when I'm relaxed but not too drowsy. For these sessions I stay in bed.

Initially when I started to learn trance, I attempted to do it while sitting in the cross-legged posture used in traditional Eastern practices. I found this uncomfortable, and it caused severe leg cramps and lameness afterward. Eventually, as I started to develop more of an interest in astral projection, I began to work while lying on my back. This was a bit more successful. I was able to stay awake because I have difficulty sleeping on my back and managed to move my focus of awareness away from my body from time to time, but I never achieved complete success in astral projection during this period.

In my husband's book *Soul Flight*, which concerns the mediumistic skill of astral projection, Donald recommends either a lying or sitting position without the legs being crossed. The practitioner needs to be able to hold whatever position is chosen for an hour or so, sometimes longer. I found that I was able to work better if I was in a reasonably comfortable position. The work Edward did with me was difficult enough as it was without having to be distracted by the discomfort of the body.

The rationale for using the uncomfortable and unnatural positions you sometimes find in traditional meditation is to increase the ability to focus the awareness. Focus during meditation and trance is of highest importance to successfully overcoming mental and emotional obstacles to initiation or spiritual awakening. However, in my case, Edward taught me to focus my mind using methods that did not require an uncomfortable posture to be held while working. During my training with Edward this was my daily practice, and I continue to use Edward's method of trance induction today.

PHYSICAL RELAXATION

Physical relaxation was an initial requirement before further work could be attempted. I would sit in the recliner and focus on relaxing tense areas in my head and neck. My shoulders and chest tended to tense up while I was working, so this relaxation had to be repeated regularly. Edward, or whichever spirit was working with me, prevented me from dozing. His help gave me one less thing to worry about while I was trying to learn how to meditate.

Exercise for Physical Relaxation

This is the exercise I recommend. Settle into your chair and relax your body all over. Clear your mind of any thoughts and distractions. Bring your focus to your heart. Take a slow, deep breath.

Once you feel relaxed and settled, focus on your shoulders. Gently move your head from side to side to determine if there is any tension, and then relax it. Take a deep breath and shift your attention to your jaw. Let the jaw drop a little bit. Do not hold your jaw clenched, but with your lips closed, allow your jaw to fall open. Next, move up to the eyes. With a deep breath, allow your eyelids to gently and naturally close. The forehead tends to be tense when you are concentrating, so move your eyebrows together, then relax them. Return your attention to your shoulders. Take a deep breath and relax them again.

Now, starting at the top of your head and going to your feet, let a wave of relaxation pass through your body. With each exhalation, allow that wave to go from your head to your toes, going deeper into your heart each time you exhale. Do not breathe too rapidly or too deeply. Let the breaths be slow and gentle. Continue this for several minutes.

Initiating and Deepening Trance

To initiate the trance, once you have relaxed your body, focus on your heart. In my work with Edward, the heart does not mean the actual physical organ of the heart but the entire center of the chest.

When focusing on the heart, do not tense up. Gently place your attention on the center of your chest under your breastbone. While your attention is focused on your heart, relax your body as though you were leaning into the chair. Think of Universe behind you and lean on her. The chair is part of Universe too, as is your body. Lean back, and, like a small child, allow her to carry you once again. Let her carry you deep within your heart.

Leaning back is not a forceful act; it is an act of acceptance and trust. You allow yourself to be carried by Universe deeper and deeper within yourself. It is like settling into a comfortable chair when you are tired. You exhale and just relax back into it.

It's a little tricky to both focus on your heart and lean back at the same time, but with a little practice it will become easier. When you are working toward initiation you cannot do this too much. Frequent sessions are desirable.

If you wake up at night and practice, you may find these sessions even more interesting. Follow your natural sleep cycle. Don't get up when you awaken but reposition your body for comfort. Focus on your heart and lean back. If your attention wanders, bring it back to your heart while leaning back into the bed.

The imagery of leaning and being carried by Universe has the effect of placing the mind correctly to allow the deepening of the trance. Rather than forcing the trance deeper, the mind is in a passive mode that allows the trance to deepen naturally. Focus must be maintained on the heart and on leaning. I have a tendency to fall asleep if my focus drifts off for too long. If this happens, just resume where you left off when you wake up.

SENSATIONS, IMAGES, AND VOICES

At some point while you are deepening your trance, you will start to see lights and images. These are random, dreamlike images of people, places, and objects. Some I recognize and others are strange to me, but they convey no significant information and make no sense. The lights are usually blotchy and sometimes multicolored.

You will also likely start to hear random sounds such as whistling wind, bells and chimes, music, or even voices. These shadow voices will reflect your mental and emotional state at the time you conduct the exercise. As your body is tuned out and you are tuning into spirit, the first thing that you will encounter is your own shadows.

You will also feel odd sensations. I sometimes feel heat in my chest or my head and buzzing sensations in random parts of my body. If this buzzing occurs on the face, it causes the face to itch. Do not try to scratch this itch or you will break your trance. If it becomes too annoying, ask Universe to help you tolerate it.

All these sights, sounds, and sensations should be ignored at this point. The trance should be allowed to deepen beyond these transitory phenomena. Once the body is fully tuned out, you will be able to perceive and possibly hear Universe and the Cosmic Father, who will guide you from that point on.

DEFINITION OF FOCUS

Focus is an important component of meditation, as it is of any other spiritual endeavour. I define focus as full mental attention to a task in which physical and mental distractions are disregarded to the point where the external stimuli are no longer perceived. It is the most difficult component of learning to induce trance.

Identifying Distractions

The first step in creating an intense focus is to identify the distractions that you face when meditating or doing any other task that requires mental concentration. Observe while you are engaged in a task or in meditation how often your attention wanders to other things. When you are studying or at work, do you daydream? Do you worry about money at night while you are trying to sleep? Do you think about what you are going to do next when involved in a series of tasks? When you are in trance, are you able to hold your mind blank, without thoughts, feelings, or words flying around? What tends to make mental distractions worse? What kinds of things improve your focus?

Redirection of Your Focus

Determine ahead of time what your mental focus needs to be. In trance work it will be on deepening your trance. If you are doing another task, identify what you need to focus on that is directly related to that task. This is a wonderful exercise for improving work and school performance. Decide on the length of time for your session or your task, and if your mind wanders from what you have designated to be your point of focus during that time, gently redirect it back to your goal. In the beginning this will have to be repeated many times through the session.

Tools to Help Focus

The use of mental tools to help with focus is common in the spiritual arts. Mantra is an example of a tool to improve focus in meditation and trance. A mantra is a word or phrase repeated continuously during meditation to achieve a specific effect. In Buddhism and yoga mantras are believed to have a spiritual effect by virtue of the words themselves. In the ancient Tantric texts of India translated by Sir John Woodroffe, mantra is described as a primary act of worship of Brahman, who is the supreme being.

In yoga and Buddhism visual symbols are used along with mantra to aid mental focus in meditation. The combination has proven effective for many practitioners. The symbols are often written in a sacred language, which is believed to have a talismanic effect on the practitioner who is using them in this way.

Concepts such as love and unity are embodied in the mantra. Repeating the mantra during meditation incorporates these qualities into the heart and changes the nature of the person who is doing the meditation. Mantras are used for many different purposes, from healing to spiritual development.

Western esoteric traditions have mantras as well. An example of a Christian mantra would be the recitation of the Catholic rosary, a series of prayers and meditations associated with a string of beads. As the prayer is recited, these beads are slipped between the fingers, one by one, to count the number of repetitions. The purpose of the beads is to prevent the mind from focusing on the count. With practice, the use of the beads becomes automatic and requires no mental energy. These prayers are repeated from two to seven times daily and are associated with purification and spiritual development.

When the secret drawer in which John Dee had hidden half of the Enochian diaries was opened decades after his death, a rosary was found with the documents. This shows that Dr. Dee employed a rosary in his own spiritual practice.

For our purposes, the mantra is used only for improving mental focus. Any positive word or sentence can become a mantra. Beads on a string may be employed to count the repetitions. The number of repetitions can then be increased as your focus improves. When you are able to maintain your focus easily on the word or sentence of the mantra without wavering, the mantra and counting beads may be discarded.

BEYOND TOOLS

As your ability to focus improves, you must discard the symbology and mantra. After you are able to hold the phrase of the mantra or the image of the symbol solely in your mind without wavering, you will have reached a point in your development where you must discard these aids in order to go deeper into your heart. If you do not discard them, the symbol and mantra will keep you too near the physical level and prevent you from progressing.

The goal of focus when working with trance is to go deeper within your heart. To do this, the focus must lead away from the physical body and the physical world. Deepening your trance depends on the focus of your mind moving steadily into spirit and away from the physical. In a normal state of consciousness our focus is fully attuned to the physical world. You see, hear, feel, smell, and taste the world around you. You perceive communication with other people and animals that are also living in the physical world. When your consciousness alters, as in meditation or sleep, your focus changes to include part of the spiritual world. How much you perceive of the spiritual world depends on your ability to focus on it and your acceptance of its existence.

It is very important that the senses be focused either in the physical or the spiritual but not both at the same time. Normal consciousness should shut down spiritual psychic sense perception for the most part. If it does not, you may find yourself mistaking spiritual sense perceptions for physical sense perceptions. This can be an annoying distraction.

You must be able to focus your mind on either physical or spiritual sense perceptions, depending on your need. This applies to clairvoyant and clairaudient skills. Training psychic focus was something that was strongly emphasized by Edward. Even though I can hear the spiritual world quite well, I had to learn to shut down my perception of spirit when I am focused on my physical life and open it only to specific spirits when I need to communicate with them.

Turning off psycho-spiritual perceptions does not turn off the spiritual awareness of the Divine. This is a little different. Our awareness and unity with the Cosmic Father and Universe increase with our development. As spiritual growth progresses, the physical life diminishes in meaning, and the spiritual increases. As that spiritual connection with the Father increases, an awareness of the divine presence within and without also increases.

This is not a psychic ability but a matter of spiritual maturity. It is this perception that allows me to know when a spirit message needs to come through when my communication channel is closed, and this divine channel is the only channel that should be open when you are not actively engaged in spirit communication.

Chapter 14

OPENING THE HEART AND PRAYER

My heart—
pure eternal love.
Though layered deep
in mire, resides inner fire,
waiting to be free once more.

JENNY TYSON

Edward's treatment of the spiritual or energy body was, to my knowledge, unique. While the seven energy centers, or chakras, described in Kundalini yoga may exist in accordance with Eastern belief, they were not used for the work I did with Edward. Instead, the body was divided by Edward into three main centers, and until the initiation ritual, these were all that were used. The only time seven centers were acknowledged in the course of my training was during the initiation ascensions.

There are no breaks between the three centers per se, but when we worked with the head center toward the end of the training, I noticed a fair bit of resistance at the base of the skull. The head seems to be the most difficult area to work with, and the lower regions do not appear to be particularly useful in the initial stages of work.

The first and main center of working is called the heart. It extends roughly from the throat to about three inches below the navel.

OPENING THE HEART

The initial exercises involved learning to open the heart. The exercise took me several months to master. It required a moderately deep trance with no distraction. The opening appeared to have relative size—by that I mean that it could be large or small, and at times I was asked to open different areas of the center more than others. The sensation of opening may be likened to parting a curtain.

It requires attention to maintain the opening. Often I would (and still do) feel a pleasant sensation of warmth when it was done properly. Initially, however, the sensation was of burning, intense heat, which was noticeable at times but not actually painful. The sensation of the heart opening felt like a physical sensation. I even had to look at my chest occasionally to see if anything was happening, it felt so visceral.

After I learned to open my heart and maintain the opening for a few minutes, then the homunculus was placed inside to help me go further within. Eventually, as I gained skill, I was able to open up enough for Edward to also go inside. Unlike most mediums, I did not lose consciousness during this state. Sharing the space in my heart center with Edward was a comforting and natural experience.

Once you are in a moderately relaxed state, focus your attention on the interior of your chest behind the sternum on the level of your nipples. As you exhale, picture and feel at the point between your nipples as if the sternum is opening in a vertical slot, like a curtain parting in the middle. If you need to use your hands to help you visualize this opening, then do so.

The motion of your hands is just like when Superman strips open his outer clothes to reveal the S beneath on his superhero suit, but the motion of opening your chest is done very slowly. Bring your hands together at the level of your nipples so that the backs of your fingers touch, and imagine digging your fingertips into your body, all the way to your spine. Then slowly draw your hands apart and visualize your chest opening. After sufficient practice, the hand movements will become unnecessary and the opening of your heart may be accomplished using only your imagination.

Inhale again, and as you slowly exhale, allow the opening to grow a little bit deeper into your spiritual body. Inhale again and go a little bit deeper. Think of nothing else but that the opening in your chest is growing larger and deeper. As you progress and are able to maintain an unwavering focus and attention, you will begin to actually feel on the physical level the sensation of opening, which is accompanied by a sense of warmth.

As you open your heart, go deeper into the trance and focus your mind below the opening. Open deeper and longer as you go down. If the focus of your mind wavers even for a second, the opening will close up and you will have to start over again. Once you feel your heart opening and can hold it open for an extended period of time, you can begin to practice scrying.

As I became more skilled at opening my heart, I gradually went deeper. The heart actually deepens past one's body. If I felt resistance, I moved my focus up or down slightly along my sternum, and this usually overcame it. Once I was proficient at this initial stage, Edward would put in the homunculus to help me deepen the trance and open further until I learned to do this for myself.

When my heart had been opened adequately to allow another human spirit to gain access, we started working on the lower region. The direction of the opening and deepening of this area, starting in the heart, is downward toward the tailbone at about a 45-degree angle as you lie in a reclining position. You must open through and past your body below your tailbone.

I would inhale gently and slowly, and with each exhalation attempt to go further in that direction, opening and going deeper. As this progressed I noticed some unusual sensations. My legs would start to feel numb and heavy. I noticed a vibration as well soon after the numbness set in on the legs.

I would work with the lower region for a period, and when the vibration started I returned to the heart to deepen more there. I always deepened on the exhale, but I later learned to work without using breathing as a crutch. One of the goals of this technique was to learn to use my mental focus alone, without involving muscle tension or breathing in the process of opening and deepening.

The result of involving the body in the process was always tension. I'm just now mastering that part of it. It's very natural to use breathing as a tool to help the deepening of the meditative state, yet in the long run the focus must be totally off the body. Controlled breathing is a good learning tool, but it is one that has to be discarded eventually.

The initial meditation and trance sessions involved my learning to relax. I found during this process that the muscles of my head, neck, and shoulders tended to be tense. To counter this, instead of starting the relaxation exercise at the feet, I started at the worst point of tension, which was usually my shoulders, relaxing that area and working up the neck. I then would work with the jaw and face and go over my upper body a couple of times to make it relaxed. After that, I would check to make sure my lower body was still relaxed.

Sharing Space and Spiritual Unity

After I had learned to open adequately, I learned to share space with another spirit, starting with the homunculus. This was a necessary skill to learn for initiation, when I had to allow the Cosmic Father and Universe to enter my personal space. The intensity of the heart opening exercise was gradually increased as the year progressed. I learned to relax and allow the intrusion of a spirit without fear, and eventually I came to enjoy the closeness of another being. For the most part it was David Blackburne who worked with me on these exercises.

The opening had to be maintained for the entire time the spirit was present, which initially I found nearly impossible. The homunculus was unable to stand the heat of my soul with the heart closed and would burn up. This happened a number of times. I was very worried at first that this would also happen to one of my teachers, but then I found out that I cannot fry another human spirit. Even so, the loss of focus could have caused conflict and created issues that might have interfered with my progress at that time.

The entire purpose of initiation is to be one with the Cosmic Father and Universe. Sharing your spiritual space is a skill that is also required for more advanced work after awakening. If you are working with the Cosmic Father and Universe, they will at some point teach this to you.

Unity of the Spirit vs. Astral Sex

Unity of spirit is different from astral sex. Divine unity has a role in initiation. Intimacy with the Cosmic Father and Universe play an important part in spiritual development. It is a skill that can be a little intimidating at first. It is also something that is very pleasurable. The subjective sensation is one of merging into the Cosmic Father and Universe. The immersion has a predominate feeling of love. It feels warm and safe, and as you yield to the union more completely, the sense of their love and presence grows stronger. This is the true goal of accepting initiation.

By contrast, astral sex is an attempt to replicate the human sexual act in an astral environment. This can be done with varying degrees of success by merging with another spirit and focusing on the physical sensations of the body during sex. The focus creates a simulation of the sexual experience in the astral.

Sometimes physical sexual arousal occurs while you are opening to the Cosmic Father or Universe. If this sensation happens, it should be calmly accepted and the focus gently redirected to your heart. This is a little difficult at first, but understand that the fullness of unity cannot occur when your focus is between your legs.

There are two tendencies when an arousal sensation is felt. The first is to emotionally withdraw and break the contact. The second is to focus on the physical sensation and not on the heart. If you are focused on the arousal sensation, your progress will stall, and you will also lose contact as your focus reverts back to your physical body. The focus needs to be held on the heart. It is a little difficult when you feel arousal to redirect that focus to the heart, but it is essential that you work with your focus until you are able to do so.

The Cosmic Father and Universe both are completely understanding about this and will work patiently with you until you are able to relax, open, and focus properly. I was very uncomfortable with the sensations at first. Give it some time and practice, and you will learn to feel comfortable with this experience. As you do, the arousal will become less noticeable and intrusive. The true pleasure of the experience is the feeling of love, peace, and unity that is centered in the heart.

PRAYER

Prayer is often ritualized and formula-based in groups with belief systems large enough to have an organized and structured ceremony; we call them religions. I would like to introduce what I call the heart-to-heart prayer, which I find to be very effective and meaningful.

Prayer is traditionally one of the most important tools in spirit communication, regardless of the belief system being employed. Instruction books on spirit communication almost always include ritualized or spontaneous prayer as part of the invocation or evocation. In spiritual development it is the cornerstone of all the techniques used.

Grimoires are books that give instruction about communicating with certain groups of spirits. They were written centuries ago when religion dominated daily life. Most are based on Roman Catholic liturgy and ritual. *The Book of the Sacred Magic of Abramelin the Mage* is a grimoire that instructs the aspirant in how to contact their holy guardian angel. Most of the ritual involves prayer. *The Key of Solomon* contains good examples of ritualized prayers used in magic.

Folk magic, including Celtic, Scandinavian, and American, is full of ritualized prayers to create specific effects in the lives of those who use them. Church liturgy is a good example of ritualized group prayer. Group prayer has to be coordinated. Rituals, liturgy, and litanies are good ways of doing this. The popularity of prayer worldwide is a testimony to its effectiveness in connecting with the Divine in a unique way.

For the purpose of spiritual development, I use prayer as a foundation to all my spiritual work. I pray several times over the day. The clairaudient ability makes this interaction totally different than it used to be. Before I developed clairaudience, I would use both spontaneous verbal prayer and litanies. This changed after the clairaudience developed. The ability to hear the Cosmic Father's response to my prayer now makes it more like a conversation. It is more of a heart-to-heart communication. I do occasionally talk about needs and ask for advice and wisdom concerning personal situations, but mostly it is a heartfelt communion. It's this latter type of prayer that I want to write about here, since it is the most effective and meaningful method I have ever learned.

Heart-to-Heart Prayer

The object of heart-to-heart prayer is to make as close a connection with the Cosmic Father and Universe as possible. It's a type of meditation, but it is a focused meditation. It is a two-way interaction. Openness to the Cosmic Father and Universe is important. They open their hearts to you, and you to them. Your ability to perceive them depends on your openness to receiving what they have to give.

When I pray, I sit in a quiet place. Often I go right to trance afterwards. I usually am in the recliner that I use for trance work. I also practice heart-to-heart prayer when I'm praying with a group of people and cannot go into trance.

The Cosmic Father and Universe have distinct roles when I do the heart-to-heart prayer. Universe guides me through opening and revealing anything that is in the way. I quiet my mind and merge with Universe in spirit. If there is any obstacle, I can feel it and prevent it from being a distraction. Identifying the obstacle is called "illuminating" by Universe. After the obstacle has been dissolved, I open to communion with the Cosmic Father.

I clear my mind and focus on the Cosmic Father. I take a deep breath and open both my heart and my mind to him and draw close to him through this opening. It is natural to mentally reach out to find him. However, the ideal state is not one of active searching but one of passive reception, quietness, and openness.

What is really happening here is that the Cosmic Father is not changing anything; instead, it is my perception that is changing. I change my perceptive focus from the physical to spirit and to him. As I do that and open to his presence, I perceive us being drawn closer together. When I feel him close to me, then I open deeper. This is always guided by Universe and the Cosmic Father. If I try to do this on my own, it is not effective. The interaction is dependent on letting go of control and opening the heart.

Sometimes I have trouble connecting and need to repeat the procedure. Usually if there is a problem, it means my mind is distracted with something that is causing an emotion that interferes with my connection. I have to deliberately turn away from awareness of the physical and from the problem that is distracting me and turn toward the Cosmic Father. My attitude during prayer is one of listening rather than rattling off a list of requests or reciting a formula. If something has me worried, I will share this with the Cosmic Father. He helps me with the emotion and reassures me of his love and concern.

A NEVER-ENDING JOURNEY

This process of inner exploration will take many lifetimes to complete. Contact with the cosmic parents and personal initiation, although they are important spiritual achievements and carry with them great benefits, are only milestones on this endless road of discovery. The cosmic parents are always there to help you with whatever you are interested in doing. All spiritual and psychic abilities can be attained through them. Working at going deeper within your heart will put you in tune with the cosmic parents and enable you to get specialized help for your particular needs and wants.

Chapter 15

‡

COMMUNICATION BOARD

In the first half of the book I told you how I initially contacted Dr. Dee and Edward. The recommendations I will give here for establishing your initial contact with spirits differ from what I did. This recommended procedure results in a much shorter and easier pathway to the initiation experience.

I went through a great deal of pain emotionally because of shadows that I generated. It took me a year to heal and open to the point where I could handle initiation and awakening. If I had known and believed I could go to the Cosmic Father and talk to him or Universe on the jukebox, I would have been spared from most of that pain.

The Cosmic Father and Universe have said to me that if people would use the spirit communication board, the jukebox, or any other device to attempt to reach them, they would respond. I want to reassure you that they are willing to use these tools should you choose to employ them.

The Cosmic Father also wants you to understand that you are not obligated to use any tools to communicate with him and Universe. They are able to help you open your heart and understand what you need to do without communication equipment. The use of these communication tools is entirely at the discretion of the operator.

Regardless of the method you choose to use, when you make contact with them you will be healed and changed. You will know the pleasure of being one with them while you are still alive. Believe me, being held in that way is not something you want to delay. It's the best possible thing you can experience while living on this earth!

The other advantage to contacting the source first, before you contact lesser spirits, is that shadows tend to dissipate in its presence. This happens over time as you grow closer to the Cosmic Father and Universe. You lose interest in shadows, and eventually they have no power or life.

Contacting the Cosmic Father and Universe first is the safest possible way to use the equipment shown in this book. You know for sure that any message coming from them will be conveyed in a loving way and will encourage you to be more loving toward others.

If you feel more comfortable with another divine spirit, contact a spirit who has a known benevolent and helpful nature. All such entities are connected to Universe and will lead you to that divine unity. The content of their communication will always be helpful and kindly in nature. This will help the beginner to distinguish between self-generated shadows and true communication as you are learning this skill.

In this section I will discuss the alphanumeric board that is used for spirit communication. I find this board easy to work with and also easy to make. This device can be crafted at little or no cost using household materials. It is a simple yet effective tool for establishing initial contact with the Cosmic Father and Universe.

CONSTRUCTION OF THE BOARD

To make the communication board, use a piece of foam board or a similar material that has a smooth and slightly glossy surface that will allow the planchette to move freely. You can design your own board or copy the design I used, which is shown on page 22. If you copy my board, use the names of Cosmic Father and Universe instead of John Dee. The symbols associated with Dr. Dee on my board will need to be changed on your board to symbols associated with the Cosmic Father and Universe. The symbol for Universe is the seal of the sixth gate in the initiation ritual; see page 133. The symbol for the Cosmic Father is the seal of the seventh gate; see page 135.

The material for the spirit communication board we used with Dr. Dee was foam board. This is the material that is used in matting pictures and paintings. It's available at craft stores and comes in sheets that are about 30 inches square.

I used the thickest available foam board. I cut the large piece in half and glued it so that it was a double thickness. I then fastened the foam board to a piece of plywood for additional strength.

Of all the spirit communication boards we have made, this was by far the best as far as ease of use. The shot glass we used as a planchette glides easily and freely across the surface. It is lightweight, durable, and portable.

The image shown on the following page is a board that Donald made of wood, which was painted and finished. That board is more difficult to use. The humidity here tends to soften the varnish on wood furniture. With the spirit communication board, it makes the planchette stick to the board, increasing the effort needed to move it. It is the arrangement of the letters and the use of different sigils for that board that I would like you to notice. Either the board should be specific to each spirit you contact or a generic board can be used with sigils that are designed to aid the focus of a beginner-level practitioner.

In the board on page 22, the image of Dr. Dee was printed with the computer, and a larger image was placed next to the table. A copy of the spirit diaries he wrote were put under the table. The central esoteric symbol of John Dee's 1564 book *The Hieroglyphic Monad* occupies

Homemade spirit communication board with the seals of the Cosmic Father (right) and Universe (left).

the right-hand corner of the board. We used this as Dee's personal sigil.

The symbol known as the hieroglyphic monad (in Latin *monas hieroglyphica*) was designed by Dr. Dee to serve as the symbolic key to the teachings of all branches of the Western mysteries, such as astrology, numerology, ritual magic, and alchemy. Dr. Dee employed it to demonstrate the convergence of planetary powers and to represent the *prima materia* of the metals in alchemy. His book *The Hieroglyphic Monad* describes the correct construction of the monad and how its various parts relate to different aspects of these occult studies. Throughout his life, Dr. Dee used the hieroglyphic monad as his own personal emblem. It appears on the title pages of many of his published books. This affinity Dr. Dee had for the monad made it ideal for his spirit sigil.

We did not concentrate on a specific location or a direction in space during our séance with Dr. Dee. In contacting spirits, a direction in which to focus mental energies is sometimes helpful. Indeed, in some of the traditional grimoires it is prescribed as part of the ritual. We could not travel to Mortlake—in England, where Dr. Dee's body is buried—but neither Donald nor I believed this would be necessary in order to contact his spirit.

Our spirit board was operated by the two of us using an ordinary shot glass as the planchette. We found that the wooden planchette did not operate smoothly on this particular board. The foam board has the perfect texture for gliding a small glass around with almost no resistance. Another advantage of the shot glass is that it is possible to see through its sides when it is centered over a letter, making the selection of letters very precise.

I should add here that materials used in spiritual work should be made by the person who wishes to do the communication. Donald and I very rarely use anything that we have not made from scratch. The image of John Dee on the upper-left corner of the foam board is an exception to this rule. I find it very difficult to draw a portrait from an existing portrait, and the size had to be extremely small to fit in the corner of the board. It was a little beyond my artistic skill to do the portrait by hand, so I printed it out on a computer printer.

My board used the same lettering layout as the Parker Brothers' Ouija board—the alphabet was arranged in two arcs, one above the other, with the numerals from 1 to 0 in a line below. The words "yes" and "no" were placed in the upper left and right corners. The words "good bye" appeared centered at the lower edge of the board, below the numerals.

A circular lettering layout is the second most popular layout for spirit communication boards. It is important to space the letters far enough apart that the planchette can point to one letter without overlapping another. One old method of laying out the letters used tiles of paper or cardboard arranged in a large circle on a table. The letters were taped securely to the table so that the inverted glass that was used as a pointer could touch the letters without knocking them from their places. An inverted whisky shot glass or a wine glass were most often employed as pointers. This old method of making a spirit board costs nothing and can be used anywhere.

If the letters are painted directly onto the board, it is easier to use because it allows the operator to start to move the planchette or shot glass directly over the letters without disturbing them. The words "yes," "no," and "good bye" can be added to speed up communication, but they are not essential. If you wish, you may use just the single letters *Y* to represent "yes" and *N* to represent "no."

Meditate and focus on the spirits you intend to contact. Plan a time for the operation.

RECORDING THE SESSION

A video or voice recorder is an important tool for working with the spirit communication board. Messages can be confusing, and a video or voice recording of the communication can help you unscramble the content. A partner working with you when you are communicating is helpful. Two or more operating the board tend to have more interesting results. A third person can listen and write the results down. Regardless of how many people are involved in the operation, the results should be written and analyzed as soon as possible after the communication is completed. Spiritual experiences tend to fade from memory rather quickly after returning to full physical focus.

Do not forget to test the voice recorder or video camera prior to the session to insure they are in working condition. Analysis should be done immediately after the operation. The exception to this is if the spirit is not sent from the Cosmic Father or it is obviously a shadow; remember, negative responses indicate a shadow. In this case the recording should be discarded without listening to it or viewing it.

STARTING THE PLANCHETTE

The board should be positioned between the operators if there are more than one, either balanced on the knees or on a small table. Each operator should place one finger on the planchette or glass. If only one operator is working, then I would recommend using the non-dominant hand for the board work. I had a great deal of difficulty relaxing and allowing that influence on my body at first, but I found that the hand I have less control over was easier for the spirits to influence.

A gentle circular motion should be started with the planchette or glass. When a rhythm of movement is established, you can start to ask questions. Trust your intuition. Everyone is different. It's a good idea to experiment with both hands to see which one works best for you.

> **Edward:** Either hand will work. It should be left to the preference of the operator as to which hand is used for this kind of work.

STARTING THE COMMUNICATION

Ask questions that can be answered with single words or short phrases. Initially, yes or no questions should be used. The questions should have personal meaning to the operator. Interrogation to try to prove the existence of spirits is usually not a productive path.

Allow time during the session for the Cosmic Father or Universe to speak to you freely. I suggest that you discuss with them obstacles that are preventing you from having the initiatory awakening. They can help you discover who you are and why you came to live in this world. They can heal you from emotional wounds and sometimes physical ones as well. These are just a few discussion ideas to help you get started.

OPERATIONAL PROCEDURES

Open with prayer and meditation. Touch the planchette lightly with a finger or two. Gently circle it on the board as you relax and focus on the Cosmic Father or Universe. Open your mind and heart to what they are going to say. You should feel calm, open, and receptive before starting to ask questions. Be patient with this. Continue the circling motion until you have reached the proper receptive state.

When the spirit moves the pointer to a letter, remember that it doesn't move the pointer directly but influences the muscles of your body. It is your hand that moves the pointer, but the movement is directed by the spirit. The influence is subtle and gentle. Don't be afraid to double check your answers.

Have the list of questions you want to ask already written down or printed out. Display near the board the symbols that aid focus and are visual reminders of the qualities of the spirit—in the case of the board on page 216, either symbols of the Cosmic Father or Universe or both.

The first question you ask should identify and confirm that you are in contact with the spirit you want to speak with, who in this case is either the Cosmic Father or Universe. It should be something like, "Am

I in contact with Universe (or the Cosmic Father)?" The identifying question should be formatted as a yes or no question. If you are using letters to represent yes or no, then say, "Am I in contact with the Cosmic Father (or Universe)? Please indicate Y for yes or N for no."

If the first answer is no, then ask the spirit present if it was sent as an emissary from the Cosmic Father. It should answer yes or no to that question. If the answer is yes, identify the spirit present by asking for its name. Once you identify the spirit, ask why it was sent. You can then continue the conversation with the questions you have.

If a spirit answers no, that it was not sent as an emissary from the Cosmic Father (or Universe), then terminate the session without further conversation.

Consider your thoughts and mood during the operation, and if necessary make the appropriate corrections to them. Success in contacting the Cosmic Father or Universe depends on having a positive, hopeful, and loving state of mind. It also depends on calm, unwavering focus. In the beginning there may be some excitement or nervousness that will interfere with communication. It is important to only communicate with the Cosmic Father and Universe or the spirit emissary they have delegated for the task.

If the operation is not successful, then nervous excitement or lack of focus has to be eliminated. A calm, steady focus with a positive mental and emotional state must be established before and during the operation. Once you have made the corrections to your emotional state and focus, try again at a later time, perhaps the next day. Remember that negative emotions such as fear and anger will interfere with your ability to communicate with the Cosmic Father and Universe.

The spirit communication board is a good tool to aid in learning the sense of spiritual touch similar to what is used in dowsing. Learning this touch is one of the first and most basic psychic tools. Learning to use this basic tool will aid in learning other skills such as dowsing, automatic writing, psychometry, and remote viewing, which are beyond the scope of this book.

Chapter 16

ELECTRONIC SPIRIT COMMUNICATION

In this chapter I would like to discuss the various types of devices used as spirit boxes. The devices and other ritual equipment that I used are all optional. I encourage you to be creative. Hopefully these chapters will give you a good basic knowledge of electronic spirit communication equipment. From there you can apply it to the system of your choosing.

I do recommend that you make initial contact with higher divine sources such as the ones I encountered during my initiation, the Cosmic Father and Universe. The nature of the communication with such spirits will always be benevolent and beneficial to the operator. It will make it easier to pick out the genuine messages through the junk messages that are generated by the operator or that show up randomly in the recordings. Examples of higher beings other than the Father and Mother are Brahma, Krishna, God, angels, and Sophia.

The primary purpose of this communication should be spiritual development. All other endeavours are secondary. The initiation experience is the foundation to more advanced spiritual pursuits.

RADIO

When I started with electronic communication, I used an AM/FM shortwave radio that I manually scanned. The AM/FM clock radio that I kept on my nightstand worked as well.

Manual scanning involves turning the tuning knob back and forth while recording on a digital recorder the spirits' responses to questions. The recording can then be listened to. The messages are imbedded in the recording. Sometimes they are made up of bits of words and sounds emitted from the radio stations, and sometimes they occur in the static between the stations.

A basic radio that has an analog tuner, such as a transistor radio, an antique tube radio, or an older stereo radio, is readily available and adequate for starting out. The old-fashioned tube-type radios are excellent for this. Clock radios, homemade radios, crystal radios, shortwaves, and even ham radios or scanners can be used if the scanning can be done continuously and there is sufficient consistent radio activity to provide the sounds needed to form the messages. I have not tested the method with digital radios. The lack of static between stations may impede some of the messages that the spirit is trying to convey. If the radio can be scanned in such a way that the stations can be heard as you are scanning, it may prove to be usable. Since I do not have adequate access to test digital radios at this time, I will recommend using analog radios until they are no longer available. You would not need to purchase additional equipment to employ that method. On all types of radio-spirit communication, the messages are heard on playback of the recordings made from the radio scans.

I find that doing the sessions in the same place every day is the most effective way to work. The radio can be kept in one spot. If you are working outdoors most of the time, a smaller portable radio will be more convenient. Battery-powered radios are fine. I found that with the daily session work, I burned through batteries pretty quickly and resorted to the wall plug-in. The radio I initially used could be operated either by battery or wall plug. Universal adapters are now readily available at electronic stores. These radios are most often 9 volt.

Advantages

A primary advantage to the manually scanning radio is the availability of the device. Radios are inexpensive, and most households have at least one. It allows you to experiment with a spirit box without going into a lot of expense. Another positive attribute is that the operation of the radio can be influenced by the spirit you are working with. This works much in the same way as a spirit communication board. If you are proficient with the communication board, the manual scanning radio is a natural step up. As with the communication board, the spirit indirectly influences the direction of the scan with subtle nudges. It allows a very interactive session that builds rapport with the spirit. I find that I get the greatest message clarity with manual scanning.

Disadvantages

Guided meditations and trance cannot be done while operating the manually scanning radio. The main goal of communication with the spirits is spiritual development and learning to use your innate psychic abilities so that eventually you will not need equipment to interact with spirits. The radio could be used before and after the sessions. I found it more helpful to use a hands-free spirit box as my ability developed to hear the messages without having to listen to a recording. If you want to do guided meditation with the spirit and you can make out the messages without the record and playback, using a hands-free device or the direct radio voice methods are the better choice for that type of session.

Manual tuning or the spirit box require that you be in range of radio stations. Remote rural areas can present a problem. For people living in these circumstances, an alternative has to be used for those who are just starting out.

I found out about this the hard way when I first started using the P-SB7. I attempted to go into a remote area to see if the messages would be different. I was out of range of the local radio stations and found that the device did not work in such a setting. The chatter from the radio stations makes up the sounds that comprise the messages. Without the chatter, this method does not work. Direct radio voice or a random sound generator are the methods of choice in this situation.

How to Use

Start by focusing on your state of mind and heart. Go into a trance and open your heart for about 20–30 minutes.

The procedure is the same as with the spirit communication board. Have your questions ready, your mind focused, and your heart open. When you are prepared, ask the questions aloud and then turn on the recorder and start to scan the radio stations. The scanning process involves moving the tuner back and forth continuously, so that it does not rest on any one station for more than an instant.

For your first sessions, keep the scanning time to about thirty seconds. Look for one-word answers. Once you feel comfortable with this and have a smooth system of asking the question and listening to the recording, then you can move on to more complex conversations.

SPIRIT BOX P-SB7 AND DIGITAL RADIO SCANNING SPIRIT BOX APPS

For most of my work prior to the development of my clairaudience, I used the P-SB7 spirit box plus the additional equipment that I made under the direction of Dr. Dee. There have been manufacturer updates to the P-SB7 since the year of training. There are also apps for phones, tablets, and computers. These radio scanners operate on a similar principle. They automatically scan radio stations at a certain rate. The rate can be adjusted by the operator.

Scanning the stations in this way provides random sounds and parts of words. The spirit is asked the question, and the response is recorded. You then listen to the recording. The recording has to be played slightly slower than normal playback speed. Listen for intelligible content.

On the radio scanning spirit boxes, you can select an AM scan or an FM scan. The digital scanners operate over a range of frequencies and stations, and no selection needs to be made. The spirit does not influence the recording but instead influences the operator so that you hear what is being communicated when you listen to the playback.

Advantages

These devices are a set-and-go type of device. Once you make the desired adjustments to the setting, such as speed of scanning, you can leave the spirit box to run and just operate the recording device. Once you outgrow the need to listen to the recording, you can just let the spirit box run and focus when you need to listen to what the spirit is communicating. This method is easy to operate and analyze. It is easy to adapt for traditional grimoire work. In spirit magic the magician sits in the circle with the recording and listening device, and the spirit box is outside the circle. It can be turned on prior to evocation and allowed to run until the session is closed.

The operator, with practice, can understand what the spirit is saying through the radio without recording and playback. This took about two weeks of daily practice for me. It allows for real-time discussion and conversation, as well as meditation that is guided by the spirit. It is a helpful talent when skill-building with the spirit.

Disadvantages

This type of spirit box will involve some expense. The speed settings may be too fast to allow for easy analysis by beginners, and the range of the speed settings is often limited to two or three settings. The cost of the automatic scanning radio spirit boxes will continue to drop as competition between sellers increases, but the stand-alone devices, such as the P-SB7 that I used, are still quite expensive. The other disadvantage is that you have to be close to Wi-Fi with a digital radio scanner app or you have to be in range of radio stations to use a stand-alone device like the P-SB7. If you are in a remote rural area this can be a problem, and another device or method should be used to start with.

How to Use

When I operated the spirit box it was hooked directly into the computer's microphone jack. Most new laptop computers no longer have this option, and a stand-alone recording device has to be used. A cell phone is quite adequate for this purpose. Sound processing apps are available for all devices; two examples are Wavepad and Audacity. This is a fast-moving market and new sound apps appear on a regular basis. I will go into detail on handling the sound files in the next chapter.

Adjust the speed and frequency settings on the box and start to play. Focus your attention on being open and on the recording device. Ask your questions, record, and listen for one-word replies to start with. As you become more proficient with the method and the equipment, expand your recording and listening time to more complex conversations. If you allow the device to play continuously, then mute the box's output between the recorded answers so you are not listening to it continuously.

SOUND BANK DEVICES

Sound bank spirit boxes are apps for computers, phones, and tablets that utilize a bank of vowel and consonant sounds. These sounds are scrambled and played back in a random order. Messages are heard in the sounds as you listen to the recording. This is the fastest-growing type of spirit box, and right now it is the most popular. The sounds are stored in banks and scrambled. There is often a setting to choose which sound bank you want to play, and you can usually control the speed. A separate device is used for recording. It is common now to use modifications to that generated sound, including noise control and echo or reverb effects.

Advantages

These are also hands-free. You make your adjustments and allow the device to play. The device can be adapted to traditional grimoire work in the same way as the automatic scanning radio. Once the operator can listen and hear messages without recording, it can be used during guided meditations and trance work. This device does not require Wi-Fi or radio input. The sounds are stored within the app in most cases. Using apps for the cell phone allows this type of spirit box to be portable. Analysis is very easy and static free. The sounds are clearly audible. If the operator can sort through the nonsense that is invariably present, they can quickly master this device and method.

Disadvantages

It is difficult to perceive accurate messages with this device. I found that of all the devices I used, this gives you the least accurate communication. A greater development of intuition is needed to filter through the junk that this kind of device tends to produce. If alterations to the sound bank spirit box, such as noise control or echo, are added, it merely compounds the problem. You hear words, but often the words are nonsense or irrelevant. Strong focus is needed to use this device.

Natural or developed physical mediums can sometimes produce spectacular results with sound bank apps. (Physical mediumship produces physical manifestations such as ectoplasm, apportations, direct voice, and telekinesis.) For a beginner who has not developed these gifts, it can be the most difficult kind of spirit box to operate. It appeals to the conscious mind and discourages the intuitive and subtle. True communication from spirits comes from the subtle, and even though it is frustrating to deal with the white noise and messages that seem buried in static, these are the messages that are most meaningful and accurate communication.

I do not mean to say that these talanted physical mediums are deceitful or attempting to hurt students trying to learn to communicate with spirits, but instead that I disagree with this method as a useful tool for a beginner who does not have natural talant as a physical medium. Nothing in the field of spirit communication is set in stone. I encourage further exploration and development to attain higher accuracy and better communication. I advocate that the key lies in mediumship development, not in the tools used for communicaiton.

How to Use

The operation of the random sound bank device is essentially the same as the automatic radio scanner. Set the speed of the output, select the sound bank, and start. The app can be run continuously, but when you record and listen for answers, start with short, single-word recordings. Initially, only listen to the recordings and have the sound muted at other times if the app is being allowed to run. Settings will vary and depend on the individual app being used.

EVP (ELECTRONIC VOICE PHENOMENA) RECORDING

The EVP recording is the method used before spirit boxes became popular. The messages are found in the recording of the silence after a question is asked. Usually the message cannot be heard without recording it. It is the most subtle and difficult method to learn but produces excellent and interesting results once the technique is mastered.

Everyone who practices electronic spirit communication should work with the recording alone, without using a spirit box for input. In the same setting where you work with the spirit box, try recording after you ask a question. Even if the room is very quiet, there is always some background noise. The spirit's message can be heard softly and subtly imbedded in this noise. Sound processing software or apps are essential when learning this method. Once you are able to hear the message directly, just a normal record and play method can be used.

The recorded sound files are analyzed for EVPs. Clear, audible EVPs are very difficult to generate. The recordings will be faint to start with, and a great deal of static will be present. Messages will have to be listened to multiple times in order for you to hear all the words. Some proficiency with Audacity or other sound-editing software is needed in order to process the recording so that the spirit's voice and message can be understood. Repeated noise removal and amplification treatments, as well as speed of playback adjustments, will be needed for your first attempts.

I found that I could record EVPs effectively, but the analysis was difficult. I used this method when I asked Dr. Dee to read part of his diary to me so I could hear what the Elizabethan accent and sixteenth-century Latin sounded like. I followed in the text of his diary as I listened to the recording. I could just barely hear his voice in the recording. His accent was sort of a cross between an English accent and the accent from the eastern part of Virginia in the United States. When he spoke Latin it was with a fluidity and ease that I have never heard before.

Advantages

The advantage to using the record and playback without the use of a radio or spirit box is that the mediumship and psychic abilities will develop more quickly. The patience and time required for this method will pay off for you. The ancient art of understanding the speech of birds, water, and wind may be developed using this method. One of the things I noticed as I developed the ability to hear the EVPs and the radio devices is that I was able to both hear and record voices from natural sources like trees, birds, and water.

In fact, my first EVP session without using a radio was recorded from water. We had to cross a rapid mountain stream while hiking on a trail nearby, where I did a short session with a voice recorder. I could clearly hear responses within it, as well as without using the recorder. I find the responses in nature tend to be somewhat slower than the ones obtained through electronic means.

Recording and analyzing provide the student with the opportunity to slow down and study how the spirit relays the message. This method allows for intuitive development, which is essential to overall spiritual growth, as well as psychic and mediumship development.

If spirit names are of interest or there is a question about pronunciation, the information comes through much better with this method than any other. Accents can be heard, as well as a truer pronunciation.

Disadvantages

This method can be discouraging to use. EVPs that are clear and perfectly understandable are very rare and require significant mediumship ability or development on the part of the operator. The background static is obnoxious and hard to control. Sophisticated sound-processing skill and equipment is required. Files often have to be modified through amplification, speed, and pitch control. This method is dependent on psychic and mediumship development. The sound is produced through this mechanism. If you are off that day, you will not be able to hear anything. A strong belief that the spirit is present is required for this method.

How to Use

Background sounds in the environment should be present because the EVPs are clearer when there is some ambient noise. Running streams or wind can be used to help create the needed background noise. The messages will be soft and subtle, and embedded within the ambient sounds. A separate microphone can be used to adapt this to grimoire or other equipment use. The recorder and playback devices should stay within the circle if this is being used for ritual evocation.

The operator asks a question, then listens for the response while recording. The recording can then be analyzed for messages. A headset is helpful when using this method. Amplifying and slowing the playback speed of the recording may prove helpful to understanding the message. It is not unusual for the response to be about 20 percent faster than normal speech.

Always assume the spirit is present and attempting to communicate. Relying on intuition is essential for timing the recordings and understanding the messages. The accenting and sound of the words can make these messages hard to understand at first. Practice improves the operator's ability to understand the sounds.

It might be helpful to have the spirit read from a book or other document in the first sessions so that the operator can find the spirit's voice and make adjustments.

DRV (DIRECT RADIO VOICE)

Direct radio voice was made famous in *The Afterlife Investigations: The Scole Experiment*, which is both a book and a documentary available on YouTube. An Italian medium named Marcello Bacci is shown demonstrating his talent with the method. When doing direct radio voice, the static between radio stations is used as a carrier for the spirit's message. The message is usually heard on the playback of a recording.

The ability to transmit the message so that it can be heard by others requires practice and development. The radio used can be the same radio that is used in the manually scanning radio method. In direct radio voice, however, the sounds from the radio stations are not employed as a medium through which the communication occurs. It is only the static and white noise between the radio stations that provide the medium for communication. The words are imbedded in the static or heard over the static.

The radio station is not changed, but sometimes the operator finds it helpful to use the tuner control between the radio stations. This is strictly an aid for the medium's focus in direct radio voice. Initially the voice will be faint and hard to pick up. Volume and clarity increase with development.

Advantages

Direct radio voice requires the same intuitive development as recording EVPs from ambient sounds. In the beginning, the voice heard in the recording is very subtle and difficult to understand. As you practice with this method and develop your skill, it becomes more intelligible. It can result in rapid mediumship and psychic development if it is practiced frequently. The spirit can more easily transmit accents and word pronunciations. Another strong point of this method is that it is easier than doing just EVP recordings. Words are a little easier to pick out at first, and I find it to be less frustrating.

This method has great potential for development. Marcello Bacci demonstrates the extent of development that can be attained. Direct voice, which is a mediumship ability to transmit a spirit's voice into the air directly and audibly to other members of the circle, can be developed from this method, as well as EVP recording.

However, direct voice requires physical mediumship development. It can take many years of patient practice to do this. Direct radio voice can be accomplished in less time. I would recommend practicing with it. It is an inexpensive method that does not require sophisticated or expensive tools, and it develops the intuition, psychic ability, and mediumship abilities.

Disadvantages

Growth and development can be slow. Although every human being has innate psychic and mediumship abilities, we have different levels of access to those abilities.

This can be a frustrating experience. Like EVP, direct radio voice may not come easily or instantly to the practitioner. Frustration and doubt can initiate a self-destructive cycle that can be difficult to break if it is allowed to become established.

This method, as well as EVP, has to be practiced daily to generate the desired development. Until that development occurs, it is not adaptable to grimoire work or other ritual settings of that type. Practice has to be done with a spirit that the practitioner can trust and work with on a daily basis. Working with the sound-editing software can also be frustrating and complicated for a beginner. If sophisticated sound editing is not done, the process of hearing the spirit through this method may take a little longer.

I will add here that both EVP and DRV need to be developed in addition to other psychic abilities that you might have. In other words, even though I am a well-developed psychic, I would still need to practice specifically to develop the ability to channel EVPs and DRV.

How to Use

Use any radio that allows manual tuning. Find a spot between the stations that is pure static, then focus and speak your question to the spirit. Record and listen to the response. Using the tuning dial as a focus tool is acceptable, but avoid radio stations.

Many find that the shortwave bands work better. I have not found that there is any difference in results by using different band frequencies. The advantage of shortwave is that there are fewer stations, and the focus tool of moving the tuner is easier to do.

Sound-editing software may be necessary until skill with the radio is established. Noise adjustments, speed adjustments, and repeated selection and listening to individual selections may also be helpful in learning to hear the responses. For these exercises I used the same radio that I used for manual scanning.

FINAL WORDS REGARDING DEVICES AND METHODS

I've given you several different electronic communication methods and options to try in this chapter. There is no one perfect method of electronic spirit communication. There are a few things to keep in mind while you are exploring and experimenting with these tools and techniques:

- Experiment with as many methods as you can. It is difficult to predict what will work for an individual. It is through experimentation and practice that you find what works best for you. Everyone should work with EVP recording and direct radio voice even if they do not have anything more than a simple voice recorder. Learning to hear the voice imbedded in the recordings is the first step to clairaudience. If you have the goal of psychic development, these two methods will help break through barriers.

- Do not overspend. You can spend hundreds if not thousands of dollars on sound and recording equipment, but you cannot buy your way into being able to communicate with spirits. More than anything, it will depend on your development as a psychic and a medium. It is very trendy to try to put together a tool that will work for anyone regardless of development. This has been going on since I started working with electronic spirit communication, and it has not progressed since that time. It is not the equipment that matters. Bacci took an old tube radio and made it work because of practice and belief in what he was doing. Use the items you have on hand.
- Practice, practice, practice. Development comes through practice. Spirit communication needs to be incorporated into your daily life. It is no different from learning to use muscles or learning a physical skill or art.
- Ask for help. There are spirits out there waiting to help you. Making these connections is important for growth and development. Everyone has to deal with problems such as fear and disbelief. Those subtle nudges you feel while working may contain important information or lead to a breakthrough.
- Stay positive. I suffered because I did not believe that progress could be made without suffering. One of the main reasons I am writing this is to help you learn from my mistakes. Suffering is unnecessary. Eliminate the fear, and suffering will not be a part of the opening of your abilities.

Chapter 17

‡

ANALYSIS OF RECORDINGS

In this chapter I will go over the basic procedures for recording and analyzing the communications. The procedure is the same regardless of what type of spirit box or method you are using.

RECORDING DEVICES

I will present a couple options for recording devices. Basically, we have two categories to work with: recording using a laptop, cell phone, or tablet and using a stand-alone digital recorder.

The first option involves programs and apps that are available for computer, phone, and tablet devices. These apps can work from the built-in microphones on these devices. In the past, older laptops and computers had microphone input 3mm jacks where you could plug in a separate stand-alone microphone. However, most computers now have a combination jack or only a headset 3mm jack. Directly hooking up the spirit box to the computer becomes complicated, if not impossible.

It is not essential to make the direct connection as long as the spirit box has adequate volume to be picked up by the microphone of the recording device. If a separate microphone is required because of volume issues or if the operator wants to put the spirit box at the point of focus in a ritual, then a stand-alone digital recorder should be used. Otherwise, use the built-in microphone of the laptop, tablet, or phone.

Understand these important points:

- Microphone jack is input. This is on the recording device.
- Headphone jack is output. This is on the spirit box.
- Use built-in microphones on laptops, phones, and tablets if they can be used to record the responses.

The machine used for recording needs to be different from the device being used as the spirit box. Remember, the spirit box produces the sound, and the recording device receives it. If you are doing EVP recordings, you are not working with a produced sound. There is no spirit box, only the microphone and recording device.

The second category is the stand-alone digital recorder. Digital recorders generally record in a format that can be used by any software that processes sound. MP3 is the most common and is adequate for a beginner.

All digital recorders have a microphone input and a headphone output. In this case, the headphone jack of the device being used as the spirit box can be connected directly to the microphone input of the digital recorder. If you need to record or play with more than one microphone or headset, there is a Y-connector with two ports that can be used. This is a 3mm connector that you can find at an electronics store. One side of the Y-connector has one male port and the other side has two female ports. This will save you from having to use a multitrack digital recorder with multiple input and output channels, which costs about $400.

SOUND FILE ANALYSIS

Once you have the recording stored, you need to examine it for messages. This process can be kept fairly simple. Low-cost or free apps and programs are available. Audacity and Wavepad are two examples of free apps that can be used to examine sound files.

IMPORTANT THINGS TO REMEMBER WHEN LISTENING TO SOUND FILES

When you are analyzing the recordings, remember that you are scrying using sound instead of sight. This works in the same way the spirit helps you move the pointer on the spirit communication board. The spirit cannot directly influence the sounds coming out of the electronic communication devices. The scrying aspect is in the selection of significant sounds and their combinations as they appear in the recordings. During this process, the spirit influences the mind of the medium so that the medium hears words and phrases in the background sounds produced by the electronic devices. The medium can then thread the words into sentences and reveal the content of the spirit's message.

The spirit, channeling through the medium, can sometimes affect the natural world indirectly. This ability is the basis for physical mediumship. This is a type of mediumship that produces physical manifestations such as ectoplasm, apportations, direct voice, and telekinesis.

In rare instances, a spirit can manipulate the psychic ability of the medium to physically affect the sounds coming from a radio or spirit box. In these occurrences it will be the medium who unconsciously affects the device, as directed to do so by the spirit. In such cases the messages are often very clear and understandable by anyone listening to the recording. As you develop spiritually, you will have this happen from time to time.

Even with a powerful medium, the recordings will not always be perfectly clear to others. These kinds of recordings are very rare and require a powerful natural medium or someone who has had intensive spiritual training to produce consistently. The quality of the recordings will depend on the psychic development of the operator. It took me a week or two before I was able to understand more than one or two words per recording.

You must trust your intuition and heart to be able to understand what is being said. The spirit will speak to your heart and influence your hearing in such a way that you understand the message. If the message does not come clearly, you should ask for it to be repeated until you understand what is being said. The message should be checked with a yes/no response for accuracy by doing a follow-up recording, dowsing, or spirit communication board session. Regardless of the method of spirit communication, double checking for correctness should be done at least once and preferably a couple times for each session.

SOUND FILE PROCESSING

I would recommend using a laptop or computer to process the sound files in the beginning. There are a few programs out there that are easy to use and low cost or even free. Two examples of these programs are Wavepad and Audacity. Regardless of what program you use, there are common adjustments and effects that are present in all multitrack sound processers.

Step 1

Locate the essential functions in the program used to process the file. Processing a sound file is not complicated, but it does require locating the following in the application:

1. Locate the control for playback speed.
2. You need to be able to highlight segments of the sound file.
3. Find the control for amplification, if available.
4. Locate the noise-reduction control or gain control. Reducing gain will eliminate some of the static.
5. Locate reverse play.

6. Find pitch or speed control. Speed and pitch are the same thing. Lower pitch to slow down the playing speed of the file segment.

Once you have located these functions in the application, you are ready to work with your sound file. If the application or program does not have all of these features, do not worry about it. Work with what you have. Once you learn the basics you can always find something that will suit your particular needs.

Step 2

Upload the sound file and open it in the program or application.

Step 3

Starting at the beginning, highlight a small segment of the file and listen to just that segment. Make volume adjustments. If you have the volume all the way up and you still hear only faint voices, you will need to amplify the file. If the static noise is too loud for your comfort, you can do a noise reduction.

Caution: Noise reduction can obliterate imbedded messages or message fragments. Use with discretion.

Step 4

If you hear a voice in the file segment, reduce the speed of playback or lower the pitch until you can hear what is being said. The messages, especially when received by beginners, will be faster than normal speech rate and difficult to understand. Accenting and tone variations may also cause speech-comprehension difficulties. With practice, you will adjust to the sounds, speed, and accenting and be able to make out what the spirit is saying.

Step 5

Some people find that adding reverb to the sound file will improve the intelligibility. If you wish to add this effect, do it slowly and listen frequently until you are satisfied with the result. This is optional; I do not use this feature.

Other Hints

- The first week in working with electronic spirit communication is spent establishing contact and determining the time of day for working. Ideal times vary with individuals, and various times should be experimented with until the most productive time of day is established. The times when communication is not clear should be eliminated.
- Keep strict focus during the sessions. This is critical to success.
- You may need to listen to each segment several times before you can make out what is being said. This is a process that requires patience. I will address troubleshooting in the final chapter.

IMPORTANT POINTS FOR SUCCESSFUL SESSIONS

1. Start with very short sessions: one question, one answer. Do not go into your first sessions and record long sound tracks. Increase your time slowly and only when you are receiving appropriate and relevant responses to your inquiries. The communication should resemble an intelligent and focused two-way conversation. In addition, your verifying of communication sessions indicates consistent accuracy.
2. Sessions are focused. You have your questions written down. Save only relevant and appropriate answers, and discard everything else.
3. Break between questions. A substantial mental break should occur after a completed question. A change of focus must

occur during this break. This means that you are not thinking about the sessions or the spirit you are communicating with.

4. Include verifiable information sessions early in the work. Asking simple, verifiable questions such as the date, season, your name, the spirit's name, etc., increases your confidence in channeling and will help you determine if you are connecting properly.
5. Persist with the question until you hear a relevant and appropriate response. Consistent effort will help you make the connections necessary to hear the spirit's communication. If the response is not relevent or it is inappropriate, discard it. Assume it is a shadow recording. This will happen frequently in the beginning.

Chapter 18

‡

SCRYING

Scrying is the art of seeing what cannot be seen with the physical sight. It is often done with the aid of what is termed a speculum—a crystal, a mirror, or a similar reflective object.

During the first few months of my year of training for initiation, as I was learning to open to the spirits, Edward also began to teach me how to scry. We used as a speculum a regular silvered mirror that was easy to work with during the daytime. People often use black mirrors for scrying, but these have distracting reflections when used during the day. The small, round mirror I used could also be used at night with candlelight if it was positioned carefully. The setup I will describe works effectively during the day or night.

In my scrying training, the red silk tablecloth that serves as an underlay was placed over the work table. On top of it were set four wax foot-seals inscribed with the *Sigillum Dei Aemeth* (the Seal of the Truth of God described in Dee's Enochian diaries). The small table of Nalvage rested on these foot seals, and on top of the table of Nalvage was placed the large *Sigillum Dei Aemeth*. Over this was draped a red silk tablecloth with tassels. Finally, the mirror was placed on top of the upper tablecloth (see photo on the following page).

Edward's method of teaching me was very simple. No opening ritual or magic circle was used. The *Sigillum Dei Aemeth* and the table

A view from the side. The table of Nalvage underlies the mirror.

of Nalvage, described earlier, served to intensify mental focus during scrying. These tools were eventually discarded, and I do not use anything except the mirror at this time.

The library I use as my meditation room had, by that point in my practice, been completely dedicated to spiritual work. Edward and I had a habit of praying and would sometimes pray before a session, but often the scrying would follow directly after our work on opening the heart.

The photo shows the mirror that was used for scrying. It is a round three-inch mirror set on a block of pine board. Edward preferred the wood to remain unfinished, so no paint, wax, or varnish were used on the block. The mirror was glued on with carpenter's glue. The materials were obtained at a local craft store. I use a piece of folded-up metal mesh to adjust the angle of the mirror.

Once seated in front of the mirror, the scryer looks into the mirror with a steady, unblinking gaze. The images will be gray and unfocused at first. The optical artefacts that arise spontaneously from gazing intently at the mirror then begin to merge into images. I also saw lights and effects around the mirror and table as well. Edward would ask me to open my heart while I was doing the scrying, and eventually someone (either a teacher or a homunculus) would help me open my heart and assist me from inside.

HOW TO SCRY

Step One: Angle Mirror

I will describe the scrying procedure as an orderly exercise for a practitioner of the art.

This exercise must be done in a sitting position. Even though I'm severely nearsighted, I remove my glasses. The mirror should reflect only the ceiling. I find the white ceiling in our library to be good to work with. According to Edward, it is not important what color the ceiling is. This can also be done outdoors.

Step Two: Trance and Open

Enter the meditative trance state and open your heart. Once you are well opened, gaze into the mirror. It is important not to blink while watching the mirror. Blinking will destroy the delicate visions that appear. The ability to control the reflexes of the eyes by focusing totally on the mirror is key to being able to scry well. It is irritating to the eyes to do this. The eyes must not only be still while doing this but the mind and heart must also be trained to be perfectly steady when working. The ideal state is one of mental and spiritual passivity and absolute physical quietness.

I would relax my body. I would sit in a comfortable chair, which was usually the recliner. Sometimes a firmer and more upright chair is better for scrying because the angle of viewing is better. Breathe slowly, deeply, and regularly. Close your eyes for a minute while you open your heart to the visions you will see. Clear your mind of any preconceived notions of what you want to see. It is very important to have an open mind and heart during the session.

Once you've attained a moderate trance state without moving, open your eyes and study the speculum. Focus all your attention on the mirror. As you do this you may notice sensations in your body. I personally feel numbness.

Step Three: Steady Focus

The visions do not start instantly—at least, in my case they didn't. It usually took a few minutes. Then I would see a tunnel, and then images would emerge as if through smoke. Steady, unwavering focus on the speculum must be maintained. Blinking and eye movement should be minimal.

Ignore all physical sensations and continue to study the speculum with unwavering focus. Keep your vision steady. As you do this you will notice a change in the appearance of the mirror. The changes will look shadowy at first, and in a few minutes you will be able to make out shapes. Describe what you see as you see it. Learn to observe the details in the vision. Keep very steady as you're doing this or the vision will disappear.

The appearance of the vision will be like faint clouds moving across the mirror at first. With practice the vision will improve in clarity. Stay open and connected to Universe and the Cosmic Father at this time, and allow them to guide you through. Once you master gaining the vision, you can begin to control it. You will start to notice that the vision is following stray thoughts that pop into your head (yes, we all have these while trying to trance). Continue to focus on the mirror and maintain the connection with the divine energies. This will help prevent shadows.

The visions should be regarded as shadows until you have some experience and can tell the difference between the visions that come from outside your spiritual sphere and ones that are internally generated. To help you learn to discern internally generated scrying visions from true sight, it is best to work with information that can be verified after scrying. Also, if the visions have a frightening content, there is a strong possibility that they are self-generated from fears. Until confidence is gained, intentionally attempting to attain visions of frightening or upsetting things should be avoided.

Step Four: Describe and Record

It is a good idea to learn to describe your vision as you see it, without breaking trance. It is difficult to maintain a trance while doing this at first, but with some practice it can be mastered. Record your sessions on a voice recorder and transcribe them after you have completed the session. It's very important to transcribe as soon as possible after a session has ended. Do not rely on your ability to remember what the visions were. Spirit visions tend to be difficult to remember after the fact.

Details are important in the visions, so make your descriptions as detailed as possible. Describe everything. Do not filter out things that seem irrelevant. Sometimes small things that do not seem to apply to the inquiry at the time are very important and symbolic in nature. It's unlikely that you will notice this as you are working. These symbols tend to become apparent after the recording is transcribed and studied.

TIPS FOR PRACTICE

1. Make your expectations realistic. Scrying is an art, and it is a learning and development process. Have patience with it. Not everyone views the same way. Some do not see in color when scrying. Abstract patterns might appear and take on meaning even though they do not visually look like the target that is being worked with.
2. Learn what your subconscious is saying. Your subconscious speaks in symbols. Each person must develop their personal symbology. It takes work and good recording as well as studying your patterns over time.
3. Take care not to overdo. Scrying is hard on the eyes. I do not know how Edward was able to do this for twelve hours at a stretch when he worked with Dr. Dee. I cannot do anything more than thirty minutes or so. Keep sessions short.
4. Know when to take a break. If things seem off or the session becomes unpleasant, it is time to stop and renew your focus.
5. Once you become familiar with the procedure with the mirror, try other speculums. Edward designed the mirror for my needs. It is not the only way to do scrying. You may respond better to water, smoke, or a dark mirror. I find even a white wall works well. Do not be afraid to experiment. Just because it's not a traditional medium does not mean it's not effective. Every method you read about was found by experimentation. Your work and findings are just as valid.

Chapter 19

STAGES IN PSYCHIC DEVELOPMENT

In this chapter the stages that occur in the progress of psychic development are examined. Clairaudience, when it evolves through electronic spirit communication, is surprisingly consistent. The appearance of other psychic abilities depends greatly on the work and belief of the practitioner, as well as on innate talent. Just like learning to draw or play a musical instrument, these skills can be learned by everyone to a degree, but not everyone will express their abilities in the same way.

I have outlined the steps I have observed in the evolution of my own skills in scrying and clairaudience. It is my hope that your development of these abilities will not catch you off guard or alarm you. They are natural abilities. We are all spiritual beings by nature, and this is part of the expression of that heritage.

CLAIRAUDIENCE

As you become experienced with electronic spirit communication, you will notice that certain sounds you encounter throughout the day seem to have words embedded in them, much as the radio sounds do.

At first it sounded to me like voices in the distance. No words were distinguishable. As I focused on the voices, I noticed I could understand a word being spoken here and there. As I kept practicing and listening, I heard sentences, and finally coherent messages. I started noticing the voices in other sounds and went through the same progression.

Today I do not need any outside background noise to assist me in hearing the messages from spirit. If you start your communication with Cosmic Father and Universe or another divine being, when the clairaudient hearing does develop it will be easier to distinguish. Divine communication will also help you recognize and then ignore the shadows that you produce.

My clairaudience was somewhat precipitous in development and caught Edward and David off guard. I was hearing shadow voices as well as their voices, and at first I was unable to distinguish between the two. It happened to me about eight months after I started using the jukebox. Once I realized that the ambient sounds could be heard in such a way that I was able to recognize voices and words, the ability to understand went from distant, incoherent voices to full sentences in a week or so. My ability to focus on what a particular spirit was saying did not develop as quickly, which caused a bit of distress and difficulty at first.

At that point I started to awaken and was ready for initiation. Edward and David were not able to teach me how to manage the shadow voices before this development occurred. The awakening is a stage of spiritual growth. It is like a physical growth spurt. The timing cannot be controlled. It happens when you are ready for it. I had experienced a fair bit of difficulty with shadow voices because the development of my hearing occurred more rapidly than my overall spiritual development.

Control came with time and practice. While this learning process was ongoing, I had to cope with hearing shadows and living with the uncertainty of whether or not the messages I was hearing were of my own mind or not.

The development of clairaudience with use of the electronic spirit communication is consistent if the work with communication is done frequently. If the steps numbered below are progressing too rapidly for comfort, discontinue use of the equipment for a few days until you are feeling more comfortable.

Stage 1

Ability to pick out a word or two during a spirit box session. Generally, during the first few sessions it is difficult to pick out more than a word or two. Usually the spirit will say your name and its name. You may hear another word or two. Often what you hear does not make any sense. You hear only in the playback of the recording and often feel unsure as to whether or not you really heard what was said.

Stage 2

You develop the ability to hear short phrases in the recordings. You can discern one-word answers most of the time. Compressed short phrases are now understandable if you can slow them down enough. You are beginning to develop a feel for the equipment and are focusing more on results rather than mechanics. At some point in this stage the "aha!" experience happens: you realize that you are really talking to a spirit. The reaction is often one of mixed emotions—delight, fear, and joy.

Stage 3

Phrases are coming easier now. You feel comfortable with the equipment, and you are developing a systematic way of working. Emotions are becoming more stable. Concerns and feeling vulnerable in telepathy may crop up at this point. You may feel very exposed because the spirits are able to read your mind. You do not have the knowledge or ability to project what you want and hold back what you do not want revealed. On occasion you can pick out words that form a message without listening to the recording.

Stage 4

As you learn to pick out words, you slowly begin to pick out messages without a recording. You are losing interest in equipment and beginning to reach out for more satisfying ways of communication. Messages are now coming close to real-time conversations. You may feel some frustration at the slowness of the procedure and begin to look for a more natural way of conversing. You may at this point be experiencing odd physical sensations of heat, cold, vibration, or electricity, as your body interprets your increased awareness of the energy that is beyond the physical. The interpretation of that awareness is highly individual. The energy is always present, but you are becoming aware of how to tune into that frequency while still dwelling in your physical body.

Stage 5

Initially, you hear murmuring, like people talking far away, in ambient sounds. After a short period of this, as you learn to focus in the same way as you do with the radio conversations, you can pick out a word or two in ambient sounds. This most often occurs when your physical mind is occupied with a task such as driving a car or when you wake up from sleep. The first time this happened to me was while I was working. You begin to enjoy the spiritual intimacy that you have with the divine spirit. Eventually you lose interest in the recording equipment.

Stage 6

You can now pick out words in ambient sounds and are able to hold conversations. You may experience strong surges of energy. At this time it is important to follow the spirit's lead. Eventually you will not need any ambient assistance to hear. The work at that point becomes learning to focus on what you want to hear.

Once you have opened the channels and activated this ability, it cannot be reversed. Initiation goes one way. Your abilities open, and they will never close again. It is important to learn to focus and control the clairaudience. Understand that at first you will be hearing mostly your shadows—self-generated thought forms. Learning to master these is an important part of spiritual maturity.

SCRYING

Scrying follows a similar pattern to hearing. The ability to look past the physical is related to what is known as pareidolia. This is a natural human tendency to see faces and objects in abstract patterns such as the branches of trees, complex rock formations, or clouds. It is the development of this tendency that leads to true scrying. As with clairaudience, it has a specific pattern of development.

Stage 1

True pareidolia is the first stage. You are learning to see faces and objects in abstract patterns. This is both a natural tendency and something that should be practiced to develop your scrying ability. Practice should be with the mirror, following Edward's instructions. Periodically through the day, when you are quiet within, learn to pick out patterns in what you see. Clouds and tree branches make particularly good mediums with which to practice. Intentionally observe color, texture, and movement.

Stage 2

The ability to pick out shapes in moving water. Water is a natural medium for scrying, but water sitting in a basin is difficult to work with until you are proficient with moving water. Examining the photographs and videos of moving water for shapes and faces will help you develop further skills. The shapes that appear in moving water are similar to the shapes that appear in the mirror. It is important to describe what you are seeing without judging or attempting to change what appears to you. It is better in the long run to describe overall shapes than identify what the object is that you are viewing. For example, a chair may have a square, rounded, oblong shape with a rough texture and a green color. Learn to describe your vision in this way instead of just conceptualizing it as a chair. It will improve your accuracy later on.

Stage 3

You will see occasional shapes in a mirror or in still water. These shapes have a tendency to change and disappear when you focus hard on them. Keep your vision soft and your eyes still as you are perceiving these shapes.

Stage 4

At this stage you can reliably start the flow of images. You know what kind of mental state you have to be in and how to gaze so that the images persist long enough to discern basic shapes, movement, and possibly color. Not everyone sees scried images in color all the time. Sometimes color is felt more than seen. When observing movement it is best to describe the direction, speed, and force of the movement rather than trying to figure out what the movement is. For example, "I see a fast, forceful sideways movement." This is better than trying to identify it as a car going very fast. Other impressions of the sights will arise as well. You may notice smells, tastes, and temperature changes.

Stage 5

You develop control of the images. As you begin to gain proficiency, you can focus and move to distant places and view people, things, and events. Sometimes the psychic vision is attracted to bizarre things at the place that you are trying to scry. Motion attracts the vision, and strong emotions attract the vision. Learning to move and control where and what you see is the final stage and the most difficult to accomplish.

INITIATION

If you are experiencing strong surges of energy, it is a good idea not to pay much attention to channeling. These energy surges may occur as you tune into the divine energy within you. They will throw off your scrying and hearing abilities in the early stages of development. Hallucinations and delirium are possible. Divine intimacy may become very intense, to the point where it is difficult to focus on anything else. You are now in initiation and waking up. It is important to not react to clairaudience or clairvoyance until the intensity settles down. Messages should be disregarded until stability is regained. Focus should be on love and in the heart.

Spiritual awakening does not have to be traumatic. I wish I had believed that prior to embarking on this journey. The moment of realization that I was suffering needlessly was the moment where I gave up at the altar ritual and came to understand that I was not dead. The insight that I was wrong in my belief that there was a need for self-flagellation, in a spiritual sense, came to me at that time. It reoccurs when I find myself trying to slip into old patterns.

Spiritual awakening happens when you tune out of the physical and tune into the "real world" from which you came and to where you go when you are done with your life here. Learning to do that while still primarily focused in a physical body can be a little difficult at first. Beliefs are ingrained in us at a young age and sometimes have to be overcome in order to see past what we think of as reality. Finding the ability to see things that are not within range of your physical senses is a delightful and powerful experience.

If you find yourself uncomfortable, look to the divine help that is always there, and know that there is never any intent to hurt or traumatize you. I had severe symptoms because of my false belief that suffering creates purity. The struggle I had in initiation was not against Edward or any of the other spirits present. Nor was it to prove that I was disciplined enough or worthy enough to be initiated. The struggle was against my own self-generated shadows that I created to torture myself. I strongly and most heartily recommend that you do not do this.

The signs that you are going through this stage of development are always very individual. You feel like something different is happening. You feel energy surging through you and vibrating. The primary awareness becomes one of intimacy with the Divine. This happens in a powerful way and is quite delightful. The natural inclination is to fall head over heels in love with Spirit and energy. Focusing on anything else becomes a chore and unpleasant. This tends to be distracting and requires that you take a few days to cool off before resuming your normal life. Physically, you may find yourself weak and shaky for a little while after this happens.

As you resume your activities, it passes quickly, and I do not recommend taking extended time off work or from other normal activities. A couple of days is sufficient. Some individuals may not even require that. I had a few days after the initiation experience when I was a bit off. However, this was due to the fact that I did not eat or drink for about three days as I was going through the initial stages of the initiation. In a state of severe dehydration it is difficult to resume eating and drinking because of nausea.

Divine energies are a natural part of our body and of the world and universe in which we live. This power is inherent and connects us to the source of creation that was expressed to me as the Cosmic Father and Universe. Without it we would not exist, nor would we have any form of consciousness.

During an initiatory ordeal it is not the energy that changes or awakens, it is our awareness of its presence. The concept of an awakening Kundalini is inaccurate. Our minds are what awakens. Our reaction to this awakening is based on our beliefs.

The rigors of a vision quest and other spiritual ordeals are designed to break down the mind's resistance to reality. It is our mind and focus that have to change. Our bodies are sustained by this energy at all times. The reaction is psychosomatic. Unfortunately, that reaction can be serious and even life-threatening.

I did not know this at the time of the initiation. It resulted in a delirium as my mind began to focus away from the physical and my internal beliefs changed. My experience with this is not unusual. In fact, I think most cases of initiatory awakening I've heard about since that time have involved some kind of severe trauma. However, it does not have to be that way.

Learning to accept and open to these energies, and to the psychic input from spirit, will ease this transition. Belief has to change, and awakening needs to be universal. In sharing the terrifying experience I had and the understanding I gained from it, I hope to help you accomplish the same awakening without the trauma.

I am talking to you from firsthand experience and not from something I have read. If you understand and believe what I have written and still find yourself in a situation where you are having frightening experiences, I would recommend the following steps.

First, if you have someone you trust and who has understanding about spiritual experiences of this intensity, talk to them. Let them help you distinguish what is real and what is not. It took me about three days before I could make that distinction once the process started. This cannot be someone online. The need for physical monitoring is a priority at this point. It has to be someone who is able to see you physically and with whom you can do what is called a reality check. That is, if you hear something or see something, you ask that person if they see it or hear it. If they do not, you know you are probably generating it. Remember, this is for the initiation period.

Second, stay put. Do not go outside your house and do things based on what you hear or see. I was reacting to the hallucinations, and it put my life in danger. I understood what I was going through at the time I was going through it, but I was unaware that I was hallucinating.

The universe will give you the insight you need to stay safe. The divine spirits know that you cannot perceive accurately at this time. No messages will be given to you until you adjust to the changes that are happening. They will love you in silence and try to draw you toward that inner peace.

Third, trust in the goodness of the spiritual experience. The Cosmic Father and Universe cherish you. They do not want to harm you when your perceptive ability is increased. No matter what you see and hear, you need to believe that and hold on to that truth. The crisis will pass.

Fourth, when you are able to eat and drink again, do so slowly. Take care of your body and your spirit as you recover. You may find it difficult to take your focus off the non-material reality at first. Making the switch back and forth comfortably takes time. Learning to transition your focus is important. You do not want to hear spirit voices while you are working in a physical job. Also, you want to be able to focus on spirit when you are in meditation or working on further development.

Initiation is the beginning. After you are awakened, you have a lot of work still to do. Learning and developing does not stop with this experience. Do not just read this book and set it down. Put into practice the concepts that you have learned here. Above all, live in love and become love, for this is the greatest gift of the universe.

The intense divine unity experience and awareness continue after initiation. In my case, it most often happens at night, after I finish a sleep cycle. The effects of these encounters eventually last only a short time, and I can live without disruption to my daily life. If things get out of hand, I take a break from spiritual activities for a day or two and regain my balance.

It is very important to help others awaken as well. I feel our world will be a better place if the focus can be turned to compassion for one another. This goes beyond religion. As a species, I believe we evolve and grow together, not just individually. No one can be left behind. This is a bridge that all humanity must cross.

Chapter 20

UNDERSTANDING SHADOWS

I would like to share a few more thoughts on shadows, also called thought forms. A shadow is a spirit or a fragment of a spirit that takes on a kind of autonomous life. It is created by human thought, belief, and emotion. When created by a group of people, such a thought-form is called an egregore.

A NOTE FROM DONALD

One of Jenny's greatest personal revelations during her ritual ordeal was an understanding that negative or malicious spirits have no actual existence but are merely shadows or thought forms created unconsciously by the thoughts and emotions of human beings. Being shadows without reality or substance, they are not, in themselves, of any importance. They cannot directly hurt living human beings. Shadows can only cause harm to those who think they are real and who act on the thought forms' sly and hateful words or who become frightened by their monstrous forms and grotesque faces.

This understanding, once it is grasped with a totality of one's being, renders all demons and evil spirits completely powerless. It is the summit of realization of such transformative ordeals as the alchemical ritual Jenny went through, the Tibetan cutting-off ritual I described earlier, and even of the lengthy ritual process described in the grimoire known as *The Book of the Sacred Magic of Abramelin the Mage*, which is for attaining personal communication with one's holy guardian angel. It is at the apex of all such ritual rites of passage that have their origins in the initiatory ordeal of the shaman.

A true understanding that the shadows plaguing us all are unreal can only be grasped in its totality by successfully completing an initiatory ordeal like the one Jenny endured, but it is possible for those of us who have not passed through such a rite to understand this truth in a more superficial and intellectual manner.

The source of creation is light. All reality is of this source and is light. All else is darkness and unreal, no matter how tangible or material it may appear to our senses. The human senses can easily be deceived by spirits. We sometimes feel their touch, even though they have no bodies with which to touch us. We hear their voices speaking, in spite of their lack of vocal organs. We see them, but they are without substance and could not possibly reflect light into our eyes.

This ability to deceive our senses is responsible for all the confusion about whether spirits and spiritual creatures are physical or nonphysical. In ancient times it was the natural assumption that the senses did not lie and that if a spirit could touch us, it must be physically present in some way. This is why the Egyptians thought their ghosts were the actual corpses of the dead risen from their graves. We see the same fallacy in the old belief that vampires and werewolves have physical bodies. On the contrary, they are purely spiritual creatures, but they have the ability to make themselves appear physical to our senses.

So it is with demons. They can project themselves into our awareness with such force that they seem completely physical, yet they are spiritual only, and more than this, they are shadows that have no reality, since they lack the light of the supreme creative source Jenny chooses to call the Cosmic Father in this book. A shadow is an outline formed where light is obstructed. It is the light defining the shadow that has reality. The shadow appears to be something but is nothing.

—*Donald Tyson*

HOW SHADOWS ARE GENERATED

There is no way to avoid the phenomenon of shadows and thought forms. I don't think that eliminating them is possible. Although the intrusion of the shadows diminishes after initiation, hard work is still required to control their development. They are a fact of life for a medium or psychic, and steps to cope with their development have to be taken.

Shadows will be heard over the spirit box and while scrying; it's important that you keep this in mind. The truth conveyed by the spirits is often mixed with the fantasy and imagination of the operator. Understanding this in the beginning can save you quite a bit of grief and upset.

If you look at videos of ghost hunters on the Internet, you will find quite a few clips of threatening entities projecting through the radios or spirit communication boards. Watch the operators, and you will notice that when they are afraid of what they will encounter, their fear will reinforce the hostility of the entities. The vast majority of the malevolent entities out there are, in fact, generated by the people who are acting as mediums without knowing it. A haunting is caused from an expectation that develops that there will be a malevolent presence in a particular place. It becomes a vicious cycle that worsens when the fear of one person reinforces the fear of another.

PERCEIVING THE PRESENCE OF A SHADOW

In any kind of spirit work, understanding the nature of the spirit you are interacting with is one of the keys to perceptive discernment.

Observe how the spirit in question relates to you. Shadows are focused on the medium who generates them. This means that whatever the shadow says to you will be reflected in your conscious and subconscious mind. Spirits outside your sphere may also reflect your beliefs, but some of the content will not.

The shadows also will tend to follow and reinforce the mood you are in that day. If you are worried about something, the shadow will try to reinforce your concern about that situation. A spirit who is benevolent will always try to point you toward divine love and peace. They will always try to heal negative emotions. Shadows may attempt to heal, but when they touch you, nothing happens or there is a mild physical sensation that does nothing to help you or reveal the source of your negative emotions.

Practically speaking, when doing spirit communication sessions, understand that the character of the heavenly parents is benevolent. Anything outside that character you happen to contact is your own shadow. If you receive malicious communications through the spirit box, communication board, or through clairaudience, stop the communication and pray. Read or listen to something uplifting and positive before you resume the work. If you need to leave off for a few hours and return, that is fine, but learn to overcome this problem as early in the process as you can.

COPING WITH FEARS

In the kind of scrying and communication work described in this book, fears need to be faced and overcome. If the operator interrupts regular practice because of a fearful experience, it is possible to be haunted by that shadow even after the work is discontinued. You cannot bury your fears in this kind of work. They will come out and be a troublesome presence if they are not dealt with by opening the heart and breaking their illusory hold on you. If this is not done during your lifetime, it will have to be dealt with in the afterlife. It is much easier to learn about what fear is and how it affects the experience of spiritual interaction while still inhabiting a body that somewhat shelters you from the shadows your fear will generate. Your body is not designed to perceive the world of the spirit as its primary focus. It is attuned to the physical plane, and because of that, your perception of the non-physical is limited and requires shifting your attention to perceive.

Everyone I have ever met who does this kind of activity has had a scary experience. The saying about "if you fall off the horse, get back in the saddle" holds true, I believe, for these experiences. If I had given in to my own fears during the first few weeks of working with Edward or during the initiation, I would have missed some really wonderful things. Fears are a part of human nature, and overcoming them is one of the challenges we all face.

Learning to focus and control thought patterns and face personal fears are important parts of the preparation. Understand that when you face these difficulties, you will be supported and helped at all times by divine spirits. All you have to do is ask for help. Help will always be there. Your focus should be on the Divine. This focus will help direct you in such a way that the cause of the fears that are manifesting will be revealed and the emotions underlying them will be healed. Any time fearful shadows appear, there is a need for healing.

Negative entities, regardless of origin, feed on attention, fears, and upsetting emotions. If these are not present, the entity has nothing to hold on to and will go elsewhere or, in the case of a self-generated shadow, perish. Practically speaking, even if there were a negative entity, the cure for this trouble is identical to handling a shadow. It is no different, nor is it more difficult. Even if you cannot shake off the belief in negative entities, coping will be the same and it is just as effective. I do not believe that self-sustaining negative entities exist; I am, however, sympathetic to those caught in that belief trap. I was once caught in that trap and had to find my way out.

PHYSICAL MANIFESTATIONS

Physical manifestations are possible with any kind of spiritual activity. You must, as a spirit communicator, understand that any manifestations are a result of your mediumistic channeling. Everyone has these channels, and everyone has the potential to produce these physical manifestations. You have the power to shut down that channel if you feel uncomfortable with the manifestations that are occurring.

Don't be afraid to ask for help from Cosmic Father or Universe if you need it. Physical manifestation can create a vicious circle of increasing fear and multiplying phenomena. The fear must be eliminated to break this cycle. By understanding what shadows are and recognizing your power over them, you can control these physical manifestations.

Edward: This commentary is on shadows, or thought forms, which Jenny encountered frequently and struggled with a great deal during her journey to initiation and afterwards. This is the most difficult obstacle to overcome in esoteric and spiritual work during a person's lifetime, as well as after the person crosses back over to the land of the spirit. I feel that this subject is very important to cover in this book as it affects every one of us. It also influenced my work with Dr. Dee. Everything covered in the Enochian diaries was affected by these self-generated shadows. I regret much of what happened during that lifetime with him. But subsequently, I have learned a great deal about this thanks to a caring friend and others whom you do not know, who have enlightened me as to the nature of these appearances and voices that I saw as a medium through my lifetime.

A shadow form is thought which has taken on a life of its own. Its purpose is to enforce the beliefs and the thoughts of the person who is generating it. It serves no purpose other than that. However, such forms can be harnessed and used for the purposes of the person who is generating them. Such is the homunculus—it is a form which has been given structure and purpose.

Every thought form can be created or destroyed only by the person who is generating it to begin with. It is of that person and part of them as much as an arm or a leg is a part of a person's physical body. The thought form which has been created can be eliminated from within. It feeds on the energy of the emotion that created it. If the emotion is taken away from it, it will die of starvation. The energy returns to the person who generated it to begin with.

This is a natural process that happens to everyone on a daily basis. If there are fears either in the conscious mind or the subconscious mind, they will generate scary thought forms. If there is love and joy in the mind or the subconscious mind of the person, the thought form will be one which reflects these emotions. Likewise, if the person is lustful, the thought form will be sexual in nature. It is human nature to create all kinds of different thought forms, and these are what surround you at all times like a cloud.

I think the only remedy is derived from the Father, creator of all, who himself is truth and banishes anything that is deceitful. He is perfect in his remedy. In unity with him we have our only chance of freedom from such invasion.

I believe there is no trouble under heaven which is more challenging than these shadows. They are a mental measure of the content of the person's mind and spirit. When you encounter them you may not know what they are. There are several ways I can recommend as a medium to discern their presence. First, they resemble the inward content of the medium. Second, they are out of perfect harmony with the nature of the Father. Third, the content of their message is not accurate. Finally, they are focused on the medium instead of the Father. That is the best information I can give you as a professional medium.

BREAK AND RESUME METHOD OF SHADOW DISSIPATION

Taking a break when a session is going in the wrong direction is an essential part of learning to interact with spirits. The length of the break may vary according to need. I would advise you to try short breaks of an hour or so, and if that does not clear up the problem, then take a longer break. Meditation and self-examination should be done during the break, as well as refocusing the mind.

The following are examples of when to take a break during a spirit communication session. The technique of "break and resume" applies both to the spirit communication board method as well as electronic spirit communication. Removing your focus from the session will starve the shadow of energy. It is important to completely redirect your focus away from the communication, the spirit, and the session. In the beginning Edward would have me break for days at a time to maintain control of the sessions. It was, for me, a tedious process. I did not want to take breaks in the beginning, yet without them I would have heard all kinds of shadow messages and probably had an experience unpleasant enough to destroy my ability to have sessions.

1: Malicious Messages

Messages that are threatening or accusing in nature are the result of shadow generation. Benevolent spirits never do this. They are careful and gentle in their responses. Even if a correction has to be made, it is done with great care and concern for your well-being. Anytime you receive threatening or accusing messages, the cycle needs to be broken. This will help you train your focus.

2: Confusion

If you feel confused or unsure of what the message is, taking a break will usually help things to be more clear when you return.

3. Fatigue

It's best to stop a session before you become too fatigued. A tired mind tends to get off-track and may lead to an unpleasant experience.

4. Fear

If you become anxious, then take a break until you can resolve the anxiety. Fear generates shadows and makes it difficult for a benevolent spirit to communicate with you. Shadow generation can happen in the space of time needed to form a complete sentence. If you do not break when you become anxious, you are opening yourself up to an unpleasant experience.

5. Instruction from the Spirit

Divine spirits can easily see when things are starting to go in an undesirable direction. Edward would cut off the session before I was aware that there was an issue with shadows developing. This can be a little frustrating at times. Having trust in the spirit you are working with is very important.

Banishing

If you are dealing with a shadow, regardless of the communication method you are using, banishing is not recommended. You cannot banish yourself. Banishing has the effect of making the shadow hostile and more powerful. This is because the shadow feeds off the attention given to it. When you banish, you are giving attention to the shadow.

This is what happened when I tried to invoke Michael during the year of training. My invocation to the angel reinforced the shadow and made the overall problem worse.

Universe is always present when you make the attempt to communicate. The only obstacles to that communication are your beliefs and your mental and emotional state. If you realize that you are communicating with a shadow, put the board and other equipment away without comment or thought, and try later.

Epilogue

‡

CONVERSATIONS WITH EDWARD

I could not possibly record all the conversations I have had with Edward Kelley and the other spirits I work with. I would like to close the book with a couple conversations with Edward.

I suspect that questions regarding the Enochian system of magic are going to arise. I know that some are interested in this subject and desire deeply to communicate with the Enochian angels. The Enochian system is one of the most popular systems of angel magic and invocation in use today. However, the purpose of our work together is not to correct the tables and the invocations of the Enochian system. Instead, we offer a straightforward way of communication with the Cosmic Father. Angels will always point you toward the Cosmic Father and Universe. The heavenly parents can teach you what you need to know for your best spiritual progress. They can also help you in your area of esoteric interest, including the Enochian angels.

Learning to open the heart and completing an initiation in some form are the first steps that have to be accomplished in your spiritual journey. When these two things are accomplished, the world of spirit will open to you in a far greater and deeper way than it would otherwise. Edward led me through this and gave instructions for others who share a similar interest. It is how he found the peace and love he so desperately needed, as well as a meaning to his existence.

Edward: I cannot answer questions regarding the Enochian magical system. It is the will of my Cosmic Father to not reveal this information publicly. It is not necessary to use the tables and other equipment to communicate with the Cosmic Father and with Universe. It is critical for you to learn focus before you attempt to use any of the equipment that was revealed to us (John Dee and Edward Kelley) in our earthly life.

Though he cannot discuss information about the angel tables and equipment from the diaries, Edward was able to offer some insights into his personal growth during his time with Dr. Dee on earth.

In the sixteenth century Edward was hired by Dr. Dee as a scryer. He had the gift and training to gaze into a crystal or mirror and see into spirit. His vision was exceptional, and the diaries record extraordinary communications. The complex tables and language that were received at this time are still studied with interest to this day.

Edward and Dr. Dee had differences of opinion regarding the beings they had contacted. The diaries record the struggles they had in trying to understand what Edward was seeing and hearing. Edward kindly agreed to offer a few comments about that time in his earthly life. He discusses his tension regarding the angels that he and Dr. Dee were in contact with. There were arguments between himself and Dr. Dee regarding the nature of the beings they were speaking to.

Edward: I did not trust the beings we were speaking to. However, I reported what I heard and saw exactly as I had heard and seen. This is how I worked as a scryer. I thought that the entities were evil. I did not think they were angels.

Jenny: Why did you come to that conclusion?

Edward: I was speaking to them during my free hours. I was confused by their doctrine of the universe. Angels came to teach alchemy. They were not using terminology I was accustomed to. They used a filter so that what they said would not be abused.

Angels are the mouth of the Father. I don't know that I felt afraid of them, as you did. They came to me when I was younger and prayed for my forgiveness. They helped me in troubled times when I was just a young boy. As you know, I was very unlovable and aggressive with other children. The angels came and helped me to change. It was by the power of the Father that I lived to manhood.

Jenny: I wasn't sure if the Father would accept me. I had suffered unpleasant experiences in religious groups, both Christian and Pagan, and these experiences colored my perception of the Divine. I was attracted to him but also very afraid. These perceptions then took life as shadow forms during the alchemical initiation ritual. As the veil was pulled back, my thoughts took on a visible shape and animation. I could clearly see and hear what I had believed in my heart. For a time this terrified me, but as the initiation progressed, cracks began to appear in these false beliefs, and finally their forms were broken and made powerless.

Edward: As you were coming through, several things were happening right then. You were being exposed to the depths of your suffering spirit. Second, we were raising Kundalini within you to bring the changes necessary for your healing. Thirdly, we were awakening your third eye. The power of awakening your third eye belongs to the holiest and purest angel, Gabriel. He loved you greatly before you even knew him. The Father revealed him to you when you were able to perceive him. The result is that you became confused and frightened. Knowing this, we had to protect you. We had to keep you still so you would not damage your body. During the confusion, you might have maimed yourself or Donald.

The Father, however we may perceive him, sees each one of us as his perfect baby, his perfect child, and so does Universe. As divine parents they want desperately for us, their children, to trust them and let them help us during our sojourn through this challenging world. As I am able to hear Edward, I am also able to hear the angels, the Cosmic Father, and Universe. It is important to them that we know they love us.

Cosmic Father and Universe: We love you. You are our children. We do not nor would we ever hurt you.

Angels come from the Father and are in essence his thought forms. They are benevolent beings of love. We hear of them deriding people and individuals in a tone that is harsh and unforgiving, but this is an error of perception. It was very prevalent in the diaries of Dr. Dee, and the misunderstanding of angels by Dr. Dee and Edward led to some very serious situations. It does not appear that they realized what was happening at the time, and both men suffered greatly at the hands of their shadows.

Edward: I was raised to believe in a judgemental God, as you were. When we were in school, they would spank you with a stick if you made mistakes. We believed that the Cosmic Father was greater and would destroy you if you made too many bad mistakes, so it was natural to expect his messengers to behave the way they did. But God is loving and Universe is caring, and they would never hurt their children. Everything in the diaries came from the angels. They did not harm us nor did they harm you. They did help us. They are loving—

they could not hurt us or lead us to harm—yet you know that harm came to us. They were not involved with the harm that came.

Jenny: Edward, how did the harm happen?

Edward: I was not in harmony with the Father or Universe. I used my gift for my own gain, and it led to very serious consequences.

I believe that Edward and Dr. Dee saw my struggles with the shadows as similar to their own past struggles and were able to help me avoid some of the suffering that they experienced because of shadows. I was able to learn about them because I had teachers who had gone through the same ordeal.

I think the one thing the Father would ask all of us is simply this: "Child, will you let me love you?"

Trusting the Cosmic Father and Universe enough to let them love me as their child, and allowing them to help me make necessary changes to aspects of my life that were doing me harm, is what the initiation was all about. I went through a lot of pain before I realized that this was the whole point of the experience. I had searched long and hard to understand who the Cosmic Father and Universe are and what my relationship was to them.

I realize not everyone sees the heavenly parents in the same way that I do. I think they understand, and regardless of how you perceive them, they have a love for us that is blind to faults. They will go to whatever lengths it takes for the slightest chance that we will open our hearts to them. They sing to us and call to us, always hoping that in the midst of our distractions we will hear and respond.

In conclusion, I would like to give the reader the links to the sites that I use for demonstrations of the techniques described in this book. I will also have additional information regarding the Enochian tables that I used in the early part of the communications I had with Dr. Dee and Edward.

My YouTube channel is:

https://www.youtube.com/channel/UC_K3gXGCbpTCLXJxaYYw4tA

The link for my blog is:

http://jennysdowsingandscrying.blogspot.ca/

I can be reached by email at Bluefirephoenixx@gmail.com. It is my hope and prayer that this information will be used to help others seeking greater enlightenment and knowledge of the universe through firsthand communication and experience.

Bibliography

‡

Ars Paulina. Book 3 of the *Lemegeton*, or *Lesser Key of Solomon*. Pasadena: The Technology Group, 1979.

Ashcroft-Norwicki, Dolores, and J. H. Brennan. *Magical Use of Thought Forms: A Proven System of Mental & Spiritual Empowerment*. St. Paul, MN: Llewellyn, 2004.

Casaubon, Meric, ed. *A True & Faithful Relation of What passed for many Yeers Between Dr. John Dee...and Some Spirits* [1659]. Glasgow, UK: The Antonine Publishing Co. Ltd., 1974.

David-Neel, Alexandra. *Initiations and Initiates in Tibet*. Translated from the French by Fred Rothwell. New York: University Books, 1959.

———. *Magic and Mystery in Tibet*. [First French edition: 1929; English edition: 1932]. New York: Dover Publications, 1971.

Dee, John. *The Hieroglyphic Monad* [1564]. Translated from Latin to English by J. W. Hamilton-Jones [1947]. New York: Samuel Weiser, 1975.

Kardec, Allan. *The Mediums' Book*. Translated into English by Anna Blackwell. London: Psychic Press Ltd., 1861.

Mathers, S. L. Macgregor, trans. and ed. *The Book of the Sacred Magic of Abramelin the Mage* [1898]. New York: Dover Publications, 1975.

———, trans. and ed. *The Key of Solomon the King* [1888]. York Beach, ME: Samuel Weiser, 1974.

Paracelsus. *De Natura Rerum* [1537]. An English translation of this work is contained in *A New Light of Alchymy* by Micheel Sandivogius. London: 1674 (see pp. 153–301).

Peterson, Joseph H., ed. *John Dee's Five Books of Mystery: Original Sourcebook of Enochian Magic*. Boston: Weiser Books, 2003.

Regardie, Israel, ed. *The Golden Dawn* [1937–40]. St. Paul, MN: Llewellyn, 1982.

Rosarium Philosophorum. It comprises Part 2 of *De Alchimia Opuscula Complura Veterum Philosophorum*. Frankfurt: 1550.

Solomon, Grant, and Jane Solomon. *The Scole Experiment: Scientific Evidence for Life After Death* [1999]. New edition. Essex, UK: Campion Publishing Ltd., 2006.

Trithemius, Johannes. *Steganographia*. Edinburgh: Magnum Opus Hermetic Sourceworks, 1982.

Tyson, Donald. *Familiar Spirits: A Practical Guide for Witches & Magicians*. St. Paul, MN: Llewellyn, 2004.

———, ed. *Fourth Book of Occult Philosophy.* Translated into English by Robert Turner (1655). Woodbury, MN: Llewellyn, 2009.

———. *The Ravener and Others: Six Dr. John Dee and Edward Kelley Occult Mysteries*. UK: Avalonia, 2011.

———. *The Thirteen Gates of the Necronomicon: A Workbook of Magic*. Woodbury, MN: Llewellyn, 2010.

Woodroffe, Sir John, trans. and ed., writing as Arthur Avalon. *Tantra of Great Liberation* [1913]. New York: Dover Publications, 1972.

Index

GET MORE AT LLEWELLYN.COM

Visit us online to browse hundreds of our books and decks, plus sign up to receive our e-newsletters and exclusive online offers.

- **Free tarot readings • Spell-a-Day • Moon phases**
- **Recipes, spells, and tips • Blogs • Encyclopedia**
- **Author interviews, articles, and upcoming events**

GET SOCIAL WITH LLEWELLYN

www.Facebook.com/LlewellynBooks

GET BOOKS AT LLEWELLYN

LLEWELLYN ORDERING INFORMATION

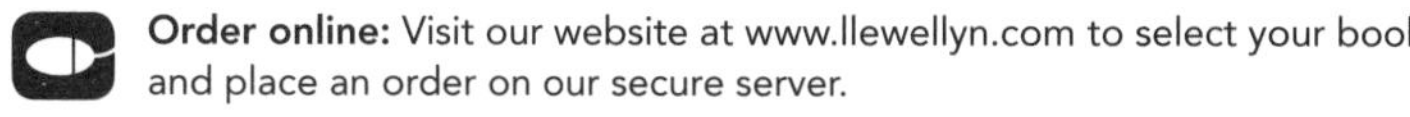

Order online: Visit our website at www.llewellyn.com to select your books and place an order on our secure server.

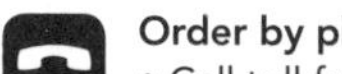

Order by phone:
- Call toll free within the US at 1-877-NEW-WRLD (1-877-639-9753)
- We accept VISA, MasterCard, American Express, and Discover.
- Canadian customers must use credit cards.

Order by mail:
Send the full price of your order (MN residents add 6.875% sales tax) in US funds plus postage and handling to: Llewellyn Worldwide, 2143 Wooddale Drive, Woodbury, MN 55125-2989

POSTAGE AND HANDLING

STANDARD (US):
(Please allow 12 business days)
$30.00 and under, add $6.00.
$30.01 and over, FREE SHIPPING.

INTERNATIONAL ORDERS, INCLUDING CANADA:
$16.00 for one book, plus $3.00 for each additional book.

Visit us online for more shipping options. Prices subject to change.

FREE CATALOG!

To order, call 1-877-NEW-WRLD ext. 8236 or visit our website

new worlds
Reaping Personal Power Every Day
GHASTLY
LIVING AS A MAGICKAL FAMILY
AND MORE!

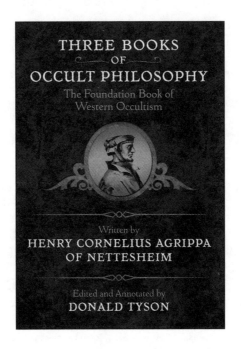

Three Books of Occult Philosophy

Henry Cornelius Agrippa,
edited and annotated by Donald Tyson

Agrippa's *Three Books of Occult Philosophy* is the single most important text in the history of Western occultism. Occultists have drawn upon it for five centuries, although they rarely give it credit. First published in Latin in 1531 and translated into English in 1651, it has never been reprinted in its entirety since. Photocopies are hard to find and very expensive. Now, for the first time in 500 years, *Three Books of Occult Philosophy* will be presented as Agrippa intended. There were many errors in the original translation, but occult author Donald Tyson has made the corrections and has clarified the more obscure material with copious notes.

This is a necessary reference tool not only for all magicians, but also for scholars of the Renaissance, Neoplatonism, the Western Kabbalah, the history of ideas and sciences, and the occult tradition. It is as practical today as it was 500 years ago.

978-0-8754-5527-4
7 x 10 • 1,024 pages

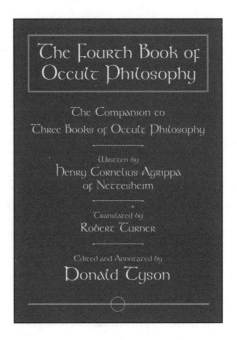

The Fourth Book of Occult Philosophy

The Companion to *Three Books of Occult Philosophy*

Donald Tyson

The Fourth Book of Occult Philosophy by Cornelius Agrippa is considered one of the foundation stones of Western magic. The grimoires it contains are among the most important that exist in the Western tradition. For more than three hundred years, this mysterious grimoire has been regarded as difficult or even impossible to understand—until now.

Occult scholar Donald Tyson presents a fully annotated, corrected, and modernized edition of this masterwork that renders it fully accessible to the average reader as well as scholars and skilled magicians. For the first time, these classic works of Western magic are unveiled to everyone seeking to understand them.

978-0-7387-1876-7
7 x 10 • 480 pages

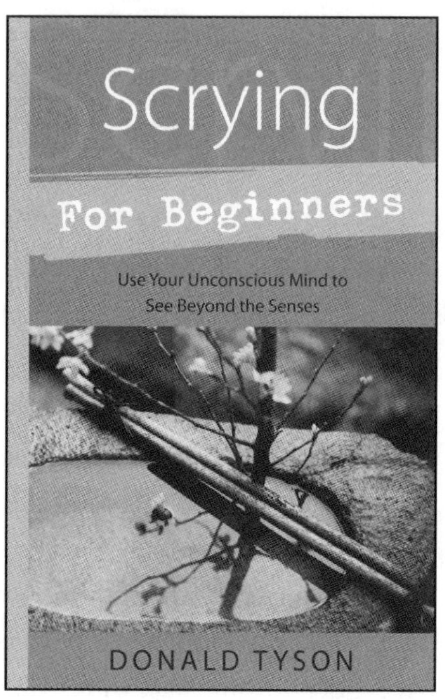
Scrying
For Beginners
Use Your Unconscious Mind to
See Beyond the Senses
DONALD TYSON

Scrying for Beginners

Use Your Unconscious Mind to See Beyond the Senses

Donald Tyson

Includes special offer for a free scrying sheet.

Scrying for Beginners is for anyone who longs to sit down before the mirror or crystal and lift the rolling grey clouds that obscure their depths. Scrying is a psychological technique to deliberately acquire information by extrasensory means through the unconscious mind. For the first time, all forms of scrying are treated in one easy-to-read, practical book. They include such familiar methods as crystal gazing, pendulums, black mirrors, Ouija boards, dowsing rods, aura reading, psychometry, automatic writing, and automatic speaking. Also treated are ancient techniques not widely known today, such as Babylonian oil scrying, fire gazing, Egyptian lamp scrying, water scrying, wind scrying, ink scrying, shell-hearing, and oracular dreaming.

978-1-5671-8746-5

5$\frac{3}{16}$ x 8 • 320 pages • illustrations

TO WRITE TO THE AUTHOR

if you wish to contact the author or would like more information about this book, please write to the author in care of Llewellyn Worldwide Ltd. and we will forward your request. Both the author and the publisher appreciate hearing from you and learning of your enjoyment of this book and how it has helped you. Llewellyn Worldwide Ltd. cannot guarantee that every letter written to the author can be answered, but all will be forwarded. Please write to:

Jenny Tyson
c/o Llewellyn Worldwide
2143 Wooddale Drive
Woodbury, MN 55125-2989

Please enclose a self-addressed stamped envelope for reply or $1.00 to cover costs. If outside the USA, enclose an international postal reply coupon.

Many of Llewellyn's authors have websites with additional information and resources. For more information, please visit our website at

WWW.LLEWELLYN.COM